November Song

Stories of Sixteen Well-Lived Lives

By Eric Anschutz

The sixteen men who tell us their stories in this book are all in or near the November of their lives. I want to thank Rachel Bingaman for allowing me to use her artwork on the cover. When my son Eric, who designed the cover, found Rachel's tree, online, he and I both felt that it portrayed the sense of "November" just as it was meant in the book's title. You can see more of Rachel's work at BingArt.etsy.com.

Ode to Aging

What a struggle to stay the same
When fleeting time's to blame.
Inside I'm filled
With hope and fear -
To stave off failure,
Keep life dear,
Keep up appearances
Year by year.

A child's disappointment
Adds stress,
Old fading love hurts – no less;
Acceptance and dependence
Conflict my days,
Bloat my calendar in foolish ways.

Wanting what I may never get,
Hiding frustrations – goals not met.
Then…the pleasure at last as things go well,
Good news to make my old heart swell.

Aging: you have a good story to tell.

> This poem, by Ben Slomoff, is taken from his most recent offering: "A Stalwart Bends."
>
> Ben has just recently celebrated his 100th birthday. His life story appears herein, beginning on page 40.

****

Copyright © 2014, Eric Anschutz
All Rights Reserved

ISBN-13: 978-1497378537
ISBN-10: 1497378532

Createspace, North Charleston, SC

Table of Contents

Page   Content

Page	Content
5	Prologue
11	John Lee
25	Bud Lembke
37	Burma Shave
40	Ben Slomoff
53	Otto Schnepp
67	Happiness
71	Lonnie Bristow
87	Bob Hanson
96	Aging
98	Ron Wyatt
111	Bobby Frankel
121	Persistence
123	Art Dreshfield
137	Duke Robinson
151	The 87% Life
154	Joe Potozkin
164	Tim Wise
177	More on Aging
179	John Gosling
191	Ralf Parton
203	Bucket List
206	Nace Ruvolo
219	Eric Anschutz
233	Desiderata

Prologue

This is a big world. Much needs to be done to provide for the seven billion of us. Farmers are crucial to our well-being, as are carpenters and physicians and police, nor can we do without bankers and plumbers and tailors. And if our world is to be beautiful and interesting, we need writers and painters and violinists.

The collection of life stories in this book tells us of the lives of a marine engineer, a teacher, a manufacturer of shoes, a journalist, a pastor, a paper-scientist, a professor of chemistry, a physician, a recreation manager, an architect, a judge, an attorney, an artist, an entrepreneur, and a hospital administrator. I include, at the end, my own life story, that of a would-be engineer who turned to diplomacy – and then to the writing of political columns and essays. Civilization is a complex organism - millions of people - each doing their part. How are roles assigned? How are the many individual contributions assembled into a cohesive entity? A city. A country. A world.

In a lecture delivered to the Harvard Phi Beta Kappa Society in 1837, Ralph Waldo Emerson said something interesting about all of this:

> *You must, he said, take the whole society to find the whole man. A man is not a farmer, or professor, or an engineer, but he is all. Man is a priest, and scholar, and statesman, and producer, and soldier.... Man is thus metamorphosed into a thing, into many things. The planter, who is Man sent out into the field to gather food, is seldom cheered by any idea of the true dignity of his ministry. He sees his bushel and his cart, and nothing beyond, and sinks into the farmer, instead of Man on the farm. The tradesman scarcely ever gives an ideal worth to his work, but is ridden by the routine of his craft,*

> *and the soul is subject to dollars. The priest becomes a form; the attorney a statute book; the sailor, a rope of a ship…. In this distribution of functions, the scholar is the delegated intellect. In the right state, he is Man Thinking…*

In assembling *November Song*, I sought to play the role of Emerson's scholar, of the "delegated intellect." So, what is brought together in these pages is meant to be more than a mere exposition of the lives of sixteen men. While it is, importantly, the story of these men, of who they are and of what their lives have been like, it is also, to cite Emerson, an attempt to "find the whole man."

Though no life is "ordinary," the lives of these sixteen are lives especially well-lived. Each of them has contributed in significant ways to the community of mankind, to bringing his strand of strength and value to the fiber of the "whole man" envisioned by Emerson.

Each of the men profiled in *November Song* lives in a Northern California retirement community, called "Rossmoor." We are neighbors, and most of us have known one another for some time – some for a decade or more. One of them is 67, one is 77, all the others are older than 80, several are older than 90, and one has just recently turned 100.

The fact that this tome tells the stories of men in the November (and December) of their lives is what brought us to the title. "November Song" has, I think, a good "ring" to it, and has the added power of truth!

The men brought together here have won neither vast fame nor great fortune; they are, however, interesting people. Indeed, the quality of being "worthy of note" was the attribute that brought their life story to these pages.

To understand more fully this special group, and to help elucidate Emerson's "whole man," I want to tell you about Rossmoor, the community in which we live. Some years ago I co-authored (with photographer John Chang McCurdy) a book about Rossmoor, subtitled "Eden in California." The following few paragraphs are taken from the preamble I wrote for that earlier book:

One must be over 55 to live in Rossmoor; the average age of our residents is early-70's. Located in Tice Valley, in the foothills of Mount Diablo, Rossmoor features a Mediterranean climate with some seven rain-free months of gentle summer weather, mild winters and just enough winter rain to sustain our verdant valley. Rossmoor's architecture and landscaping are beautiful, for which we owe a vote of thanks both to those who designed it some 50 years ago, and to those who maintain it today.

Almost ten thousand of us live here in some 6,500 "manors." We are all of "a certain age," a common ethos, a remarkable élan, at least a trace of the wisdom that comes with age, and an almost universal generosity of spirit. Each of us brings to the mix that is Rossmoor some six or seven or eight or nine decades of life experience. There are among us former university deans, physicians, CEO's, diplomats, clergy, attorneys, nurses, truck drivers, schoolteachers, engineers, mechanics and shopkeepers. We are from every state in the union, and from all over the world. Most of us are parents, many of us are grandparents, and not a few are great-grandparents. Many of us have served in the wartime military. We are politically divided roughly 60-40 among Democrats and Republicans. But, each of us, whatever our professional background, our politics, our life experience, our religion - or dissent from religion - tries to avoid open dispute over conflicting views.

Many of us are actively linked to the Internet, exchanging emails to keep one another abreast of the latest jokes and wisdom of the day. We Google daily; we read blogs and newspapers and journals from around the world, and many of us find ourselves learning more online than we ever learned during our years in colleges!

Just as our schooling, our marriages and our professions gave shape and purpose to our lives, so do the communities in which we were raised, in which we worked, and to which we retire. For those lucky enough to spend retirement years in a community such as Rossmoor, life offers a special opportunity for the sort of companionship and intellectual growth that can bring the individual into the "whole society" and integrate him into wholeness as a man. In our "November" and "December" years, many have the opportunity to rise from *"farmer"* to *"Man on the farm."* Our working lives are over, and we now have the time and the broader view needed to appreciate *"the true dignity of our ministry."* That ascent, from *"farmer"* to *"Man on the farm,"* is in a sense the purpose of this book. I hope too that committing these life stories to print will serve to enrich our understanding and appreciation of one another.

Genesis and Writing

The inspiration for this text is a book authored in 1996 by Pulitzer-winner Studs Turkel. Entitled *Coming of Age: The Story of Our Century by Those Who Lived It*, Turkel's book weaves together the voices of a number of very different people to provide a panorama of American life.

I was inspired too by the breadth and depth of experiences brought together in this great community of ours, and by the collective wisdom assembled here. I am again and again delighted and inspired by the generosity and humor and good will that are the currency of life in our Rossmoor. I have long wanted to assemble some of this between the covers of a book, and the life-stories collected in these pages provide what seems to be the perfect format.

I wrote each of these life stories in the voice of the person who lived it. Each is based on interviews and discussions; in some cases, the person being profiled wrote some parts (and in three cases most) of the text for me to integrate with my own writing. To ensure fidelity to the facts, the several iterations of each profile were edited and scrutinized by the subject so that the final product is exactly as he wished it to read. Terkel said this about the process used to create his *Coming of Age*; I would say the same for my own modest undertaking:

> *"What I bring to the interview is respect. The person recognizes that you respect them because you're listening. Because you're listening, they feel good about talking to you. When someone tells me a thing that happened, what do I feel inside? I want to get the story out. It's for the person who*

reads it to have the feeling . . . In most cases the person I encounter is not a celebrity - rather the ordinary person. "Ordinary" is a word I loathe. It has a patronizing air. I have come across ordinary people who have done extraordinary things."

The Essays

To enrich the life stories of our sixteen men, I have written a number of essays designed to give perspective to the times in which we lived. One of the essays, about those once ubiquitous Burma-Shave roadway signs, will remind us of drives along pre-turnpike country roads. Essays about *Happiness* and *Aging* remind us of the joys found in the America of our autumn years. Another essay visits pianist-comedian Victor Borge as he relates a story about *Persistence* and its importance to a successful life.

Essays at their best are aimed at getting to the truth. Essayists seek to bring relevant facts and opinions together, trying thereby to illuminate the topic in ways that will lead to deeper understanding. I have long found that writing essays is the best route to learning. We all have thoughts on such topics as happiness and freedom, but when we do the thinking and research required to turn thoughts into essays, our views and beliefs invariably widen and extend and sharpen beyond their original form.

Acknowledgements

My brother Bob, my son Eric, and my daughter Kari have been important in bringing this book to life. Bob edited the text as it was being written, improving grammar and honing the wording. Eric designed the book's beautiful cover, and helped to bring both text and cover into a format appropriate for publication. Kari did a final reading to find and correct remaining typos.

Dedication

I want to dedicate *November Song* to my wife, Sidsel, for her love and affection, for help in editing, and for keeping our home life serene and on a steady course through the months it took to create this book. It is dedicated too to the fifteen men (I myself am the sixteenth!) who opened their minds and hearts to tell me about their lives, and then allowed me to publish their life stories.

Parting Insights

Three gems of wisdom capture the élan and essence of the lives presented here. First, from Steve Jobs: "We seek people who bring both mind and heart to work." Second, from Romain Roland: "A hero is a man who does what he can." Third, from Helen Keller: "The world is moved not only by the mighty shoves of heroes, but also by the aggregate of the tiny pushes of each honest worker." And, last, from Albert Einstein: "Living life is like riding a bicycle, if you stop working at it you fall off."

****

John Ming Yee Lee

Born in Shanghai, circa 1938, John and his parents moved to Hong Kong in 1947, before the ascension to power of Mao Tse Tung and the communist government. Educated at Amherst and Yale, John is an architect of note, and one of Rossmoor's leading tennis players!

The Beginning

My parents came from opposite ends of the Chinese social structure. My father, born into a well-to-do Shanghai family, had been educated in Massachusetts at Amherst College. Upon his return to China, he taught political science at a university in Shanghai. After a time, my father left teaching to take over from my grandfather management of the family printing business.

At the time he met my mother, my father had long-been married to another woman, and with her had a family of three children. My parents came together in an "entertainment house" - to which my mother, a beautiful teenage woman, had been sold by her parents, poor peasants who lived in the countryside outside Shanghai. Captivated by my mother's beauty, and perhaps also motivated by my impending birth, my father bought out my mother's contract, put her (and me) into an apartment, and then promptly left our lives because of the Sino-Japanese conflict. He was able to visit us only rarely for the first seven years of my life.

My mother was quiet, shy and gentle. I saw her parents on only one occasion. Knowing that she was being supported by a relatively wealthy man, they visited my mother in an effort to extort money. My mother's younger sister was brought along on that visit, and the parents had the audacity to suggest that to relieve their financial distress that daughter too might have to be sold to an entertainment house.

I was born circa late 1938. In those days, births were not always registered, birth certificates were not issued, except to established families, and the exact date of my birth is therefore not certain. I learned, informally, that I was born on the Chinese New Year's Eve of a lunar leap year, probably in 1938.

My father's printing business included printing bank notes (paper currency) for the Chinese nationalist government. At the time, late 1930s, the Japanese occupied Shanghai and much of the rest of China. Because of difficulties with Japanese authorities, my father had moved himself and his business, in 1938, to Chungking (not then occupied), remaining there until 1945 when the war ended and the Japanese were ousted from China. Thus, during that seven-year period his visits to my mother and me were very rare.

To sustain us, my father provided funds, delivered to us on an irregular basis by his brother. The funds were just enough to cover our most basic needs; when on occasion delivery of funds by my uncle was late or disrupted, we had barely enough to eat. Because of our fear of the Japanese occupiers, my mother and I left our apartment only once during the first seven years of my life. That one outing was necessitated by the need for urgent medical care for me. Because servants cost almost nothing in those days, we had a maid living with us who did any needed shopping. Since she and my mother had similar backgrounds, both from peasant families, the two bonded, developing an empathetic relationship. After the war, my father rewarded the maid, and saw to her return to the countryside.

During these early years of my life, my mother and I had no legal or even informal link to the Lee family. The relationship between my mother and my grandmother, the domineering grand dame of the family, is best described as one of benign neglect.

A Major Turn for the Better

In 1945, a major turn occurred in our lives. My paternal grandfather, whom I had never met, died, and my grandmother invited my mother and me to attend the funeral – thus acknowledging for the first time our inclusion in the family. Thereafter my grandmother and mother had a sometime relationship, not close, but now real. All of this made my mother happy, both for herself and especially for me, that she and I now had a place in the family. Also, in 1945, as the war ended, Japanese occupiers were ousted from China, thus enabling my father to return from Chungking to Shanghai.

In 1946 my father, leaving his official wife and family behind, took my mother and me on what was first intended to be a vacation visit to Hong Kong – but as it happened, we stayed on, never returning to Shanghai. While in Hong Kong, my father was involved in real estate, including purchase of several houses, one in Repulse Bay, another in Deep Water Bay, and a third at the Peak.

Because life for our moneyed and educated family was increasingly seen as unsustainable under encroaching communism, and Mao's impending rule, the rest of our branch of the Lee family left Shanghai in 1947, moving one at a time to join us in Hong Kong. My grandmother, my mother and I, plus assorted aunts and uncles, moved into the house on Repulse Bay; my father and his official wife and family took the house on Deep Water Bay. Because of relentless fog, the house at the Peak came to be considered undesirable; eventually it was sold to the Canadian Consulate.

About a year after moving to Hong Kong, my father went into the movie - making business, specializing in dramatized documentaries depicting people important to China's history. For a time, there was a ready market throughout China for films of that kind. However, in 1949, after the communists took over the country, some of those lionized by my father's films were deemed by Mao to have encouraged westernization of China, causing the new government to block distribution of the films on the mainland, and thus effectively throttling my father's business.

My father was well liked and highly regarded by his friends. Advised by them against venturing into the treacherous movie enterprise, he nonetheless persisted with the belief that film could be an important tool for mass education. It failed, but many of his friends remained loyal to him to the end.

In 1948, my mother died in childbirth, and I, then about ten years old, was brought to live with my father and stepmother. I had until then never attended school of any kind. Upon my move into my father's house, a tutor was engaged to teach me English, and I was enrolled in a boarding school run by British missionaries. Though I stayed at that school until graduation in 1954, the six years there were among the worst of my life, both because I was totally unprepared, and because I lacked the social skills needed to deal with teachers and classmates. I was insecure and lost.

During the year before my mother died, when we were all under one roof at Repulse Bay, there were a couple of developments worth mentioning. It was the first time that I received some modicum of pre-school education, and it was from my grandmother. Every weekday, my cousins and I were assigned one hour of traditional Chinese calligraphy with brush and ink. She would review our work and reward us five cents for each character that met her strict standard. With that training, I learned at least to appreciate the discipline and beauty of the Chinese brush artistry.

The other development was that for the first time of her life, my mother had a genuine friend - with one of my aunts. My mother was in charge of taking care of my grandmother's needs. My aunt understood well how demanding that could be since she had been in a similar position before her marriage. She would advise and help my mother on the side. After my mother's passing, and after my aunt's family moved into their own home, she would invite me there during weekends. When I was ready to leave Hong Kong after high school, she financed my journey to this new land. My cousin also was my dearest relative during those Hong Kong years.

My Schooling

Though of Chinese parentage, born and raised in China, the circumstances of my early years were such that I was never educated in proper Chinese, including calligraphy, except for the lessons given to me by my grandmother. To this day my ability to read and write Chinese is very limited. Among those who are wholly literate, writing and speaking in classic Chinese is beautiful. Those educated in classic Chinese learn poems and stories, and when speaking or reading, scholars of the language always know in depth what is being said because references to earlier writings are integrated into the exchange of ideas to enrich the dialogue. This aspect of the Chinese culture is of special importance in business and official interaction. Unfortunately for me, I was never fully initiated into that aspect of Chinese culture.

In 1955 I entered Amherst College – the school from which my father and my oldest step-brother had graduated. By then, my father's businesses were mostly defunct, so my Amherst fees and living costs were paid by scholarships and summer work. I should note that at the time of my matriculation annual cost for housing and tuition at Amherst was about $1200 - nothing near the obscenely large fees now standard at good colleges in America; Amherst's annual total fee today is $63,000, even with substantial subsidies from the endowment fund.

At Amherst, I began with a major in mathematics, and survived for a couple of years. I found myself, however, to be wholly outclassed by other students in the understanding of advanced mathematics. Not cut out to be a mathematician, I changed my major to art, learning techniques and art history. During a beginner studio session, the class was asked to enter a competition for a poster for a Bach concert – and I won.

For me, Amherst provided a great education; the school was relatively small; my class size was about 300. The entire student body today totals 1800. During my years at Amherst, small-group seminars were numerous – and always enriching. Importantly, too, there was constant out-of-class interaction with faculty, including numerous enriching and supportive visits to our teacher's houses. Every summer, I worked at hotels in nearby Cape Cod, washing dishes, bussing restaurant tables and helping to maintain the grounds. Needless to say, money earned there helped to pay my living expenses at Amherst. I graduated from Amherst, with honors, in 1959.

Professor Ted Soller, of the Physics Department, and his good wife Nina, were especially caring for me when I was at Amherst. On many weekends, and during the holidays, like Thanksgiving, they would ask me to join them for evenings with some other faculty members. There I was introduced to the college theater and a few of the fine arts professors. Later, after Yale, when my application to be a resident in this country floundered - repeatedly being lost by the bureaucracy - Nina solicited her brother, a Senator, to help me stay in this country as a resident. In due time, by then living in New York, I became an American citizen.

While a student at Amherst, I was in this country on a student visa. To avoid deportation, I needed immediately after graduation to enter into graduate studies. My second half-brother, a recent graduate of the Yale School of Architecture, suggested that I enroll there too. I did that, was awarded a full scholarship, and graduated from Yale in the spring of 1963 with a BArch. What I liked especially about the Yale program was its emphasis on the architectural thinking process. Technique, yes, but conceptual thinking too. I was fortunate that at Yale a Chinese professor took interest in my design works, encouraged further efforts, and helped me financially by offering me part time jobs on interesting small projects at his one man office. It was at Yale too that I learned from the great teacher Louis Kahn who elaborated the importance of "form follows function."

I need to pay special tribute to my second step-brother, Billy, who took charge of me immediately upon my arrival at the New York airport from Hong Kong in the fall of 1955. He showed me the riches of the Big Apple during the holidays, and introduced me to his friends and the few relatives living there. When I was about to graduate from Amherst, he convinced me to apply to Yale Architecture School. After finishing there, he helped to find me a position at the Metcalf office in D.C., and later on at Barnes in New York City. The importance of a wide and loyal network of helpful family and friends can hardly be overstated.

Metcalf Architects and Solari

Following graduation from Yale, I joined Metcalf Architects, a firm located in Washington, DC. In those years, Metcalf specialized in medical facilities (hospitals, clinics and the like), and the design of residences for US ambassadors. My initial assignment was the design of animal quarters associated with medical schools! My next assignment was design of a residence for the US ambassador in Gabon.

After one-plus years with Metcalf, with some savings, I decided I needed to see the rest of America. Finding an aged Chevy, I bought it and set off from Washington, first for the south and then the west with no specific destination in mind. After some months of wandering, I wound up in Scottsdale, Arizona, which at the time housed a summer camp for the Solari Studio. I spent some six pleasant weeks there. Solari might be described as a hippy architectural guru! His dream was to build a community of earthen structures, constructed by forming hemispheres made of piled dirt, covering them with wire mesh, pouring cement over the dirt, and removing the dirt once the cement had hardened. Voila: a shelter! Since those early days, Solari has acquired a large site, and established a complex; it might be called a commune. He has named it "Arcosanti," a term meant to combine two words: Arcology and Solari. Solari is also well known for bronze and ceramic bells, beautiful in both appearance and tonal quality; the bells have become an important source of income for Solari.

One of the other young architects at the Solari Studio was a Japanese who arrived in Scottsdale to partake in the Studio experience. We became good friends, joining forces to tour together in my increasingly tired Chevy. Our trip was destined to last only a few miles; something happened to cause my car to crash and flip, and we both landed comatose in a Flagstaff hospital. Mrs. Solari came to our rescue, taking the Japanese fellow back to the Studio, and giving me enough money for a Greyhound bus ticket from Arizona back to Washington. Upon arriving in Washington, I rejoined Metcalf – where I stayed for two more years.

Marriage and Children

In mid-1965, my first year back with Metcalf, I met Barbara Peck, the woman destined to become my wife! Born and raised in England, Barbara had come to Washington just a year earlier, and was employed as a secretary by Burlington Textiles. Following a very brief courtship, we two married in the summer of 1965. We had two sons: Justin - born in 1966, and Misha - born in 1970. Justin is a graduate of Kenyon College, works in information technology, and lives in Berkeley. Misha, a graduate of Ripon College, lives in Madison, Wisconsin where he works as a government-relations consultant for insurance companies.

Before my wife came to this country, she had been assistant to the principal of a high school in Yorkshire. Though her parents could not afford to send her to university, she had been encouraged at the school to self-educate, learning to write well-enough to do much of the writing for the principal. When the principal, of whom Barbara was especially fond, contracted Parkinson's and needed to retire, she decided to leave England.

Barbara was a good wife and mother. I took pride in her ability to recite many of Shakespeare's plays. During our marriage, she picked up piano again and taught herself French, well enough to read French newspapers and novels by Colette. Our marriage was on the whole a good one. I think that most marriages can be good when there is a resolve to make it so. I have seen some marriages that are held together mostly by the determined efforts of the parties; very few marriages are the product of a magical unending attraction. Sadly, my wife was afflicted, in the early 1990's, with a virulent form of Alzheimer's. Confined in her final two years to a Madison, Wisconsin nursing home, located near our son, Misha. Barbara died in 2003.

Some time after my wife passed away, my step-brother Billy, at one of his traveling exhibits of Chinese children paintings in this country, introduced me to my present companion, Barbara Phillips. Barbara has become an important and valued part of my life. While we do not live together, we have dinner together most days, we travel together, and have a shared social life. That kind of relationship is in some ways easier than marriage. The parties have time and space for personal undertakings, and a sense of freedom denied to couples in a marital relationship. We have managed together to enjoy fully the best of our golden years.

Edward Larrabee Barnes

Upon my departure from Metcalf in 1967, I moved my growing family from Washington, D.C. to New York City, joining Edward Larrabee Barnes, a well-respected firm employing some 60 architects. Specializing in institutional and residential architecture, Barnes had been a student and devotee of Marcel Breuer, the influential Hungarian architect and furniture designer, who taught at the Bauhaus in Germany, and later at Harvard. I was attracted to the Barnes organization by the quality of their recent work, including the design of houses for the Rockefeller family and campus buildings for the State University of New York. Barnes was later awarded the prestigious Gold Medal from the American Institute of Architects for his body of work, putting him in the company of such eminent architects as I.M. Pei and Phillip Johnson.

Ed Barnes was a charming urbane gentleman. His wife Mary was also an architect; she graduated from Cambridge and participated in the Bloomsbury group. In the office Mary was not active in design or business matters, but took interest in knowing every one in the office in a very warm personal manner. Often invited to be on the jury of Yale students' design presentations, Ed and Mary were always mild and encouraging – in contrast to other jurors who tended to intimidate the students. The same attitude extended to the office. During my twenty-five plus years there, I do not recall the office firing anyone. Of course, most of the designers there treated the years as stepping stones to founding their own successful practices.

Just as I joined Barnes, the firm was awarded a major urban development project to be done in Kansas City, Missouri. The project was to take place in an area of Kansas City that had fallen into urban decay. Redevelopment of that area was to center on construction of a large complex next to the administrative and manufacturing headquarters of Hallmark Cards. Anchored by the Hallmark building, the redeveloped area was to include new apartments, hotels, a shopping center, and additional office buildings.

As I took my place at Barnes, I initiated the construction of study-models of the complex. As my proposed plan took shape, Mr. Barnes was impressed. With modifications and improvements by him, the plan was presented and accepted by the client. From that time forward I was the project's main designer, under Barnes. It also served as my ticket to being made an associate in the firm even though I had yet to qualify for an architect's license.

Joyce Hall, Hallmark's founder, had begun his career by selling postcards at the Des Moines train station. In off hours, he penned inspirational phrases on the cards, mostly taken from the bible. The strong demand for "message cards" led eventually to the founding of Hallmark Cards, which became the company we know today.

Other projects of note in which I was involved include an IBM office building and the Asia Society building, both in Manhattan. Our company also worked for Boston Properties on a Manhattan office building, and on the Federal Judiciary Building in Washington, DC. In 1983, I was made the firm's full-partner, and the firm became known as Edward Larrabee Barnes and John M.Y. Lee.

In 1993, Larrabee Barnes and I closed our firm upon his retirement. I then opened a new firm, in my name, partnering with Michael Timchula. My new firm, with a staff of twenty architects and designers, carried forward some of the Barnes-Lee work, and we took on new work for the University of Texas SW Medical campus. Through my step-brother, I learned of some Chinese, educated in America, who had returned to China; that connection brought us a contract to design a headquarters building for the China Merchants Bank in Shenzhen, China. Shenzhen, across the border from Hong Kong, was the first Chinese new economic zone established by Dong Xiao Ping whose economic policies propelled China to its present status. We also won a competition for design of the Citizen Center there, as well as the regional headquarters of Legend, a computer company that eventually took over the IBM personal computer Division.

It had been agreed between my partner Michael and me that as I carried forward our work in China he would find new work for us in the United States. He failed in that effort, and my work was complicated by difficulties getting paid for some of the projects in China. For these and other reasons, our firm was dissolved at the end of 2003. I have continued on a small scale as a design consultant on the University of Texas SW Campus, and to do a very modest amount of teaching, but in essence I am now fully retired.

On Happiness

I think that happiness comes in large measure from acceptance of what life has brought you. It comes too from being moderate in your expectations, and from appreciation of small things. And it comes from a readiness to make something out of little or nothing, of an interest in transforming the ordinary to something special.

My training in art, my Chinese heritage, and possibly the deprivations of my earliest years, may have combined to shape my readiness, even eagerness to embrace and enjoy and love simplicity and moderation. My home is replete with small works of what I call art, things created at no cost and with little elaboration. The window from my small living room looks out at a woodsy hillside. Across the width of that large pane, to a height of 30 inches or so, I have placed an array of dozens of clear plastic cylindrical tennis ball cans. Each can is stuffed with a plastic shopping bag, some red, some blue, some yellow. The effect is colorful, affords a modicum of privacy, and changes as the sunlight changes at different seasons and time of day. Another display on a shelf in my living room comes from a set of cardboard cylinders, one-time centers of paper towels. These paper towel cylinders are each wrapped with a number of rubber bands, many different colors. Simple and visually effective.

I believe that commitment to, and enjoyment of uncomplicated and undemanding things, helps to bring about a sense of ease and openness and serenity in life. Once embarked on this dedication to simplicity, a walk down an urban street can become an adventure as you see intricate patterns and splendor where others might see blight and decay. I think it brings too a sense of respect for people different from me.

Many find happiness and self-respect in the practice of their craft or professions. A life of accomplishment can of course be rewarding. For myself, though I take some pride in my professional and personal accomplishments, I see all of that as a fleeting thing. Some who achieve success in business can be mired in misery and unhappiness when their child is afflicted with serious illness or their marriage is one of despair and gloom. As I see it, accomplishment aside, if you are happy to be a bum, God bless you!

Religion, War and Technology

On the question of whether or not there is a God, I am agnostic. Because none of us can know whether or not there is a divinity, whether there was a guiding hand in creation of the universe or of earth or human beings, I find it fruitless to contemplate the question. What is, is. What will come after death will come. No amount of study or discussion can bring conclusions or even yield insights. So, to me such questions are of no real interest. I think that religion, and the zealotry that it can bring, has been the cause of much of the conflict among people and among nations.

War has been present in our lives on a more or less continuing basis for much of my lifetime. For what? America's apparent readiness to go to war may result in part from the fact that our homeland has experienced little of the devastation that wars bring.

Most now agree that the wars in Vietnam, Iraq and Afghanistan were tragic mistakes. They were not only futile; worse, they were counterproductive. Many killed, so many more maimed, trillions of dollars wasted. Our infrastructure, education and health care are third rate – even behind some of the developing countries – as we divert energy and funds to building and sustaining a military that Americans proudly and incessantly proclaim as second to none. Again, for what?

Continuous invention and innovation are the motor of western civilization. Progress is what we term it, even though some may argue that on many occasions, they set us back. We are facing the explosion of new digital technology. No one can argue against the wonders of the search engine at one's finger-tips. The same applies to the ease of communication. But it is more than irritating for one to be bombarded with the avalanche of undisciplined social networking.

At an event, even in a classroom, it is not uncommon to note many paying more attention to the gadgets than to the speaker or to each other. On public transportation and in restaurants, one is surrounded by cell phone yakking, not of messages of import but mindless nonsense. Society has yet to apply some rules of civility in dealing with these behaviors. On the more serious front, military industries and establishments are producing ever-more lethal killing tools with new technology. We Americans are still the prime manufacturer and exporter of weaponry. The other puzzle is while a small number of countries are accelerating and prospering, along with the digital revolution, the overwhelming majority of the world has been unable to afford minimum education and food to survive. How are they to catch up? Are we in fact creating another caste system of the haves and have-nots.

Architecture

In 2000, I became a Fellow in the American Institute of Architects. Because I am an architect, and because I think that good design of houses and cities and workplaces affects happiness, productivity, public demeanor and even economic well being, I will close this life essay with some thoughts about architecture.

I consider architecture first and foremost to be a service profession. An architect serves the client by understanding and identifying his/her visions in a clear program. As with a house, the husband's needs and expectations in his experience of the house are different from the wife's. There are variables. Working together with the clients, it takes effort and time for the architect to come up with a comprehensive program that meets the needs and expectations of all concerned. The next step for the architect is to develop models and sketches to test the program. More often than not, the initial program needs to be modified once the client has plans and pictures and models to modify his/her vision. After the schematic design is confirmed, the more technical phases can proceed to deal with such factors as budget, design and construction detail.

Another most important issue, especially in a dense urban area, is how a project relates to the surrounding environment. It is important to have a good master plan to create a larger context and community. I believe that there is a simple reason why we flock to the old cities where there is a visual cohesiveness and a connected life style. There are landmarks with plazas to provide identity and order. Of course there are people who prefer the vibrant chaos of a Times Square. Except for temporary relief, I find it hard to live 24/7 in such an environment. It is also often disconcerting to see structures of different functions having the same visual expression. A museum too often looks the same as a concert hall or even a library. Instead accepting the challenge to express each one's unique story line and interior function, a surface decoration masks all of them. There is often a disconnect between the inside and the outside that disturbs my platonic taste. Or maybe I am still mentally tied to the old principle of "form follows function?"

****

Daryl "Bud" Lembke

Bud Lembke is, at this writing, past 91. With a full head of pepper and salt hair and a jaunty mustache, he looks far younger. More importantly, he has the energy and demeanor of someone still seeking to accomplish new things, to stay active and involved. Child of the depression years, veteran of combat in World War II, accomplished journalist, and a playwright of local renown, Bud remains a force to be reckoned with.

My Background

I was born in 1922, in a farmhouse near Mantorville, population 427, in southeastern Minnesota. My parents divorced when I was a baby; my mother left me with my grand-parents, and soon thereafter moved from Mantorville for a new life in Minneapolis, some 85 miles from our farm, working there as a beauty operator.

I was raised and parented entirely by my grandparents. My father disappeared from our lives; I met him for the first time when I was sixteen, but never during the years of my childhood. I did see my mother periodically. Though I had no siblings, I did have playmates among a number of cousins who lived nearby on adjacent farms.

None of my relatives, including parents and grandparents, had much education. But my grandmother, a good and loving woman, was innately bright, worked diligently beside my grandfather on the many tasks associated with farming, and was renowned for her cooking. Though not well read, she encouraged me to get a good education, to read, and to work toward a better life.

The Great Depression began in 1929 when I was seven years old, and went on until about 1939. So, much of my boyhood took place during those economically bleak years. Unable to keep up with mortgage payments for his small farm, my grandfather lost the farm in the early '30s, causing us to move to a small rental house in Mantorville. Rent for that house was $10 a month. Fortunately, the Social Security Act passed into law in 1935. Those small monthly payments, together with vegetables harvested from the garden my grandmother kept in the yard of our house, kept our three-person family afloat. I remember with great affection my grandmother canning vegetables and storing Mason jars in our basement "fruit cellar." Altogether, I remember my childhood years as happy ones. No big city attractions, but altogether a wholesome and fulfilling boyhood.

My elementary school was a good one. The teachers, as I remember them, were competent. My high school, however, because it was poor and small, did not offer much in the way of science and foreign languages. Teachers carried a double load; for example, the high school football coach taught geography. I remember, however, that we had an excellent English teacher. One good thing about small high schools is that every student got to do everything. I got to play football, though at my weight of 120 pounds, I would never have gotten to play in a big city high school. I also got to act in school plays. My senior class, 29 of us, was the biggest up to that time. We had some smart kids in that class -- I was not the valedictorian or salutatorian; I was a bit lazy, coming in as third or fourth in my class standing, as I remember it.

I should mention that in the summer between junior and senior years, I had no transportation for going on dates – big problem! So I went to nearby Rochester (home of the famed Mayo Clinic) and bought a car for $20, a very used Chevrolet. I drove it home, and my grandparents refused to sign papers permitting me to own and drive the car. I remember going around the house bawling and yelling; my grandfather finally gave in and signed, though he could barely write his name. My dating opportunities immediately improved! Our town had a central telephone system, everyone on the same line. So when anyone of us made a call, all the rest on the line would know about it. This made calling girls for dates a matter for public discussion.

Macalester College

On graduation from high school, in 1940, my grandmother, on whom I relied for guidance in such matters, urged me to get a job at Bohlanders's Department Store, the only "big" store in town. But, somehow, I did aspire to something more. Having saved some $50 from work I had done during summers at nearby farms, and at the local gas station, I enthusiastically reviewed bulletins from various colleges advertising their offerings. One that especially intrigued me was from Macalester College, in St. Paul. Part of the allure was that Macalester was in a large city, a different world. As I remember it, the annual cost, including tuition, board and room, was $600. Though I had only the $50, I applied, got a modest monthly stipend from a youth program, and was given paying jobs at the school - -such as using a stabber to pick up waste paper and other debris on the campus, and cleaning the ice rink. Later, I got a job as night watchman in a wholesale appliance store, which offered a small wage plus a spare room in which I slept. All of this combined to sustain me through my first year, though it slowed my social life pretty much to a halt.

The second year at Macalester, I got a good student job, working for a wealthy family in St. Paul. Their house was just a couple of blocks from the campus. The job, for which I got room and board, plus a monthly stipend of $100, was to serve dinner every day, use the family's station wagon to take the family's four kids to their four different schools every morning, and to clean the house every Saturday. Though the job left little time for social life, there was enough time and flexibility for me to participate at Macalester in band and drama, as well as to carry my full load of sophomore classes. I also worked on the school paper, writing a column on school sports. It was called "Out on a Limb With Lembke."

Macalester has become widely known in recent decades for its program in international affairs. Kofi Annan, former UN Secretary General, is a graduate of Macalester.

Fighting in World War II

World War II started in December 1941, at which time I was midway through my sophomore year at Macalester. I was able to finish my sophomore year, but was drafted into the Army in September 1942.

For reasons unknown to me, I was put into the Medical Corps, and went through Medical Corps basic training at Camp Barkley in Abilene, Texas, learning how to give shots and apply tourniquets, and other medical techniques. Because I was turned off to the idea of dealing with blood, I applied for duty in the Air Corps. Rejected for pilot training, I was placed into training as a radio operator. I might have tried to become a navigator, which would have led to being commissioned as a Second Lieutenant, but my sense of direction is terrible; when I go into my doctor's office I wind up in a broom closet as I try to find my way out! As a radio operator, I rose to the rank of Tech Sergeant.

In mid-1943, I was shipped out to the Air Corps radio school in Sioux Falls, South Dakota. That schooling took about twenty weeks; we learned the Morse Code, and I was taught how to build a radio. I then went to gunnery training in Las Vegas, Nevada, because flight radio-operators were required to man one of the plane's guns during combat.

After that training, I was assigned to a crew; I would be with that same crew throughout my time in the European Theatre. Our plane was a B-17, the famous Flying Fortress. We were sent to Sioux City, Iowa, and trained together. We flew that airplane all over the US, training again and again in every aspect of our operation, bombing mock targets. The crew-training period lasted three months, with our final training at a base in Kearney, Nebraska. All of this training added up to about a year.

In May 1944, we shipped out on a transport ship from Newport News, Virginia. It happens that we arrived in Oran, Algeria, on D-

Day, June 6, 1944. After ten days there, seeing the sights, we were put on another ship, and transported to Naples, Italy, and then by train to Foggia, near where our airbase was located, and at which we were to be based for the rest of our time in the combat theatre. We were in the 15th Air Force, assigned to bomb enemy targets in Southern Europe.

My job, as radio operator, was to stay in radio contact with the base, mainly to receive target updates and to receive recall messages if the weather turned bad over the target area. By this time, mid to late 1944, fighter aircraft opposition had been greatly diminished because the Germans were running out of aircraft fuel. Anti-aircraft fire, often intense, was our main concern. The Germans deployed up to a thousand anti-aircraft batteries at some of the more important targets.

During our bombing missions, our plane was frequently hit by flak; throughout the many years since the war, I have kept a piece of flak that had come close to hitting me. On one mission, to the Hermann Goering Tank Works, in Linz, Austria, an engine on our left side, of which I had a clear view, caught fire. Our pilot was able to feather that engine and the fire died out. However, because that engine was unusable, we fell out of formation and needed to jettison everything loose so that we could limp our way to an emergency field on the island of Yts, off the coast of Yugoslavia. In a kind of party atmosphere, we loosened the nuts and bolts that held the heavy ball turret and succeeded in jettisoning it, and we dumped ammunition and expensive though bulky radio equipment.

On the mission to the Goering Tank Works, our long-time co-pilot had been assigned to another B-17, as a step toward promotion to first pilot. The plane on which he was flying was directly ahead of ours when it received a direct AA hit; the shell exploded inside the plane. Some years after the war, the pilot of that other plane was on a visit to San Francisco, and we had lunch together. He told me that while the explosion had literally blown him out of the plane, he had parachuted safely onto German territory, living the remaining months of the war as a POW. He had, however, before his ejection from the plane, seen that the copilot had been killed instantly and had gone down with the plane with five other crew members.

Our bombing armada would typically consist of up to 500 aircraft, a mix of B-24s and B-17s. Our targets included several missions each to Vienna, Munich, the Ploesti oil fields in Romania, the Tank Works in Linz, Austria, and a place on the German-Polish border at which the Germans were developing synthetic petroleum.

Though our bomb group flew exclusively in B-17s, we never had the same airplane from one mission to the next. Damaged aircraft were quickly repaired, and we started each mission with a plane in good condition.

After flying 50 missions, crews would be returned to the states. "Milk runs" against lightly defended targets, such as railroad marshaling yards and ports would count as one mission. Missions thought to be especially dangerous, such as Ploesti and Munich, would count double. So, at the end, I was credited with 51 missions, but got to that number with only 36 sorties; my 49th mission was against the tough Blechammer artificial fuel plant along the German-Polish border, for which I got double credit. I was sent home in October 1944, having spent only a bit over four months in combat. On coming home, I was assigned to instructor's school in Pueblo, Colorado to teach gunnery on a B-29, a job about which I knew nothing. The B-29 had a gunnery system entirely different from the one we had on the B-17. Before teaching, I had to go through the school myself. The war ended in August 1945, and I was released from the Army in October.

The bombing experiences were easily the most suspenseful and dramatic of my long life. Fear gripped me from head to toe on some of our missions. To see the sky ahead black with little clouds of exploding AA shells as we approached "bombs away" and knew that we had to go through that was bad enough. Then the flak kept peppering our plane, making sounds like a shower of little pebbles striking the tin roof of a house. No place to run or hide! In 1997, I self-published a 186-page book, "Ups and Downs in a Flying Fortress," about my war experiences. It sold about 900 copies. I have, however, recently reissued it.

One of our crew-members, a waist gunner, came out to the plane for our mission one morning and just could not force himself to climb aboard. It would have been his 41st mission. He was sent to the flight surgeon, who authorized his return to the United States for treatment of battle fatigue. I quoted in my book a statement from a good buddy of his, our crew's tail gunner: "I could see that {fatigue} building up in him for a month before he actually blew his stack....We had just got back from another mission. He had been so nervous at debriefing. I can see it now. He was smoking a cigarette. His hands were shaking so badly that he could hardly guide the cigarette to his mouth. On the way back to our squadron from group headquarters, I kept asking him, 'Are you sick?' He kept saying, "'I'm all right. I'm all right.'"

My combat had far less risk than those experienced in Air Corps actions at other places and in earlier periods of the war. Not to mention the Army infantrymen who underwent long stretches in combat in often miserable conditions. But my relief knew no boundaries when I reached that 51st mission and could go home.

Finding My Way After the War

Upon release from the Army, in October 1945, I enrolled at the University of Minnesota, staying only for a quarter. My mother was living in Los Angeles, and because we had maintained a relationship, I decided to move to California. I was able to get into Stanford, but stayed there for only three months because some of my earlier college transcripts could not be transferred to Stanford.

The GI Bill was great for financing the last two years of my college work. Because I was in a hurry to graduate and get out into the world, I transferred back to Minnesota, graduating in 1947 with a degree in "radio-speech." I had hoped to become a radio announcer, but getting a job proved to be difficult. Still using the GI Bill, I enrolled for what turned out to be a short time in a summer-theatre school in Rhode Island. I then went back to Los Angeles to live with my mother, enrolling in the Pasadena Playhouse for more training as an actor. That lasted two weeks, at which point I finally realized that finding a career in theater was going to be a long shot for me.

For about a year I worked as an "investigator" for a retail credit company, going door-to-door in LA neighborhoods getting information on people applying for insurance. My job was to ask friends and neighbors whether the applicant was reliable. I was scheduled to do sixteen of these reports every day! Most of my colleagues were faking the answers, generally asking the subject, rather than neighbors, to get enough material to fill in the report and to have something to turn in. I soon realized that that career too was not one for me.

Finally, the Job of My Dreams

My next job was as a reporter for a small semi-weekly newspaper in Santa Ana, California, in the center of Orange Country. I worked there for a year, and went on to a number of other newspapers in southern California. Finally, in 1959, I was able to land a job with the *Los Angeles Times*, the job of my dreams! I started as a general assignment reporter, working the night shift from 3 to 11 p.m., covering crime, fires and local events. The daytime crew generally covered the big stories, but on occasion I would get to do follow-up work in a story that was being worked on by one of the paper's senior reporters.

My timing was good. The *LA Times* was just beginning, in the late 1950s, to move upward as a national newspaper; it aspired to be on a par with the *New York Times,* the *Chicago Tribune* and the *Washington Post.* The *LA Times* had been ultra conservative under Norman Chandler, its long-time publisher, but the tide turned when his son, Otis, took the reins. Otis Chandler was determined to make the paper's news and columns politically neutral, and to report the news objectively and honestly. Otis sought quality journalists, and began to establish bureaus in important places around the country and the world.

Though most of my reporting during the first year or so with the *LA Times* was of relatively insignificant events, I was able to do a couple of important stories. In early 1961, I was assigned to our bureau in Sacramento, the state capital. My principal job in Sacramento was to cover the California state senate; two other reporters in our bureau covered other important branches of the state government. These were exciting years in our state's governance. Jess Unruh was speaker of the state assembly. Pat Brown was Governor. And they were frequently at odds with one another.

After I had been in the Sacramento bureau for some 18 months, Otis Chandler and his editors decided that the *LA Times* needed a bureau in the Bay Area, and in August 1963 I was appointed San Francisco Bureau Chief –- though there were no Indians! In that capacity, I covered not only the Bay Area, but also all of northern California and as far north as Oregon and Washington. I foraged far and wide, even doing stories from Hawaii and Alaska, neither of which had a bureau. I did several major stories from Canada.

I was with the *LA Times* San Francisco Bureau for 13 years, and in 1976 was transferred back to the LA area, assigned to report on politics in Orange County. This was presented to me as a special challenge; the *Times* was seeking to expand its Orange County section, to in effect create a newspaper to compete with the Register, then the dominant paper in the Orange County area.

While in San Francisco, I had gone through a divorce. On phone calls daily to my boss in LA, I talked to Mary Theisen, an attractive and intelligent executive secretary in the LA Times offices. Because Mary was 20 years younger than I was, it took time before I worked up the nerve to ask her for a date. She did, however, accept a dinner invitation, and we have just celebrated our 38th wedding anniversary. Mary had been with the *LA Times* for a short time; most of her career had been in teaching, a career that she returned to upon our marriage.

I have a daughter, Nancy, from my earlier marriage. Nancy lives in Oakland, with my grandson.

A Newspaper of My Own

I had long aspired to own and operate a small newspaper of my own. So, in 1980, I took early retirement from the giant *LA Times* and started a small weekly newspaper in Dana Point, California. My wife, Mary, who was teaching in a special needs school at that time, wrote a cooking column for the paper; her column was probably read more widely than the general interest column I wrote. The paper, which was dedicated exclusively to coverage of local issues and events, was distributed free to all residents; circulation was about 8,000.

There had been a housing boom in Orange County, leading us to hope for a strong revenue stream from real estate advertisements. Our timing, however, was terrible. Because mortgage interest rates had risen by 1981 to as much as 16%, the housing market collapsed, as did our revenue from that market. We gave the paper up after about 18 months, selling the business to our advertising director. The loss to us was about $100,000, which wiped out our savings.

We moved back to San Francisco, and then to Sacramento, where we spent 22 years. In 1985, I started writing the *Political Pulse,* the "Newsletter of California Politics and Government." I did all the work on it for about five years, after which I took on an editorial partner. The annual subscription rate for the newsletter was $85 at the start, rising over time to $285; it came out every two weeks to about 600 paid subscribers. I worked on that newsletter until 2005, at which time my partner and I sold the business.

My Life Now

I am now, in 2014, well past 91 years old. Life remains good, but there are changes that have come with the advancing years. I find myself now being typecast by younger people, patronized by some and treated with special kindness by others. I am from a different world from the young, particularly in computers and entertainment. We have different interests in television, music, magazines and books. As a younger man, I watched all of the weekly TV shows -- and now the current crop bores me. I watch none of it. The computer world has left me behind. I do write emails and look at the *Sacramento Bee* on the computer.

My days remain full. Some years ago I turned to playwriting, and I like to spend an hour each day on that. Two of my plays have been produced as readings here in Rossmoor, and I am currently rewriting a third. I was, for a time, on the board of the Drama Association of Rossmoor, an organization that I helped found. I get up at 6:45 every morning. We get three newspapers: the *Contra Costa Times*, the *San Francisco Chronicle,* and the *New York Times.* I take a fitness class three days a week at our Fitness Center; it starts at 8:45 in the morning. Mary and I go often to see plays, in San Francisco and Berkeley, as well as locally. Our schedule has been on hold in recent months because of Mary's serious illness, but she is now pretty much on the mend, and we have moved back from a care facility to our condo in Rossmoor.

I think the key to happiness is learning. It is a joy for me to learn new things, which happens every day when reading my newspapers and books, and in doing research for my playwriting. We are especially blessed here with the many museums and our parks -- all of these provide learning opportunities. I continue somehow to be driven to create, to accomplish new things. Retirement has a bad connotation. I confess that the fear of dying hangs over me now. I don't fear the prospect of a painful death, because medicine can abate that. I don't really fear death so much as I regret that I will not be here to see the future, to see what promising things pan out and which challenges, like global warming, do not.

The hard part is leaving everything behind. Leaving my wife and my friends will be terrible. I would like to know who will be elected president in 25 years, and because I am now 91, I will not know that. I assume that in 25 years most cars will be electric. I would like to see that. I think we will one day have high-speed rail in California. I will miss seeing that. The future will be wholly lost to me. I regret that more than anything.

I did once believe in an afterlife, one that would enable me to look down from heaven to see how things develop. I no longer believe in any kind of afterlife. I no longer believe in the power of prayer. I now think it is over when we die. I do continue to have some notion that there might have been a master planner of the universe. It is all so wonderful and amazing that it seems to me unlikely that it just happened, without an architect and without a builder. I respect people who have a faith, and I respect those who do not. For myself, I am simply not sure, one way or the other. That philosophy fits in with the Unitarian Universalist church to which I belong.

I do wish I had more time to read books. I devote about an hour a day to reading, and that is simply not enough. There is so much available to read. The *New Yorker* magazine alone, if I were to read it thoroughly, would take all the time I have.

I have been a little lazy from time to time in my life, but always had ambition and big dreams. One, for example, was to go to college when it was rare for those in the little town where I grew up, and when I had no money to finance it. I was always ambitious to move onward and upward in my newspaper career. And I was rewarded when the *Los Angeles Times* assigned me to some big stories.

Covering Bobby Kennedy in the final two weeks of his presidential campaign was a career milestone –- though it ended so tragically when I phoned the City Desk to report that he had been shot following his victory speech at the Ambassador Hotel in Los Angeles.

Doing an "enterprise story" for the *Times* was another career milestone: I had discovered while reporting from Fairbanks, Alaska that a private pilot who flew polar bear hunters in northern Alaska had built a home and a little airport halfway between remote Barrow and the remote North Slope, and was living at the top of the world with his family. He was unreachable by phone, so I gambled that he would be there, spent $8,000 of the *Times* money to rent a private plane and pilot, and flew to this isolated site. Luck arrived, as it has many times in my life. He was there with his wife. After a two-hour interview, I flew back to Fairbanks and wrote a story that made Page One of *The Times*

And then there was playwriting, which I began doing many years ago while still at the *Times* San Francisco Bureau. The results were pitiful, but I remained an aspiring playwright. I have improved after taking numerous classes and by bowing to Mary's painful (to me) but productive editing. My most recent play, "Arthritis be Damned," drew 300 people at three readings held in the Mount Diablo Unitarian Universalist Church, in Walnut Creek. It was a parody about a 9,000 resident retirement community, like Rossmoor, where we live. No one toilet-papered the flowering tree at our front door, in protest, even though the play poked fun at some of the failings of life in this beloved place where we live. As I said, I'm a very lucky guy, in finding Mary those many years ago and for many other joys of this life.

****

Burma Shave: Memories Of an Earlier America

THE BEARDED LADY – TRIED A JAR – SHE'S NOW – A FAMOUS - MOVIE STAR – BURMA SHAVE. Most of us of a "certain age" will recognize this great little verse as a Burma Shave message.

Beginning in 1925, pre-turnpike highway roadsides across the nation were dotted with sets of signs intended to sell Burma Shave, a brushless shaving cream. Eventually, there were some 7,000 sets of Burma Shave signs. In 1963, most of the signs were taken down – but a few remain, even today. The signs were ubiquitous during the early years of many of the men who tell their life stories in this book, and are a memorable part of the America of that time.

Those who founded Burma Shave needed a way to bring the merits of their new product to the shaving public. Because the introduction of Burma Shave coincided with the growing use of automobiles, the notion of roadside signs was adopted. The formula was both simple and unique to the world of advertising: place six consecutive signs, about 100 paces apart. The consecutive signs, each with just a few words, commanded the attention of those reading them longer than any single sign could ever hope to do.

After a time, drivers looked forward to seeing them. The humorous signs helped make long journeys more entertaining, and people became addicted to reading them. By having the rhymes build suspense until the punch line, always carried on the fifth sign, Burma Shave forced those reading the signs to focus their attention on the full series of signs so that the message could be understood and savored like a good joke.

The signs proved to be so successful that Burma Shave was one of the few American companies that sailed unscathed through the years of the great depression. Here are a few of my favorites, taken in part from a book by Frank Rowsome, called *The Verse by the Side of the Road:*

USE THIS CREAM – A DAY - OR TWO – DON'T CALL HER – SHE'LL CALL YOU – BURMA SHAVE

EVERY SHAVER – NOW CAN SNORE – SIX MORE MINUTES – THAN BEFORE – BY USING - BURMA SHAVE

WIITHIN THIS VALE – OF TOIL AND SIN – YOUR HEAD GROWS BALD – BUT NOT YOUR CHIN - USE – BURMA SHAVE

SHE RAISED CAIN – WHEN HE RAISED STRUBBLE – GUESS WHAT – SMOOTHED AWAY – THEIR TROUBLE – BURMA SHAVE

HENRY THE EIGHTH – PRINCE OF FRISKERS – LOST FIVE WIVES – BUT KEPT – HIS WHISKERS – BURMA SHAVE

BIG MISTAKE – MANY MAKE – USE THE HORN – INSTEAD OF – THE BRAKE – BURMA SHAVE

SLEEP IN A CHAIR – NOTHING TO LOSE – BUT A NAP – AT THE WHEEL – IS A PERMANENT SNOOZE – BURMA SHAVE

IF YOU THINK – SHE LIKES – YOUR BRISTLES – WALK BAREFOOTED – THROUGH SOME THISTLES – BURMA SHAVE

SHE EYED - HIS BEARD – AND SAID NO DICE – THE WEDDING'S OFF – I'LL COOK THE RICE – BURMA SHAVE

WHY DOES A CHICKEN – CROSS THE STREET – SHE SEES A GUY – SHE'D LIKE TO MEET – HE USES – BURMA SHAVE

WHEN THE STORK - DELIVERS A BOY - OUR WHOLE - DARN FACTORY - JUMPS FOR JOY - BURMA SHAVE

IF YOUR PEACH – KEEPS OUT – OF REACH – BETTER PRACTICE – WHAT WE PREACH – BURMA SHAVE

THIRTY DAYS – HATH SEPTEMBER – APRIL, JUNE – AND THE – SPEED OFFENDER – BURMA SHAVE

A CHIN - WHERE BARBED WIRE - BRISTLES STAND - IS BOUND TO BE - A NO MA'AMS LAND - BURMA SHAVE

PAST SCHOOLHOUSES - TAKE IT SLOW - LET THE LITTLE - SHAVERS - GROW - BURMA-SHAVE

MANY A FOREST - USED TO STAND – WHERE A - LIGHTED MATCH - GOT OUT OF HAND - BURMA SHAVE

During the 1950's, sales of Burma Shave began to decline, perhaps because cars were driving faster and country roads had become turnpikes. The once-beloved signs were no longer effective in attracting customers, so in the early sixties, the decision was made by American Safety Razor Products, the new owner of Burma Shave, to remove them.

A piece of 20th Century Americana has been lost. By posting here just a few of the Burma Shave verses, we can document and be reminded of something that once provided amusement and a sense of community to those of us who lived during those earlier times.

****

Benjamin Slomoff

Having recently celebrated his 100th birthday, Ben Slomoff continues to this day to do important work in arbitration of financial disputes. After a highly remunerative life in various aspects of the shoe business, Ben decided at age 79 that it was time to go to college, earning first a BS in Urban Studies, then an MS in Conflict Resolution. He served during World War II, in the Air Force, rising to the rank of Lt. Colonel. Just before this writing, Ben published his first book of poetry. He is at work on the second.

My Background

I was born in 1913, in Pittsburgh, Pennsylvania, the second child of six. My parents were both immigrants from Lithuania. My mother came to America at age 16; my father was 19. Both arrived around 1900, and settled in western Pennsylvania. They arrived here separately, met in this country, and married at a young age. Neither of them could speak English on arrival, but they soon adapted to the American culture and learned enough English to get by. It was a good marriage; they loved each other deeply.

My parents' income was meager, but in time they had saved enough to enable them to buy a very basic house. We had a large extended family living nearby; my father had a number of sisters, all of whom had come to America soon after my father did. He had a brother, too, who died in an accident soon after arriving here.

My father did various things to earn a living for his growing family. He bought a horse and wagon, selling fruit and vegetables along a route in our town. My mother did sewing in a garment factory. During the years of my childhood, we lived in New Kensington, Pennsylvania.

When I was five years old, my father was badly injured in an accident; a streetcar ran into his horse-drawn cart, killing the horse and severely injuring my father. The injury required him to be hospitalized for an extended period, and left him a lifelong cripple. The accident brought us a small monetary settlement, enough to make it possible for my parents to buy several modest rental properties which provided a small income.

My mother found it necessary during my father's hospitalization to place me and my two siblings (there were three children at that time) with various relatives. I spent a period of several months living with my grandparents, nearby. Though my grandmother was a sweet person, my grandfather was a religious orthodox zealot. He was a difficult person, one who especially disliked children. My grandfather took no interest in my presence, spending his days reading the Torah and praying. I slept in a cold room, on a cot, and developed a lasting fear of being deserted. That episode was for me an unhappy one; memories of it are still painful.

As a child, I liked to read. I was, however, a bored student. School never interested me. My high school years were a total disaster; I hated everything about it. Because I read so widely, however, I was self-educated. I found the school's curriculum boring, and beneath me. The teachers were second-rate political appointees.

I graduated from high school in 1931, at the age of 18, in the midst of the Great Depression. There were few jobs for adults, and virtually none for youngsters; wages were very low for the few jobs available. I did manage to get a job jerking sodas at the local drug store, working from 8 am to 4 pm and from 4 pm to midnight on alternate days. Sundays I worked all day. My weekly total wage was seven dollars. To supplement that, my brothers and I went to the local golf club to seek jobs as caddies. For 18 holes, carrying bags for two golfers, we would get 75 cents.

Getting into the Shoe Business

Those were bleak times for all of us. But I had dreams, one of which was to become a journalist. I enrolled at the University of Pittsburgh -- lasting only half a semester before I ran out of money. For the next few years I worked at a variety of jobs, doing menial work. Through my brother, who was working in a shoe store, I was introduced to a sales representative of the Brown Shoe Company; that led to my getting a job as the Sales Rep's assistant. The arrangement was for me to help on weekends in Brown's hotel-based showroom. There was no cash pay, but he offered me three meals on both weekend days. I took an interest in the shoe business, and learned a great deal about it during my weekend work in the showroom. That seemingly inauspicious and unpromising job was to become a major turning point in my life. It was now 1935; I was 22 years old.

One day, a Brown sales executive came from the St. Louis headquarters to visit our showroom, and after some discussion I was invited to come to Brown headquarters in St. Louis to enroll in company's one-year-long training program. That program would give me insight into every part of the business: manufacturing, purchasing, credit, sales and more. There was no salary, but I was to be provided a small hotel room in which to stay, and all meals. I jumped to accept the offer, and was given a first-class train ticket on the Spirit of St. Louis, a ticket I promptly cashed in and exchanged for a coach ticket, pocketing the $45 difference, more money that I had ever seen! This experience began in 1936; I was 23 by then.

The training program, for a large group of trainees, began on my first day in town. Each of us was asked which department we would like to begin in. I asked for the Sample Room, which turned out to be the best decision I ever made! That room was the place to which the company's salesmen would come to see what was available, and where deals were made. I quickly learned about the various styles, what sold, where discounts were given, and was after a time able to provide suggestions to the visiting sales reps. From them, I learned the shoe business from the sales point of view. At the end of our year of training, there were only a few of us left from the original group of trainees. Soon after completion of the training program, in early 1938, I was hired by Brown as a salesman, and assigned a territory that centered on Detroit. I was given an office and a weekly drawing account of $75, an enormous sum in those days.

Marriage and Kids

Before exploring further my business career and my later education, let me speak about my marriage and kids. I met Sylvia, my wife, in 1932, at a party to which we had both been invited. I was 18 at the time, she was 16. We were immediately attracted to each other, began dating, and were committed to each other from that point forward. Our marriage needed to be delayed until we could afford family life, and until Sylvia completed her education. As my job with Brown Shoes became increasingly successful, and after Sylvia graduated from Indiana State Teachers College, we got married. The year was 1938; Sylvia was 23 - I was 25. Her family had purchased a large farm where we lived for a time while I recovered from an earlier automobile accident.

On graduation from Indiana State Teachers College, in 1936, Sylvia took a job in Washington as secretary to the head of Social Security. Sylvia was very bright, an accomplished potter, and an artistic craftsman, making baskets and other objects. She loved to play cards and liked to gamble. Despite her many accomplishments, she was extremely shy, always diverting attention from herself. In the early 1960s, because I was doing so much traveling for business, Sylvia went back to school, this time as a grandmother, to get a degree in speech therapy. She graduated as valedictorian. After winning that degree, from Emerson College in Boston, she practiced at Mass General Hospital for a while, before we moved to California.

Our first child, Judith, had been born in 1941, the year I went into the Army. Judith, always a good student, graduated from Sarah Lawrence, where she majored in education, going on to work for some years as a teacher. She soon met and married a young Yale graduate, and moved to Washington where her new husband worked for the Department of Transportation. They had two sons, now grown; one became a banker and the other a physician. But that marriage ended in divorce, upon which Judith returned to school. She got a Masters Degree in Journalism, which earned her a job with the Washington-based National Geographic Magazine. After some difficult years as a single mom, Judith remarried, this time to a solicitor in England, who had come to Washington on assignment. Upon arriving in London, Judith went on to more schooling, studying psychotherapy. She worked for many years as a psychotherapist in a London hospital. Judith, now 72, will retire this year.

My son, Mark, was born in 1946, while I was still in the service. Most of his early schooling was at St. Luke's, a prep school in New Canaan, Connecticut. He did his undergraduate work at Cornell, and continued through Medical School at Down State Medical University in Brooklyn, He did his internship in New York City, and went on to a residency in San Francisco. Together with a fellow physician, Mark ran the Haight-Ashbury Free Clinic for several years. He then joined the staff of John Muir Hospital, in Walnut Creek, where he has for many years been a senior E.R. Doctor. Mark's wife, Dorothy, is an ObGyn Physician in San Francisco. They have four grown children, one a filmmaker, one a medical research assistant, one now in medical school at Berkeley, and one an equestrian.

My Years in the Military

While living in Detroit, I had learned about an officer training program then being conducted by the Army. It was mostly book learning, requiring only one day a week (every Saturday) of actual military duty. Much of it involved the trigonometry associated with artillery firing. Having never mastered trig in high school, I found it difficult. During this time, Sylvia remained at her job in Washington, so I would send her the math problems by mail; she was able quickly to solve them, and by return mail got the answers to me in time for my next Saturday session. In early 1941, I was commissioned as a Second Lieutenant in the Army Reserves, and very shortly thereafter was called to active duty, and assigned to the Quartermaster Corps.

I was sent to Maxwell Field, an Army Air base in Montgomery, Alabama. After a very short time there, I was transferred to Dothan, Alabama. My job there was to help the Army Corps of Engineers build a new airfield that was to be made available for training of British pilots. On arrival in Dothan, I was transferred from the Quartermaster Corps to the Corps of Engineers, and received promotion to First Lieutenant. After the Dothan work was well advanced, many of the more senior Corps of Engineers officers were transferred to other construction projects, and I wound up being responsible for the project. That job called for a Captain, so I was promoted yet again.

In 1942, it was decided to break the Air Corps away from the Army, and to create a new branch of service, the United States Air Force. I was transferred back to Montgomery, this time as Assistant Chief of Staff to the Commanding General of Maxwell Field. I was responsible for managing support facilities for the Southwest Training Center, which managed a number of USAF training bases. By this time I had been promoted to the rank of Major. In 1946, I left the active service as a Lieutenant Colonel, and went into the Air Force Reserve where I stayed for 16 more years.

Back to the Shoe Business

After leaving the service, I planned to go into the construction business with my brother, Jerry. I had accumulated some cash, as had my brother. He and I drove together to Los Angeles, where we were joined by a third partner, a friend of my brother. To get started, we bought a hardware store. That proved to be a bad idea; we discovered too late that neither one of us was interested in running that store.

After leaving military service, I had written to the Brown Shoe Company telling them that I would not be returning to them. Just after realizing that the hardware store venture had been a mistake, I got a letter from Brown acknowledging my resignation letter, but inviting me nonetheless to come to St. Louis at their expense to discuss a possible arrangement with them. I accepted their invitation.

On my visit, Brown offered to rehire me as a sales representative. The lure was twofold: I was offered the relatively lucrative

Philadelphia territory, and the offer included consignment to me of a very large quota of shoes. The quota allocation was especially important, because shoes, like many other commodities, had been rationed during the war years and shoe retailers were for some years after the war hungry for new shoes to put on their shelves. For these and other reasons, I agreed to Brown's offer. The year was 1948.

By judicious allotment of quotas to my territory's top shoe retailers, I was able in a very short time to sell my full allotment of shoes. I did set aside 1000 pairs, and offered them to a small department store that theretofore had not sold shoes. This arrangement was dependent on the condition that they allow me to set up and operate a shoe department on their premises, giving them a share of the profits.

My brothers, who had also just recently come out of military service, asked me to join with them in buying and operating a small chain of shoe stores. The store for which my younger brother had been working was part of the chain we sought to buy. I bought a 25% interest in the company. That proved to be a good deal; the chain expanded rapidly, and was soon worth far more than we had paid for it. As all of this was happening, I was asked by the Brown Company to transfer to New York and to take over that territory. I agreed to do that on the condition that Brown would give me the right to retain my key accounts in Philadelphia. They agreed.

Upon arriving in New York, I found that Gimbel's was selling a variety of shoe lines. On approaching them, I proposed to provide them with a quota of some 100,000 pairs of shoes if they would agree to make Brown shoes their standard line. Acting on that arrangement, Gimbel's opened a shoe department in a top spot on their first floor. I made similar arrangements with leading shoe sellers in Brooklyn and on Long Island.

After many years, the management at Brown Company was changing in ways that I did not find acceptable. I had heard about a small shoe factory, called Milford Shoes, in Milford, Massachusetts, that was looking for someone to run it. I told them that I would do that if they would sell me a 25% interest in the company.

After a rocky start with Milford, I was approached by the Melville Shoe Company and contracted to build their line of casual shoes for the next season. Later they asked me to build their new line of Hush Puppies. My son Mark, who was at the time a college student traveling in England, sent me a letter urging that I should build "Beetle Boots," then the rage in England. We did that, and they proved to be increasingly popular as the Beetles became a sensation in this country.

Milford Shoes flourished, so much so that the majority owners decided to sell the company. After long, complicated and often acrimonious discussions, the company was sold to Morse Shoes., a very large nationwide shoe retailer. The majority owners got cash for their share, and I got the equivalent of my share in the form of equity in Morse Shoes, a much larger company. I continued to run Milford Shoes, for some ten years, with Morse now both my boss and my major customer. For Milford, I began to outsource some of our shoe manufacturing to Romania and Taiwan, thereby enabling me to diversify and bring our prices down.

After retirement from Milford Shoe, in 1983, at age 70, I became a consultant to Morse. Because that job turned out to be both uninteresting and undemanding, I soon resigned to start my own consulting business for the shoe industry, doing that until 1991.

College at 79, a New Career in Arbitration, and a Spot on TV

In 1992, I enrolled as a student, at age 79, at the University of Massachusetts. I was able to enroll as a junior because the University gave me credit for life-experience and for extension courses I had taken at Harvard. I graduated in 1994 with a BS in Urban Development, and went on, still at UMass, to get a Masters Degree in Conflict Resolution, graduating in 1997. That Masters degree launched my career in arbitration, something that I still do now, at the age of 100. Most of my arbitration work has to do with resolution of financial disputes for the New York Stock Exchange, NASDAQ, and the Financial Institution Regulatory Administration.

For my master's thesis in conflict resolution, I was assigned by Boston's mayor to the Boston Redevelopment Association as a mediator for the air rights over the Massachusetts Turnpike, as part of the famous Big Dig. Mayor Menino rewarded me for my contribution by establishing a "Ben Slomoff Day," and awarding me a commemorative inscription designating me as an Honorary Bostonian, no matter where I lived.

As I was about to graduate from my Master's Program, NBC was doing a special program on Adult Education. I was by far the oldest person then enrolled at UMass, so was asked to participate in the NBC program. That led to interviews and videotaping at various places on the UMass campus. Later, in class, to my great surprise, the NBC crew, with two reporters, came into the classroom, a complete surprise to me, to tape part of the ongoing class session. They had of course made prior arrangements to do that, of which I had not been told. One of the students, a pretty blond girl, was asked her thoughts about being in class with a man old enough to be her grandfather. She answered with a smile: "Who?" A perfect response! The entire tape was shown on NBC that night.

A Poetic Side, Too

My lifelong interest in literature led me in recent years to a special interest in poetry. I have now, for some years, been writing poems, publishing just last year a book of my recent writings. I am working on a new collection, and am hoping soon to publish my second book of poems. I like to describe my poems as "narrative poetry." They are meant to tell stories about my life, my wife, my mother, and my friends. A poem of which I take particular pride is called "War Shadow." I include it here:

Why are those dark clouds
Obscuring our golden daffodils
Making our new day gloomy?

A long bleak winter we've survived;
Nature has signaled
Welcome spring is on the way. The message seems clear
Warm happy sunny days are near.

Yet, shadows, ominous shadows appear.
Though one war has ended,
Another goes on endlessly.

The news is bleak; maimed and
Wounded soldiers are returning.

Have we lost interest?
Or are we so self-absorbed
That we deny brutal war exists?

The Rewards of Marriage

Let me return briefly to my life with Sylvia. It was successful, due in large part to her competency in managing our household, especially with our children. As we age, as our marriage evolves into an ever-closer partnership. I completely respected Sylvia's business judgment, especially in home buying.

Our life together was a long one, and a strong one, beginning in our teens and lasting through our 69-year marriage. Sylvia died in 2007; she was 92. I miss her.

We were both always active and involved during those long years together. Even now, at 100, I continue to work as an arbitrator and mediator. I could have retired long ago, but would find life dull without the stimulation that comes from the demanding work I do. It is not full-time, but it keeps me engaged in life. I still have a sense of ambition and am driven to do meaningful things.

In addition to continued involvement, I think that the secret to continuing happiness is being happy in yourself, accepting yourself for who and what you are. You need to be honest with yourself. Look in the mirror and know that this is who I am. As we age, we need to reinvent ourselves, not by becoming someone else, but by acquiring new skills and new interests. My mother, who was a very able person, used to tell me that her mind had worn out four bodies! Same for me!

Having been born in 1913, we of course had no telephone, no radio, and no cars during the very early stages of my life. The explosion of technology since then has changed the world. Mostly for the better, I think, certainly better in terms of creature comforts such as central heating, indoor plumbing, automobiles, jet planes and antibiotics, to mention just a few. But the price we pay for all of this is a kind of loneliness and self-isolation. Far too many people would rather watch TV or send text messages than engage in extended conversation. Endless TV cable news has played a role in creating and sustaining political warfare.

I helped Sylvia write her valedictory speech when she got her second degree, as a grandmother. We wrote something to the effect that *"Our education has been designed to **make** a living. What we need too is education **for** living."* What we meant by that is that our society has not solved the human equation. Speaker Tip O'Neal, from Massachusetts, was fond of saying that all politics begins at home. Yes, but we have not produced a body-politic that yields policies devised to improve everyday lives. National security has less to do with NATO than it does with high quality urban transportation, good schools, full employment, safe streets and beautiful parks.

Views about the Future

I have two views about the future, one positive and one negative. On the downside, unless the American political divide is somehow bridged, we face a continuing decline in our ability to deal with issues important to the country. An obsolete and inadequate infrastructure is having a growing impact on our global competitiveness. My biggest concern is climate change. Oceans will rise and coastal cities will shrink or even disappear under the encroaching oceans.

On the upside, the demographic changes underway in our country will change the political landscape to one in which progressives will have the opportunity to devise and pass progressive legislation needed to bring our country into the 21st century, to end senseless militarism, and create an America of great cities. All of this will require several terms of Democratic Presidents, Democratic majorities in the House and Senate, and a post-Scalia/Thomas/Alioto/Roberts Supreme Court.

When I was in the military, we were instructed that war results from the breakdown of diplomacy. Wars today seem to no longer be between states. Rather, they are conflicts among small splinter groups. Mostly, it seems, the small but very hot wars of today result from deeply felt hatreds between religious groups. In our lifetime, religion has ceased being a positive force; it is now a negative one.

A Personal Summing Up

But, putting aside these monumentally important issues, my life has on the whole been blessed. It has been, and remains, a good life. One of the accomplishments in which I take special pride is my decision to return to school in 1992, at age 79, and to stay with it through the Masters degree, awarded in 1997. I am now on the Board of Overseers of the University of Massachusetts, the school from which I received those two degrees. Sylvia and I endowed a Visiting Professorship at UMass, in which we subsidize annual lectures by a distinguished persons Last year, for example, we brought former Senator George Mitchell to the school to deliver a lecture and talk with students and faculty about his experiences as US Special Envoy, first to Ireland and then the Middle East.

Speaking of books, I am reminded of some years during the mid-sixties when I taught a weekly Great Book course to a group of 45 prisoners in the Danbury Federal Penitentiary, in Danbury, Connecticut. This was during the time that my family and I lived in nearby Westport. Because Danbury Penitentiary was a prison for people convicted of white-collar crimes, most of the prisoners had been found guilty of such crimes as fraud. My group of 45 included lawyers, CPAs and other educated people--though a few had been imprisoned for drug-related crimes. For all of them, these Great Book discussions became important. We met every Saturday afternoon, entering into spirited discussions about the many books we dealt with.

I know that courses like this are done too for hardened criminals, and they might be of even greater importance in helping to refocus the lives of people who had somehow gotten themselves into trouble. For me, the experience was enriching and informative. I remain a proponent of the Great Books series for every reader.

I have always read a great deal. Even now, I want to expand and enrich my knowledge. I seek to learn new things every day. Here I am, now 100 years old. I do think often that the end is near. I have, as we all must, come to terms with it. My greatest fear is not dying - it is being buried alive. I have instructed my son, Mark, a physician, to be absolutely sure that I am dead before action is taken on the disposal of my body. I will be cremated, not buried. I do not believe in an afterlife. This is it. One life and when it's over it's over. I do think about it, we all do, but you can't do a damn thing about it. So we accept the inevitability.

For the past four years I have been blessed with a warm companionship. For several years after Sylvia's death I spent many lonely nights. Then I met Rheta Daggs, who not only filled a void, but energized me to experience many new pleasures. Though we live apart, we've enjoyed dining, theatre arts, movies, dancing and even a wonderful cruise to Alaska together. During my recent illness, Rheta was not only supportive but inspiring. She has become important to my life. How fortunate I have been to find and hold such a wonderful person as a close and loving companion.

****

Otto Schnepp

Uniquely interesting, quietly modest, and extraordinarily wise, Otto Schnepp was born and raised in Vienna, Austria. At age 13, he and his family fled the brutality of Nazi occupation and the onset of the Holocaust, emigrating from Austria to Shanghai. Coming to the U.S. in 1948 for graduate school at Berkeley, Otto went on to become a professor of chemistry, first at Israel's Technion, and later at the University of Southern California, Los Angeles.

The Early Years

Born in 1925, in Vienna, I was just 13 years old when in March 1938 Germany announced its "Anschluss" with Austria, annexing Austria into a "greater" Germany. In August 1938, to escape the encroaching Holocaust, my sister, Herta, then 16, was sent to live with an uncle in Kenya. My parents left for China in November 1938, and, by prearrangement, I joined my parents in January 1939. Our small family settled into the International Settlement of Shanghai, where we were to remain for the next nine years, living mostly in abject poverty, in a series of rented rooms with shared kitchens and bathrooms.

Shanghai during those years housed a considerable number of Jewish immigrants from Europe, mostly Jews fleeing Hitler's Nazism. Earlier in the century a sizeable Jewish community had been established, consisting of Jews escaping from pogroms inflicted by Russia's Tsars, and then later from the civil war following the Communist revolution.

In fleeing Austria, my parents were unable to take money or any valuables, so we arrived in Shanghai essentially destitute. My father, a physician, established a small practice, earning just enough to sustain our family. I first attended the "Shanghai Jewish School," where classes were conducted in English, a language then new to me. I attended this school for two years and then changed, for the last class of high school, to a school conducted by the British and administered by the Shanghai Municipal Council.

Shanghai was chosen as a refuge by some 20,000 Jews from Germany, Austria and Poland because it was at that time the only place in the world where people without means could immigrate without the requirement of a visa. This was so because Shanghai was in part an international city – not part of any country. This unusual arrangement was an outgrowth of the nineteenth century Opium Wars that had ended with the victorious British inflicting trade and territorial demands on the Chinese.

Prior to arrival of the Jews escaping from Nazism and Stalinism, the Jewish community in China consisted of two distinct sections: Sephardic Jews from Iraq and Ashkenazi Jews from Russia. These two Jewish communities, some of whom had achieved economic success and even considerable wealth, organized and formed committees to receive and extend aid to the new arrivals.

The Piano Recital

Before recounting our family's exodus from Vienna, I want to say a bit about our lives before Nazism inflamed and contaminated Austria and much of the rest of Europe. Here, in the next few paragraphs, is a brief vignette from our family life, prior to the Anschluss.

We had a grand piano in the living room of our apartment and Mother played occasionally. Herta, my sister, three years older than me, had studied piano for two years with the same woman teacher who had taught our Mother. Herta practiced her music assignments at home, and I had become accustomed to hearing music in the house as well as on the radio. Also, my father had had some musical education playing the violin, although Mother considered his achievement to be on a lower level than hers. When I turned ten, it was my turn to be sent to study piano with the same teacher. I was not really enthusiastic, but I accepted the idea that music was a legitimate part of education.

It was a rainy Sunday afternoon in the fall, and this was a rare occasion: all four of us were at home, even Father, who was usually busy, even on weekends, with his medical practice, working at some hospital clinic, making house calls, or seeing patients in his clinic, which was part of our apartment. My sister and I were reading or doing homework. "Wow! We are going to hear a concert!" Herta exclaimed.

Indeed, Mother had sat down at the piano, and Father was in the process of opening his violin case after extracting it from the storage place where it lay, forgotten most of the time. "This was a beautiful piece by Beethoven," Herta commented for my benefit as the two of us sat on the couch, listening. "We are lucky to have a culturally rich atmosphere at home. Not all of my friends have parents that well educated. I wish they would play more often," Herta then continued in a whisper, "I really enjoy music. Mother quite often plays by herself, but when they play together, it adds something special!"

I soon joined Herta in taking piano lessons, though I never achieved anything close to her level of excellence. When I had studied the piano for ten months, the teacher planned a recital for her students to demonstrate what they had learned before an audience composed mostly of families and friends. The program was announced, and we were all busy preparing our parts. To my surprise, I was also to participate. I felt some fear of playing in front of the public, no matter how friendly. When the recital came, Herta performed beautifully, and I managed to survive.

This was my first and last concert performance. A year or so later, in March 1938, the German annexation of Austria ended the musical aspirations in our family. My having to give up piano was no great loss to society, but Herta did have some talent, Mother said. The grand piano was sold for a pittance before we had to give up our apartment and move in with my grandmother. Soon thereafter, all four of us fled the country, Herta to Kenya in East Africa (to live with my father's sister) and I with my parents to Shanghai. I did not see my sister again until 1952, 14 years later.

I did acquire some lasting basic knowledge of music in the short course of my studies, and to this day, some 75 years later, I enjoy concerts. In fact, the incentive to tell this story came from attending a concert of the San Francisco Symphony Orchestra recently. As I watched a pianist perform, I was reminded of my experience.

Nazism and the Holocaust

Because my family fled Austria in late 1938, and WWII started in September 1939, it is clear that my parents and I left Germany in the nick of time. Those times were turbulent, terrifying, brutal, confusing and chaotic. There just was not much time to make decisions to uproot lives, and to raise the means necessary for fares. The voyage to Shanghai took four weeks and was commensurately expensive, and it was difficult to complete all necessary formalities with the Nazi-appointed authorities – who were by then administering Austria. And this is not to speak of the courage and determination it took to go to foreign and distant shores, facing a future devoid of certainty. I turned 13 in July 1938 and did not confront the question of survival, but my parents must certainly have faced that question. It is to my father's credit that he pushed for our leaving with great energy, and that he had the foresight to understand that the greatest danger to our survival would be to remain where we were. As it turned out, my father's judgment proved accurate, and I am indebted to his wisdom for my survival.

I had witnessed the Viennese welcoming German troops with enthusiasm in March 1938. Later, when Hitler himself visited, he was greeted on the streets of Vienna as a liberator. Jews, by edict and by the evidence of cruel and suppressive actions, had been declared an underclass, without rights. We were now fair game, exposed to random and capricious physical attacks.

One day, a group of four or five boys followed me. They called out, in turn: "Dirty Jew, coward, stop and fight! We ought to kill all you Jews!" Two of them then attacked me. I took a number of blows to my body, and one landed on my face in the area of my right eye. I did not try to defend myself. With that they turned and left. My grandmother and parents, later noting the black eye, expressed their concern, but my father avoided asking for details. I got the message that it was best to make light of the experience. Even now, some 75 years later, I carry in me some remnants of sadness and fear as I think about the relentless terror of those days, and relive them.

Bands of teenagers could and often did attack young boys like me. I had begun to admit to myself that nobody, including my parents, had the power to protect me. I felt rudderless, unworthy and confused; in retrospect, I believe my parents did as well.

Because my father was allowed now to practice as a physician only for Jews, our family had been obliged to give up our apartment; we moved in with my grandmother. On the night of November 10, 1938, a night that soon came to be known worldwide as Kristallnacht (the night of broken glass), my Aunt Mitzi, burst in on the rest of our family. Breathless with anxiety and concern, she said "They are arresting Jews all over the city. They have burned synagogues. They have broken into all Jewish stores and have emptied them." The events of Kristallnacht marked a major shift for the worse: an open no-holds-barred attack on all Jews and Jewish property, inflicted both by Nazi authorities, and too often by people in general.

By then, the existence of concentration camps, and the harsh treatment prisoners experienced there, were common knowledge. The word Dachau sent shivers down my spine.

As we all lived in a state of bewilderment and fear, it had become clear that Jews had to try to leave to save themselves. Though my father had somehow escaped arrest, my parents looked for opportunities with renewed vigor and settled on plans to leave for Shanghai. My parents, my sister and I did get out in time. My grandmother never did. Though we are not certain of her fate, we believe that she died in Theresienstadt, a concentration camp.

The Voyage to Shanghai

As I noted earlier, my parents left Vienna for Shanghai in November 1938. Just two months later, in January 1939, I left Vienna to join them. I was 13 years old. A small family group came to the train station, Vienna's Sudbahnhof, to see me off, including my Aunt Mitzi, her son Gert and my Uncle Gyuri. My grandmother stayed at home – I had already departed from her, tearfully. I was confused about my feelings. Though glad to be on my way to rejoin my parents, I was sad to leave behind the place where I had lived since birth.

My parents had prearranged for me to travel to Shanghai in the company of a couple with whom they had exchanged tickets. The train was to take us on an overnight trip across the Alps to Genoa, in Italy, where we were to embark on the ocean liner "Conte Biancamano," of the Italian Lloyd Triestino shipping line, that would take us on a four-week voyage to Shanghai.

As the train approached the Italian border, we got our documents ready for inspection. I experienced a few minutes of panic because I could not locate the tax document I needed to show. To my relief, I finally found it. I felt an immense relief when we crossed the border into Italy, leaving Nazi Germany and Austria behind.

On the ship, I was quartered in a 3rd class cabin, shared with three women, including the woman with whom I was travelling. The steward who served us meals spoke broken English. Sometimes he brought some dishes from the "fershta classa." Another higher-level crew member spoke an equally broken German.

We passed through the Suez Canal, and there, on the banks, I saw my first camel outside a zoo. I remember it well – an impressive sight silhouetted against a clear blue sky. We were not welcome to go ashore in every port where the ship anchored. I assume that they did not want to host several hundred poor refugees, none of whom were good prospects for making purchases, but I never found out what these decisions were really based on.

Most of the time, we had good weather and calm seas, but we also encountered storms on the way. I was seasick at these times, and in those days, there was no Dramamine to help. I could not stand up, but never threw up. I just had to keep still, and then I was all right. Some grown-ups took pity on me and helped me find a place on deck, and the fresh air also helped. People said I should eat to feel better, but I could not move.

The ship anchored in Colombo, then the capital of Ceylon, the island just south of the Indian peninsula, now called Sri Lanka, and we were allowed ashore. As I left the ship with my guardians, a kind elderly local with a white beard approached us. "May I offer you and your son some drinks?" he inquired in English while looking at me. "I would like to do a kindness to the young boy," he added. All of us understood the question and the couple quickly consented. They did not explain that I was not their son. The man led us to a nearby drink bar, and I recall getting a lemonade served in a tall glass. The drink was delicious, and I sipped it happily from a straw. There was something luxurious about this drink, and it obviously made a deep impression on me. This happened 74 years ago, and I still remember the experience clearly.

We encountered a final storm, a cyclone they called it in the announcement over the PA system, between Manila and Hong Kong, and I experienced another bout of seasickness. We then sailed north through calm seas, sheltered by the Chinese mainland coast, to Shanghai. Shanghai does not lie on the ocean front, but is accessed by way of the Huangpu River, one of the waterways making up the delta of the Yangtse River.

The ship anchored offshore; we were taken in small boats to the custom-house on the Bund, the riverside road in the International Settlement. The customs officers were all Europeans, and were, in fact, British. I had my passport ready for inspection, but to my surprise, nobody asked for it. The customs officers were only interested in the baggage. And then – I saw my parents waiting for me! For me, and I think also for them, this was a deeply emotional moment. I hugged my mother, and we both shed tears of joy. I must also have hugged Father, but I do not recall how I greeted him. He was mostly a well-controlled man, although I had seen tears in his eyes when my parents left me behind in Vienna.

Beginnings in Shanghai

My parents lived in a single room in a ramshackle house in the French Concession of the International Settlement, with bathroom and kitchen shared with other renters. The day after my arrival, my mother took me to the Shanghai Jewish School that was about a ten-minute walk from our place, and I was duly registered. This school, which was supported by the Jewish community, followed a syllabus modeled on the English educational system. I was interviewed by Mr. Kahan, a senior teacher, who determined that I was advanced enough in algebra to be placed in a class designated as "Upper Five." The teachers at this school were all recruited from the local English-speaking Jewish communities, except for the teacher of English language and literature who was hired from England. Her name was O'Dwyer. There were four other refugee students in this class and Mrs. O'Dwyer referred to us collectively as "the German children."

I was the youngest student in the class. In the school there were probably more than fifty refugee students spread over a variety of classes, most of whom were bused in from the area called Hongkew (Hong Kou in Mandarin), a distance of about half an hour travel.

Everything was strange to me, including the language of instruction. During the first two weeks I understood very little, which understates the situation. Better said, I understood next to nothing. I was, however, helped by the other "German children," who tried to keep me informed as to what was going on. All this difficulty was resolved within a few weeks, and I could then stand on my own two feet. For quite a while, I needed to ask for explanations at times, but the trauma of living in a bubble separate from my own environment was over, and from then on I made steady progress and soon placed within the first three or four scholastically in a class of 30.

I should mention that I had studied English as a foreign language for a year at school in Vienna, and Father magically produced (in Vienna) a private teacher with whom all three of us – Father, my sister and I – studied more intensively for a few months. But none of these efforts prevented my living for a few weeks in a bubble separate from my fellow students and teachers.

Life soon became routine, and we adjusted as well as we could. My father had opened a medical office downtown, and his income was such as to barely support our low level of existence. For myself, I progressed in school and soon began to read a lot using the school library. I joined the Boy Scout troop attached to the school and made some friends.

University

Completing high school in December 1941, at age 16, I worked at odd jobs for some two years. My father's Shanghai medical practice, never sufficient to our needs, declined further after Pearl Harbor and the Japanese takeover of Shanghai. My job as salesman in a men's accessories store brought an income that, though meager, was for my parents and me essential for our survival.

"You are wasting your time selling in that store! You should be studying at a university to advance your education." Mr. Kahan, then principal of the Shanghai Jewish School, was speaking to me emphatically, carefully enunciating every word. I was taken aback and stunned. The subject of my future had come up tangentially as I was explaining my first attempts to study Chinese. The turn of the conversation took me by surprise. "But I need to earn money to contribute to the family income. My father's medical practice has suffered significantly since the Japanese takeover of Shanghai after Pearl Harbor," I responded.

Mr Kahan spoke up. "As you know, the Public Schools of the Shanghai Municipal Council have closed down, and we have a number of students who have transferred to our school: some need help to adjust to our curriculum. I can refer these to you for tutoring, and I am sure you can earn enough to substitute for your present income." My heart gave a leap at this unexpected opening up of a possibility to pursue my ambition for higher education. I left Mr. Kahan's house walking on air. My dream had suddenly come within reach.

I returned home that day, feeling high with optimism in the midst of our really miserable circumstances. It was September 1943.

Our diet was poor and sometimes inadequate. There was no end in sight in relation to the war in the Pacific. At 18, my wish for life could not be entirely suppressed, but I had not had the luxury of thinking of a future.

Upon informing my employer of my intent to leave the store, I received an offer to double my salary if I stayed. Tempted by that good offer, I began to do tutoring during off-hours, and found that full-time tutoring would bring in more money than my store clerking ever could. But the most important outcome of my tutoring experience was that it led me to renewed determination to seek higher education.

I soon found myself with a good-sized tutoring practice, teaching high school students and a Chinese group in science, math and English. With the income derived from tutoring, I now had sufficient resources to enroll at Shanghai's St. John's University in February 1944. American missionaries had founded St. John's, a good school, decades earlier. I graduated in 1947 with a BS in chemistry.

After Pearl Harbor in December 1941, and the Japanese surrender in August 1945, all of Shanghai, including the International Settlement, was under Japanese army occupation. In March 1943 the Japanese issued a proclamation requiring all stateless residents who had arrived in Shanghai after 1937 to move into a "designated area." This proclamation affected mainly the Jewish refugees and caused a great deal of suffering. I was able to continue my studies at St. John's University, but needed to obtain a pass from the Japanese authorities to leave the designated area; the university was located a good distance from there. Our liberation from the Japanese occupation was for us a most important event, as it allowed us to plan for the future and to leave Shanghai

While studying at St. John's University I interacted with many Chinese fellow students. I found them to be good and loyal friends and had satisfying personal relationships. After leaving Shanghai, these friendships continued and we spent many hours together during my later visits to Shanghai and Beijing. I also had the opportunity to host some of my former fellow students when they visited California.

Upon graduating from St. John's, I was admitted to the University of California at Berkeley, starting there in February 1948. I had heard about UC Berkeley from other foreign and Chinese students who were planning to go there, or knew of others who had gone there. Upon starting at Berkeley, I was required to complete two semesters of undergraduate studies; I was then given a BA and admitted to the graduate school, from which I graduated in September 1951 with a PhD in Chemistry.

My Teaching Career

I stayed at Berkeley for one post-doctoral year, and in October 1952 went to Israel to teach chemistry at Technion, the Israel Institute of Technology. Founded in 1912, Technion, located in Haifa, is the oldest university in Israel. Starting as a Lecturer in Chemistry, I stayed with Technion for 13 years, rising in time to a full professorship.

In 1957 I was granted a two-year leave from Technion. The first year was spent at Duke University as a Research Associate on a professor's grant money; the second year was with the National Bureau of Standards, in Washington, DC. In 1965 I left Technion to accept a professorship at the University of Southern California in Los Angeles.

I was to stay at USC for the rest of my teaching career, retiring in September 1993. I did, however, take a two-year leave from USC in 1980 to serve as Science Counselor at the US Embassy in Beijing, China. My work as Science Counselor was aimed at nurturing the growing goodwill between the two countries that began with President Nixon's world-shaking 1972 visit to Beijing.

My specific efforts there were directed to monitoring and facilitating implementation of the US-China Cooperation Agreement in Science and Technology that had been signed in 1978 by President Carter and the Chinese leader, Deng Xiaoping. In addition, I visited research and academic institutions and reported on the status of S&T in China. The Chinese gave this program high priority after their isolation following the establishment of the People's Republic by Mao Zedong in 1947. They were eager to send research personnel to the U.S. under the agreement to receive training while participating in cooperative projects. It is worth noting that the Chinese officials with whom I dealt on these matters were almost always competent and cooperative. Though our relationships were formal and businesslike during these interactions, many have matured into genuine friendships in the years that followed.

Returning from China to USC, I co-authored a book about US/China Technology Transfer.

Marriage(s) and Children

In 1950, while still a doctoral student at Berkeley, I met and married Miriam, who had been a student of mine in Shanghai. She had been born in Shanghai, where her parents belonged to the Russian Jewish Community. They had moved before her birth from Harbin, in northern China, to Shanghai, where her father had a piece-goods store. I had tutored her in math and physics following her transfer from a Shanghai Municipal Council school to the Shanghai Jewish School. She spoke Russian with her parents, but all her schooling had been in English. Our meeting in Berkeley was a happy surprise for both of us, and we soon married. Miriam and I had two daughters together: Deborah, born in Haifa, in 1953, and Tamar, born in Washington, DC in 1958. We ended our marriage in 1966.

I was subsequently married three more times: to Virginia from 1974 to 1977; to Judith from 1977 to 1988; and to Eileen, in 1989. My last marriage lasted for 21 years, until Eileen died from cancer in 2010. There were no children from these last three marriages.

My older daughter, Deborah, began her school studies in Hebrew. We moved to Los Angeles in 1965 when Deborah was 11; after that her education was, of course, in English. After graduating from high school, and three quarters of studies at UC San Diego, she returned to Israel to do her army service. After completion of her army service, Deborah stayed in Israel, married and studied at Tel-Aviv University, returning to Hebrew. She graduated with a BS in applied mathematics, and worked at an Israeli company as a software engineer for many years. She has three children: two sons and one daughter. They live in Haifa. Her husband is a pediatric neurologist. She recently retired.

My younger daughter, Tamar, was born in Washington, DC, in 1958, when I was working at the US National Bureau of Standards, on leave from Technion. Tamar eventually followed the example of her older sister and returned to Israel to do her army service. She returned to live in California, graduated from UC Davis with a BS in biology, and then continued her studies at UC Berkeley, obtaining an MS in public health. She is married, has two children, a son and a daughter, and they live in Oakland. She has worked at a Non-Profit in Marin County, in Northern California, the Service Employees International Union (SEIU), and currently works with Kaiser Permanente.

Secret to Happiness

Though pursuit of happiness is our right, as stated in the Declaration of Independence, its realization is left for us to achieve, and each person must chart his own path to that realization. For myself, happiness requires that I have a woman companion; I want some love – somebody to hold and be held by, to love and be loved. Some sexual turn-on is important. It is important too in a man-woman relationship that each be a good companion to the other. Experiences and thoughts, to be fulfilling and satisfying, need to be shared, best on an intimate basis.

Companions need to know how to really listen. I have learned a lot about listening to others and find deep listening to be a valuable asset in any relationship and friendship. I learned that from my activity of peer counseling. Done under the guidance of a licensed counselor or therapist, I provided counseling to seniors who have problems with adjusting to aging. I have found it an especially blissful experience to listen and be listened to in interacting with a special woman companion. It is important to be prepared to be completely honest and truthful while sharing feelings.

A sense of achievement is another important component of happiness. I take pride in my professional accomplishments, including 80 Publications in peer-reviewed and review journals and one book; 10 post-doctoral research associates; 25 Ph.D. students; 5 MS students; research grants from the National Science Foundation, the National Institutes of Health and the Petroleum Research Fund. I am proud too of the role I played in establishment of the Science and Technology Section at the U.S. Embassy in Beijing (1981), and of my contribution to implementation and facilitation of the US – China Science and Technology cooperation program while at the U.S. Embassy in Beijing. And I take special pride in receiving, in 1978, the USC Award for Creative Scholarship and Research and, in 1982, the Superior Honor Award from the Department of State at the termination of my tenure as Science Counselor at the U.S. Embassy in Beijing.

Another ingredient of happiness is to be willing and available to perform a public service and assume responsibility for community functions. When it was appropriate, I was willing to become president of a large and active club at Rossmoor (Democrats of Rossmoor). After that I accepted responsibility for producing the club's newsletter – a function I perform to this day. I find it satisfying to be active in positions where I am significant – particularly after retiring from my professional activity.

I have had a lively interest in technology and have had the advantage of encountering it in my professional activities. I enjoy the use of my iPhone, my iPad and, of course, my personal computer – which I have updated about every 3-4 years. I hope to continue doing this and learning new software. I have become proficient in new software for producing the newsletter for Rossmoor's Democratic Club. I now hope to learn to create and maintain Websites.

I am happy these days writing memoirs of my life. Reading gives me great pleasure, both fiction and non-fiction. Having lived in China and Israel, it is of special importance to me to closely follow events in China and in the Middle East. Understanding the Middle East is particularly important at this time.

The continuing presence of war in our lives is a source of great distress to me and, according to recent polls, to the majority of Americans. Mini-wars rage too, on our city streets. Unfortunately, we have not yet learned enough about settling disputes by peaceful means. We need to include in education skills of dispute resolution starting at an early age.

****

Happiness: Bhutan Leads the Way

We all strive for happiness and success. Most of us, however, are never quite sure what they are, or how to achieve them. We do know that financial and professional success can be empty and meaningless when achieved at the expense of an unhappy family life. Too often, professional success demands endless work and frequent travel, both of which can adversely affect family life. The question then becomes one of trade-offs. Who is happier, the modestly paid school-teacher, home every night, summers off, who can take pride in bringing literacy and numeracy to inner-city kids, or the senior partners of law firms whose satisfaction may come from accumulating billable hours – devoted too often to representing clients where legal maneuvering can take priority over moral virtue? Whose work is more fulfilling, the carpenter whose tangible creations emerge daily as he practices his trade, or the auditor who spends his work hours staring at and manipulating numbers on a computer screen? In the last analysis, happiness and success stem from pride in the work we do, the esteem of our community, and in the love of family and friends.

Philosopher Eric Hoffer wrote that the unending and relentless search for happiness is one of the chief sources of unhappiness. Another old adage tells us that life is what is happening while we wait for happiness. Since what we have may be as good as it gets, we must make an effort to appreciate and to find joy in the current situation. OK, enough of folklore. We need now to take a more serious look at what happiness is all about, and how to make it happen.

According to the 2013 World Happiness Report, released by Columbia University's Earth Institute, a survey of 156 countries ranks Denmark, Norway, Switzerland, the Netherlands and Sweden as the world's happiest countries. But, Fellow Americans, bad news for us: the United States came in at number 17, lagging behind Canada (6), Australia (10), Israel (11), the United Arab Emirates (14) and Mexico (16). The report ranks the United Kingdom as the 22nd happiest country in the world. Other major nations in the report included Germany (26), Japan (43), Russia (68) and China (93).

The search for happiness has of course always had high priority with individuals. It seems, however, that now, as a matter of public policy, increasing attention is being given to what constitutes happiness – and how to best go about realizing it. In fact, the United Nations has invited member states to "pursue the elaboration of additional measures that better capture the importance of the pursuit of happiness and well-being – with a view to guiding their public policies."

"It is important," said the World Happiness Report, "to balance economic measures of societal progress with measures of subjective well-being to ensure that economic progress leads to broad improvements across life domains, not just greater economic capacity." Columbia's Report comes on the back of a growing global movement calling for governmental and other policy makers to reduce their emphasis on achieving economic growth, and to focus holistically on policies that can improve people's overall well-being.

The concept of "happiness economics," first proposed in 1972 by Bhutan's former King Jigme Singye Wangchuck, has in recent years gained traction in countries across the world, including the UK, Germany and South Korea. The UN first encouraged member countries to measure and use the happiness of their people to guide public policies in July 2011.

Because Bhutan was the first to grapple with the idea of measuring the happiness of its people, and the first to link its happiness index to government policies, it is worth having a look at how they go about it. The King of Bhutan, with his 1972 decree, declared that Bhutan's Gross National Happiness (GNH) index was henceforth to be more important than its Gross National Product (GNP).

Bhutan's 1972 declaration is built on its 1729 legal code, which asserts "If the government cannot create happiness for its people, there is no purpose for the Government to exist." Bhutan's happiness policy is not for them a mere pie-in-the-sky aspiration. Their GNH index is measured and used on a continuing basis to orient the people and the government toward happiness.

Emphasis is less on improving the happiness of those already happy (they are assumed to be on the right track), but rather to identify those who are less than happy, and then adjusting policies in a way that will improve their lot. When the lot of happiness "have-nots" is improved, the whole society benefits: everyone's happiness improves.

Bhutan puts it this way: As measured in the GNH index, happiness is not *"the fleeting, pleasurable 'feel good' moods so often associated with that term. We know that true abiding happiness cannot exist while others suffer, and comes only from serving others, living in harmony with nature, and realizing our innate wisdom and the true and brilliant nature of our own minds."*

Bhutan accepts the notion that people are diverse in the ways and means they can achieve a fulfilling life. GNH is determined by regularly measuring nine weighted "domains" that in Bhutan's view cumulatively determine happiness:

- **psychological well-being** – *family well-being, safety from crime, generosity, compassion, contentment, serenity*
- **time use** – *the balance between paid work, unpaid work and leisure are important for personal well-being*
- **community vitality** – *a sense of belonging, supporting community programs, interacting positively within the community, volunteering and donating*
- **cultural diversity** – *language, arts and crafts, festivals, events, ceremonies, drama, music, dress, etiquette and spiritual values*
- **ecological resilience** – *harmony with nature, conservation*
- **living standard** – *income level, housing, job security*
- **health** – *both physical and mental*
- **education** – *in addition to reading, writing, math, and science, students are measured for creative learning and expression*
- **good government** – *voting and attendance to community meetings*

Individuals are deemed to be happy when they have sufficiency in 2/3 of the nine (weighted) indicators. Higher scores indicate extensively happy or deeply happy.

British Prime Minister David Cameron has gotten aboard the happiness train. The UK's Office for National Statistics has started the National Well-Being Programme. It includes household financial and "human capital" analyses, various quality-of-life measures (job security, relationship satisfaction and environmental conditions) and self-assessment of well-being by individuals. The intent of all of this is to activate an "invisible hand" mechanism that will spur localized efforts to improve scores. Towns are asked to compare their scores with one another, and when scores lag to find ways to improve things,

German Chancellor Angela Merkel said recently that Gross Domestic Product isn't the only important marker of Germany's success – individual and collective well-being also matter. Germany ranked a very low 26 in the World Happiness Report, a matter of some concern to Merkel, who has said that her government is determined to help Germany turn that around. It has been said that the plan may include the following: take time to slow down to enjoy life, get back to nature, invest in holistic health care, and provide aggressive support of the arts (music, theatre).

The UN too has weighed in on this: Secretary General Ban K-Moon stated the "[Gross National Product] fails to take into account the social and environmental costs of so-called progress. We need a new economic paradigm that recognizes the parity between the three pillars of sustainable development. Social, economic and environmental well-being are indivisible. Together they define gross global happiness."

John Dunne saw it this way: "No man (or woman) is an island." Each of us is part of the whole. People need people – it's pretty simple. Yes, food and shelter are imperative, but after the baseline has been met, happiness varies more with the quality of human relationships than income.

We in the United States, where the right to pursue happiness is written into our Declaration of Independence, might well take note that the pursuit of happiness is being taken very seriously across the world. Perhaps we can learn to raise our happiness score from 17th to something higher. How about Number One!?

****

Lonnie Robert Bristow

Lonnie is a physician of special note. He served for many years, and at various levels, along a path in organized medicine that eventually led to him being elected President of the American Medical Association. He has received a long list of awards and honors – including four honorary doctorates. And he has written widely on issues in the fields of both medical practice and medical ethics. Lonnie is an active member of the Institute of Medicine of the National Academy of Sciences. Though long retired from clinical practice, he remains active as a consultant on the many complex sociologic and economic facets of health care for Medical Education institutions and for various State and Federal governmental bodies.

The Early Years

I was born in New York City, in April 1930, and grew up in Harlem. My parents had moved, just prior to my birth, to New York from South Carolina. During the early years of my childhood, there was a steady stream of their friends and former neighbors, themselves making the move to New York, who would stay with us while acclimating themselves to the city, and searching for places they could move to. I remember that stream of visitors with special pleasure because it made for an active and genial social setting. I have one sibling, a brother some five years younger. I went to New York City public schools, through high school.

My father worked for Standard Oil of New Jersey. After starting at a filling station as a mechanic, he obtained work after only a few years as a messenger in the office of the company's president, Winthrop Rockefeller. I should add that I, then 15-16 years old, worked part-time in that office during my summer vacations from school, and had occasion at times to interact briefly with Mr. Rockefeller. That fact would prove valuable years later; when, in 1953, I needed references to gain admission to the NYU School of Medicine. Mr. Rockefeller, a major benefactor to the school and a Trustee, sent a note to the dean. Only two sentences were needed - here's what the note said: "I know this gentleman. Any favors you can do for him would be greatly appreciated." Not very long after, I learned I had been admitted!

During those years, my Dad went to Divinity School at night. A deeply religious man, my father had for some ten years served as a deacon in a very large Baptist church in Harlem. After completing his studies at the Divinity School, my Dad was ordained and formed his own church, the New Zion Baptist Church. Small at the start, the church soon grew, and my father left Standard Oil to become pastor of his church on a full-time basis.

My mother worked for several years as a family domestic, and later went to night school to study nursing. At the age of ten or so, I would work with my mother during her homework study sessions. We two were learning medicine together. My growing interest in medicine came in part from that experience. My mother went on to become a licensed vocational nurse, working at a hospital not far from our home. When I was about twelve, she was working the evening shift in the emergency room, getting off at eleven at night. My father was working on the night shift, so it became my duty to go to the hospital before eleven so that we could walk home together. I was so intrigued by all that was going on in the hospital that I went early, sat in a corner to watch it all, and to absorb as much as I could. To me, the doctors and nurses were people who had magic in their hands. That became a world that I wanted to be part of. In later years my mother left hospital work and worked primarily with private patients.

By the time I entered kindergarten, I knew my alphabet letters and colors, and had a modest ability to read. Throughout my school years, my parents took note of my progress, and were intolerant of anything less than good grades. During the years of my childhood, the country was beset with economic depression. But, throughout those years, both my parents were always employed. Wages were low, but we were always able to live in reasonably good neighborhoods. My New York City public schools were multi-racial.

I had a happy childhood. My grammar school annually awarded a medal for good scholarship, given by the Daughters of the American Revolution. At the end of the sixth grade, I received that award – an important moment, because it was the first indication to me that I had special talents. The schooling was good; I remember that we had a class in music appreciation where we learned a good deal about how to appreciate and enjoy classical music as well as about the contributions made by different instruments.

Morehouse College

Like many young men, I wanted to get away from home--and to broaden my world, so I decided to go to Morehouse College, a good school, in Georgia, with an entirely-black student body. As a matter of some interest, I came to Morehouse as a freshman when Martin Luther King was in his junior year there. I knew him, though not on an intimate basis. King had entered Morehouse at the tender age of 15 or 16, but from the start was a big man on campus – fun-loving, very gregarious and outgoing. His father was a well-known pastor at that time, with traditionally conservative Baptist views; he frowned on social dancing, which his son loved to enjoy. Upon graduating from Morehouse, with a BA Degree in Sociology, King went to the Crozer Theological Seminary in Pennsylvania, and then to Boston University where he obtained a Doctorate in Systematic Theology.

Morehouse admitted only male students at the time, and felt itself to be unique. The school believed that, at the core, its mission was to create "Men (always with a capital M) of character," and that Morehouse students were educated to "be of service." We students were admonished to never lose appreciation for our gentle side, but to be aggressive in pursuing our purposes in life. I majored in biology, knowing from the start that I wanted to become a physician.

Every freshman, at the beginning of his freshman year, was obligated to have tea with the college president's wife. She would have us in groups of six or so; each of us was expected to learn and practice good manners and mature behavior in both social and life situations. In the first year, going to chapel every week was mandatory; attendance was taken to monitor compliance with that rule.

The recurring theme at Morehouse was that to really be a "Man" requires character. One of the songs we often sang was "Be Strong, Oh Men, Be Strong." The lyrics were "We are not here to play, to dream or drift. We have hard work to do, and loads to lift. Shun not the battle, face it - 'tis God's gift. Be strong, oh men, be strong."

I remember once when the college president, who had been away for a week or so on a fund-raising tour, returned to learn that there had been a stone-throwing tiff, with no resulting injuries or damage, between Morehouse students and students from nearby Clark College, located just across the avenue from one another. At the first chapel after his return, he sat at the rostrum for a good 20 seconds, which to us seemed like forever, just looking grim. "It has come to my attention," he began, "that over the weekend there was an altercation between the Clark <u>boys</u> and the Morehouse <u>Men</u>. I <u>never</u> want to be so embarrassed again." Because we all revered him, the words had a huge impact. That memorable moment typifies the dignified atmosphere at Morehouse. We were taught to be responsible; set high standards for ourselves, and live up to them. Now, almost seventy years later, though my stay at Morehouse was short, I look with pride at my fellow alumni for the impact they had on all of us.

I did not, however, catch fire intellectually; though I had no trouble with the scholastic content, I became lazy as a student. On coming to Morehouse, I was very young, and immature; I did not apply myself. I found many of my classes to be too easy – I was bored. I did manage to get through the first year, albeit with mediocre grades. But during my sophomore year I began really goofing off – not paying attention to my studies. I fell into the bad habit of skipping classes. As I got close to the end of my first semester, the dean called me in to tell me that I was in danger of flunking.

The Navy

Rather than run the risk of actually flunking several subjects that semester, I chose to join the Navy, and did so in February 1948, leaving Morehouse in the middle of my second year. At the time the Navy had a program that allowed recruits to spend one year on active duty, followed by six years in the Active Reserve. I opted for that program and spent only one year on active duty. I went through training for submarine service, and then spent the rest of my year assigned to a submarine as a Seaman First Class My duties included being a lookout when the ship ran on the surface, and operating the stern diving planes when we were submerged. My year of service was just prior to the Korean War. I did go to sea for war-game exercises and greatly enjoyed that entire year.

As a sidebar, I should note that in 1948, the year before I went into the Navy, President Truman had, by executive order, racially integrated the American military services. Where black sailors had before then been placed into jobs as cooks and stewards and the like, they were now given the same opportunity as all others to apply for any specialty for which they might qualify.

Truman, who will for that and other reasons remain my favorite American President, had sent to our New London, CT base a senior civilian official of the Navy, perhaps an Assistant Secretary of the Navy, for an extraordinarily camouflaged mission, simply to meet with all of the African-American sailors at the submarine school. So, just a few months after I enlisted, I found myself one of six who were assembled to meet with the official to respond to the President's questions: How was racial integration working? Was it successful? We assured him that racial integration in our part of the Navy was a complete success – that each of us was not only allowed, but was actually encouraged, to seek jobs in the Navy that would allow us to use whatever talents and interests we might have.

City College

Upon discharge from the Navy, I enrolled at City College of New York. Because the grades I had gotten at Morehouse were not good - and to avoid having those mediocre grades attached to my record, I enrolled at City College as a freshman. At about that same time, to help with my living expenses, I took a part-time job with a watch-making factory in New York. Now enrolled in school, I wanted to avoid the monthly drill requirements of the Active Reserve, so I persuaded the factory to declare me an "essential" worker, a status which allowed me to transfer from the Active to the Inactive Reserve. That proved to be a fortuitous move, because had I still been in the active Naval Reserve a few months later, I might well have been called back into service during the Korean War that began in June 1950. Once matriculated at City College, I did apply myself very seriously to my studies, and to make up the lost year at Morehouse I pushed myself to graduate in three years.

NYU School of Medicine

Upon graduation from City College, I applied to and was accepted by the New York University School of Medicine, from which I graduated in 1957. As I've already mentioned, Winthrop Rockefeller very likely played a role in my gaining entry into Med School! Though I might well have gained acceptance without his letter of endorsement, I feel quite certain that it did not hurt! To support myself during the four years in Medical School, I continued to work, finding jobs like filling-in at the post office during the Christmas holidays, or as a dishwasher for the Horn and Hardart chain of restaurants, and later as an on-call night lab technician in the clinical laboratory of a hospital on Long Island. One vivid memory from that experience is that I was once called to draw a routine blood sample from a woman patient who turned out to be Lena Horne! In addition to the income from these jobs, I required additional money to pay tuition costs – so by the time of my graduation I had accumulated a number of student loans that were later repaid in full. That I was able to get these loans is something for which I'll be everlastingly grateful.

At one point during my first year in Med School I was falling behind in my studies. Never a fast reader, I needed help to get through the large tomes that comprise the med-school literature.

So, I took the Evelyn Wood speed-reading course – and found it to work as advertised. I increased my reading speed threefold. Using the same amount of time, I could now go over the material three times instead of once, resulting in much greater retention of content. I had no further worries about scholastic performance.

My Practice

While in med-school, I had at first aspired to specialize in pediatrics – but I soon decided that I had a better talent for adult medicine, so I switched my goal to becoming an internist. I think of all medicine as being similar to Scotland Yard: its officers are very good at solving crimes, but when Scotland Yard can't solve the crime they call in Sherlock Holmes. In the same way, internists are the Sherlock Holmes' of the medical world! One indication of this is that most physicians, when they themselves are ill, go to internists to learn what ails them, and what needs to be done to restore wellness! Internists are diagnosticians, trained to collect evidence and to solve the problems of illness in adults: what is it – and what causes it? It was my early appreciation for that fact, and my admiration for and interest in the diagnostic or sleuthing function, that caused me to select internal medicine as my specialty.

When I finished my medical training, I worked for a year at Stockton State Hospital, a California State institution for the mentally ill. Following that, I next found employment for more than two years at Kaiser Permanente in Richmond, California. I enjoyed that time with Kaiser, because I was able to focus all of my time there in the practice of medicine. Kaiser, one of the better Health Maintenance Organizations, relieves its physicians of much of the paper work and of all administrative chores. However, as I neared completion of the three years of employment that are required by Kaiser to become eligible for Partnership in the group, I decided I could better achieve my goals as a physician in solo practice. I have never regretted that decision.

It is my strong belief that, over the last 30-40 years, health insurance companies and hospitals have joined the pharmaceutical industry to become increasingly driven by the profit motive. Profit first, service second: Control the largest "market share" and the stockholders will prosper. With this change in the landscape, it has become increasingly difficult for physicians in private practice to be treated fairly. Insurance companies tell physicians what they will pay for particular services. Individual doctors have little recourse but to accept the proffered rates if they want to have insured patients. I think of this as the corporatization of the Health Care enterprise. Almost the only path left open to physicians in private practice is to become part of a group practice, and hope it is large enough to legally negotiate on a more equal footing with the large insurance or hospital industries.

The personal accountability and continuity of care traditionally provided by physicians in private practice is often being seriously eroded and undermined by this insertion of the "corporate perspective," which seeks to maximize profits for the investor. A not-for-profit insurance program will have lower administrative costs. For example, the Medicare program has administrative costs approximating 3%, as compared to the typical private health insurance administrative costs of 17% (all before the profit margin is added on). These changes have significantly diminished the enjoyment of practice for many physicians.

After some years, I began to sub-specialize in Occupational Medicine, also known as Industrial Medicine – which is the identification and treatment or prevention of work-related injuries or diseases, such as those caused by exposure to hazardous materials like asbestos or toxic chemicals. I studied and acquired particular expertise in identifying and measuring disability related to such injuries. Because of this, I was often called upon to provide evidence and testimony when individual claims were adjudicated by courts, or the larger questions of potential legislative controls were being considered by state or federal governmental agencies.

In 1974, many states were beginning to focus on the disease of Sickle Cell Anemia, a genetic illness prevalent in the black community. Well-meaning individuals in California reportedly were considering writing a law to require that the sickle status be tested on every black person who might be admitted to any hospital in the state. There were no accompanying provisions for how that information would then be utilized to benefit the patient who had been tested. There was an enormous potential for unintended harm to be done to people who simply had the "trait" gene but not the full-blown illness for anemia. For example, in some parts of the nation communities had mistakenly advised sterilization procedures for young girls because of poorly thought out "testing programs."

Because of my concern for the potential harm here, I wrote an article in the *Western Medical Journal* entitled "The Myth of Sickle-Cell Trait," warning against the dangers of a poorly designed state law in this area. The article came to the attention of some in the legislature. Hearings were held, and the proposed law was scrapped. I was then asked to lead a committee to make appropriate recommendations for the problem. One year later, those recommendations were enacted into a law, and that law became the model adopted by many states across the nation for the proper way to obtain and utilize sickle cell testing information to the benefit of those being tested.

In 2006, the U.S. State Department requested that I go to Africa for Black History Month (February). There is a terrible problem with AIDS throughout Africa – but particularly so in South Africa. It would be helpful, the State Department told me, if you would go there to offer to share insight from our American experience that might guide their government and their medical community to policies that would help them with that problem. That proved to be an important and successful assignment – I was there for a month, speaking every day, sometimes several times a day, to South African physicians, school children, Medical schools, Universities, Churches, and civilian health officials on methods used in the United States to first get our arms around the AIDS epidemic and then get it under control. The key to successfully halting the spread of HIV infection is voluntary testing, with treatment and counseling for those identified as positive for the presence of the virus.

Just as we had learned in the U.S., the biggest impediment to success is the stigma associated with the disease. This limits willingness to participate in screening programs and must be overcome. Other strong, very unique cultural factors in Africa add to the difficulty and must be respected and factored into the solution. This has to be an "African" solution, not an imposed American replica. I shared tactics used in the U.S. (for example, having notable personalities like political leaders show their willingness to be tested, etc.). I also shared how remote areas away from major cities can be linked to the medical centers by using Telemedicine communication methods the U.S. currently uses to connect with remote Eskimo villages in the arctic. It was an intense experience for one month and included the Kingdom of Lesotho, which is an enclave nation within the Republic of South Africa. I think our work there did help the South African medical community to find ways to deal with that problem. My wife Lyn accompanied me on one of my trips to Africa.

The American Medical Association

One of the high points in my professional life has been to serve, in 1995-96, as President of the American Medical Association. That office is not one that can be attained by seeking it. Certainly I did not seek it. My long road to that office began in the mid-1960's when I joined the Alameda-Contra Costa County Medical Association in order to learn best practices – and to share my own ideas. The same reasons led to my membership in the California Society for Internal Medicine and the American Society of Internal Medicine in the early 1970's, institutions in which I also later became President. In 1978 the American Society of Internal Medicine sent me as one of its two representatives to the American Medical Association's House of Delegates. That body is very much the equivalent in the medical profession to the U.S. Congress in its function as a representational government. In that body, I was elected to the AMA Council on Medical Services, and a few years later was elected to the AMA Board of Trustees, of which I became chairman in 1993-94. From that position, I became the President of the AMA in 1995-96.

Let me share a bit of what that AMA experience was like:

During an AMA Meeting of the House of Delegates in 1994, a major concern was the Health Care Reform plan being written under the guidance of Hillary Clinton. It was essential that the medical profession have a clearly articulated, constructive, overarching strategy. The AMA Board presented its report to the House of Delegates, setting forth the current policies that would be used, which included advocacy of mandated employer health insurance as an important and necessary component in achieving universal coverage for all Americans. Per the usual process employed for these meetings, a Reference Committee had reviewed and then affirmed the Board's report and the strategy it proposed. If anything, they made the language even stronger before recommending that the House of Delegates vote its approval. That body then began debating the report and its recommendations.

Not surprisingly, there are some individuals who honestly view any governmental action that would mandate insurance coverage for everyone as being tantamount to socialism, and they oppose it on that basis. The delegates were considering several minor possible amendments to the Board's language. During that ongoing discussion, Dr. Ed Annis, a popular and charismatic former President (from three decades earlier) of the AMA, rose to state his strong opposition, both to what he believed to be the Board's support for the Clinton initiative, and to any kind of government involvement in the provision of health care to our citizens. He was passionate and very eloquent and seemed possibly to be swaying the delegates toward removing this policy and going back to the position the AMA had held in by-gone years. Such a reversal of policy would have placed the AMA in a position similar to someone showing up at a gunfight with a penknife. Someone needed to rise in opposition to the speech by Dr Annis. Since I was Chairman of the Board, I rose to speak in support of the Board's action, and in strong support of the Reference Committee's recommendation that we have a positive platform for our Association to use in engaging the Clinton initiative. My impromptu speech was given to keep us on course and not revert to a stance that was no longer appropriate for the time.

The proceedings were all recorded, and I quote my speech below as taken from the DVD:

My colleagues, it is not strange that on December 7th there should be an aura of conflict. But make no mistake about it, Americans have been able to deal with that in the past, and they will in the future, and we will handle that today.

I am reminded of the fact that in this month, some 217 years ago, 1776, specifically, two nights before Christmas, Thomas Paine sat down and wrote, in a room lit by candles, "These are the times that try men's souls, and the summer soldier and the sunshine patriot will, in this time of crisis, shrink from the service of his country, but he that sticks it now will deserve the love and thanks of every man and woman. "

These are extraordinarily difficult times. Your Association is committed to pursue aggressively, with all proponents of health system reform, universal coverage, quality, cost containment and freedom of choice of patients and physicians. Your Board believes that the reference committee has strengthened the report the Board has submitted to you. It has added to it. They also give us the flexibility that we need. And we hope that you will support the recommendations of your reference committee as they have been written.

You know, two nights later, after Thomas Paine wrote those words, George Washington led a poorly equipped outnumbered army across the Delaware to take Trenton and turn the events of that war around. Now, fortunately for all of us, there was no one in that army who said "You know, General, I don't think we need the few cannon that we have, even though they served you well during the previous battles." And, thank goodness there was no one in that army who said "we are an army, what do we need with boats? Why don't we burn them for fuel?" Well, they didn't, instead they wrapped their feet in bandages and pulled on those oars and they went to Trenton and took it.

Why did they do that? Certainly not for the pay – that they really weren't getting. Certainly not for the food that they weren't getting to eat. But it was to give a heritage to their sons and daughters, one which each of us here enjoys today. The American Medical Association has an opportunity to also provide a heritage for our sons and daughters in the years ahead. Support your reference committee. Don't take away our cannons. Don't burn out boats.

Three minutes later, the delegates responded with a resounding support of the Reference Committee's recommendations.

One of the great personal joys about my time in AMA leadership positions was dealing with the letters I received. People with concerns about their medical situation wanted at times to reach out to someone, to express their concerns to someone who might provide advice or help. So, sending letters to the AMA seemed at times to provide a straightforward target. I would often see those over the transom letters. I will always remember one in particular that touched me to my core. A man from down in Texas wrote: "I don't know whom else to write to, but I want someone to know about my doctor. I have AIDs – and my doctor is so wonderful - she must be the sister of Jesus." As I read letters like that one, I knew that this doctor, this patient, and all those like them were the kind of persons that I, as AMA president, was working for – and in behalf of.

Another important AMA function is to identify and disseminate best practices. As a physician, my personal goal was to try to make a difference in the lives of my patients as best I could. Being in the AMA leadership gave me the opportunity to help not just my few patients, but to make a difference in the lives of people far beyond the boundaries of my reach. It was an honor, as an AMA leader, to enable and facilitate the wide and deep body of good work that the AMA did.

The Physician's Obligation to the Patient: C,C,C, and H

I have very strong views about the obligation of those who are physicians to their patients. Health care professionals should be guided by a set of core principles: I call them "C, C, C, and H. The first "C" is for Compassion. You must care _about_ the person, not just _for_ them. All human beings respond to being cared about. You can't fake it for long, but you definitely can learn and improve it from observing a good mentor or role model.

The second "C" is for Competence. That's why you've chosen to enter the health care profession, and gone on to gain the knowledge and skills we've talked about.

The third "C" is for Courtesy. I'm not talking about simply saying "please" and "thank you." Those are important, but only constitute what I call "common courtesy." What I'm talking about is "cultural courtesy." You must make an effort to learn about and respect the _cultural_ background of those to whom you give care. It will enhance your effectiveness enormously, and it will surprise you by the enrichment it will bring to your own perspective on life.

Finally, you owe them "H" for "Honesty." By this I mean, be honest about what you know, and honest about the limits of what you know and, if you have your own limitations, be willing to guide patients to the help they need. That, of course, means that you have to first be honest with yourself. Patients do not expect you to know everything there is to know, but they do expect you to be honest and, first and foremost, "Compassionate."

Family

I am in my third marriage. The first was undoubtedly due to a rash decision on my part when I was very young, and lasted less than a year and there were no children. The second took place in my mid-twenties, lasted for four years, and produced a daughter, named Mary Elizabeth. I am sorry to say that after the divorce, I lost track of her for many years. However, just a few years ago we found one another, and are now enjoying a well re-established father – daughter relationship.

My third marriage has been to Lyn, more than fifty years ago, and has yielded two wonderful children. Lyn, a former nurse, has always been "the wind beneath my wings" - and together we have soared to heights far beyond anything we ever thought possible. Our son Robert has become a physician of world renown. As Director of Gynecologic Oncology, he is a Professor at the University of California, Irvine, and is frequently invited to travel to universities in many countries to teach the advanced techniques he has developed for the treatment of cancers of the female reproductive organs. Robert and his wife, also a nurse, have three children. The first is a boy, now 12 years old, while the second and third children are beautiful girls, one 9 and the other 6 years old.

Our second daughter, Lisa, is married and also has three children, two daughters ages 12 and 9, and a son age 6. She owns her own small housecleaning business to bring in a modest supplement to the income provided by her husband, a fine young man, who is assistant manager in a large grocery chain.

Philosophy of Life

I am a Methodist, and am very comfortable in the belief that this universe of ours is so vast, and yet so orderly, that there must be some grand design – and that God exists and we infinitely small humans struggle to understand our relationship to this universe and God as best we can.

I chose to be a Methodist (after many years of being a Baptist) because I encountered a charismatic Methodist minister in Richmond, California shortly after I came to the Bay Area. He responded to a cross-burning on the lawn of a black family in that community by putting his life on the line; he announced his intention to sit on the porch of that home the next several nights, challenging any of those who burned the cross that they would have to face him if they returned. That was the kind of man I could follow anywhere, and I soon joined his church. Since then, it has been my good fortune to see the same kind of willingness to become engaged in the trials and needs of everyday living in many other Methodist ministers and congregations. That's the kind of faith I believe in – you must "live" your faith by your actions on a day to day basis, otherwise it seems of little use to me.

My job is to do what I can with the opportunities that occur within my reach and within my field of vision. Like that Methodist minister back in Richmond, I judge my own performance and try to live by my own standards – that's what I learned at Morehouse.

As a physician, I have found that being able to make a difference in the life and health of someone else is enormously satisfying, just as I imagined it would be in my boyhood dreams. That satisfaction increases logarithmically when you can make a difference in lives well beyond your personal reach or line of vision. God has been good to me and given me that opportunity. That's why I usually choose to go through those doors.

I don't fear the day of my own demise, but that is because I perhaps have an advantage over other people. During my career, I have served as a director of a Coronary Care Unit in the hospital in my community. As to be expected, on occasion patients have had cardiac arrests and "died" despite the best standards of care. Sometimes, we were able to successfully resuscitate such a patient – to "bring them back", so to speak, after several minutes of no spontaneous heart action or breathing. In a small percentage of those resuscitated cases, perhaps a dozen times, I have found a patient who subsequently remembered what they had experienced during that time of "death." Without a single exception, they have all described a very pleasant experience - of being somewhere that was beautiful, like a meadow or field with flowers, and with something "positive" way out in front of them toward which they seemed to be moving. Without exception, that recollection is transitory, and within a day or two they all lose the memory. So, I don't know what happens after death, but it seems to me it is not necessarily unpleasant or to be feared. Once again, when one door closes, another door opens.

****

Robert Fred Hanson

Bob Hanson's email address is "DoctorOutdoors," a label that fits him perfectly! With a PhD in Recreation Management, Bob has built a career of great success in the creation and direction of sports programs at YMCA, university, and summer camps. He owned and operated his own camp, and has created a camp sales realty brokerage. But Bob's most important contribution is his effective and relentless dedication to world peace.

The Early Years

The Hanson family farm in Bowbells, North Dakota rang with joy on July 19, 1931 as I was born! The birth certificate read "Baby Boy Hanson" for a time, until my parents finally came up with Robert Fred. I was the second of four children: sister Doris was #1, sister Erma was #3, brother Lyle was #4. Times were tough across the country in the early 1930's; adding to the economic travail, our farm suffered one bad crop after another due to dust storms, hail, rust, drought, grasshoppers, gophers and various combinations thereof. But, at the age of three or four I had no thought of bad times: that's just the way things were.

Third grade was for me a milestone. I was fitted with glasses, caught smoking in back of the school, skipped school to read stolen comic books, and engaged in other such forms of rebellion. At the age of ten or so, a transformation: I became a charter member of the "Over-all Boys" 4H Club. Raising beef cattle became a passion, and my second steer won the grand championship at the Burke County Fair. But, just after I had purchased a wonderful Hereford heifer, intending for it to be the start of a herd and future life, my farm life came to an end as my parents announced that they were selling the farm and our family would move to the west coast. After two or three good crops, they had paid off their debts and chose to leave farming rather than take a chance on a return to bad times.

I was twelve when our family moved to Enumclaw, Washington. Just a year after our move, my father died of a heart attack, giving my mother the burden of breadwinner in addition to raising us four kids. Shortly after our arrival in Enumclaw, I joined Troop 422 of the Boy Scouts, which would prove to be a major positive influence in my life. At the age of 15, I achieved the rank of Eagle Scout and served two years as junior assistant scoutmaster prior to high school graduation. In my junior year, the Boy Scout Council decided not to have their annual camporee. Unhappy with that decision, my friend Dean Duncan and I organized an invitational camporee, inviting all the troops in the Council. Amazingly, we pulled it off — I have a patch to prove it! After graduating from high school, I organized and led a backpack trip on the Wonderland Trail – a 96-mile circumnavigation of Mount Ranier. In spite of our being raided by a bear, and one of the boys walking most of the way in stocking feet because his shoes could not be put on over blisters, all eight of us accomplished the feat.

Football was my other high school passion. I was never very good because of my diminutive size (148 lb. guard in senior year!), but the coach liked my spirit and I was awarded a letter for each of three years. My main contribution to the team was to run off and on the field to deliver play-instructions to the quarterback. I also lettered in golf, though I was even worse there; I made the team because only two boys at the school had ever played the game before and the school was committed to field a five boy team. By every measure, my biggest success in high school was in the home economics classroom. As the first boy ever to take cooking at EHS, I was consistently first in the class. That achievement did nothing to improve my social life!

Washington State College

As my older sister Doris had gone to Washington State College (now University), there was little question where I would go after high school. When I got there, I found that Doris had signed me up for Pine Manor, a student cooperative dormitory. Living there made it possible for me to work my way through college without help from home. Everyone at Pine Manor had a work assignment; I served variously as janitor, table waiter, and (my favorite) breakfast cook.

I would have majored in Forestry, but learned that Forestry grads could not find work at that time. So I stumbled into Recreation; I enjoyed the course work and went on to a degree in that field. I attended a YMCA-sponsored Freshman Camp at Lake Coeur d'Alene. The Student "Y" would prove to be a major influence on my life because of my association with Stan Rheiner, the director. During my five-year association with the Student "Y," I served progressively as social chair, community service chair, president of the student council, and, during my fifth year, as Associate Director.

Military Service – Such as it Was

I graduated in 1953 with a BA in Recreation Management, and earned a Masters Degree in Recreation Management in 1954. I had been in the ROTC program at WSC, and in June 1954 was ordered to active duty as a Lieutenant in the Signal Corps. The Korean War had by then wound down, and I entered basic officer training at Fort Monmouth, New Jersey, and was then posted to serve at Fort Ord in Monterey, California. On the way west from New Jersey I stopped in Michigan to visit my uncle Bob Jordan, owner of a Mercury Car dealership. I drove the rest of the way home in a beautiful 1953 Mercury hard-top, my first wheels!

Soon after arriving at Fort Ord, I asked for a few days leave to attend the YM-YWCA yearly meeting at Asilomar in nearby Pacific Grove, where I met June Dawson, who would become my first wife and mother of my three sons. My heart was not with the army, and by all standards I was a failure as an officer. I hung with enlisted men, all of whom called me Bob. Our alcoholic Company Commander was offended that I and the other junior officers would not spend time with him at the officers club. Not having any skills related to communications, I was given assignments such as motor officer, supply officer and mess officer. For my entire time in the army I attempted to get into Special Services so that I could use my recreation training, but was always turned down. Not surprisingly, I was never promoted to First Lieutenant, and cheerfully accepted early discharge after 21 months.

Marriage and a Doctorate

About a month before discharge, June and I were married. After release from the army, I took a job as physical director of the "Y" in Ellensburg, Washington, where I would spend the next 2½ years teaching swimming, volleyball and exercise classes, and serving as the city's summer recreation director.

Since I was entitled by my short military service to GI Bill education benefits, I decided to go for a doctorate. So off we went to Bloomington, Indiana, where I attended Indiana University and completed my course work in 1959 with a Doctorate in Recreation Management. During the same time, my wife earned a Masters in French, also at I.U. I note, with pride, that sister Doris and brother Lyle had also earned Doctorates.

Because there were few college teaching jobs available upon my graduation, I accepted a position with the Olympia YMCA as physical director and camp director. After a year I became the Y's acting general director, at an annual salary of $4,800. In 1962 I mailed resumes to about 50 colleges and universities, and was delighted to be offered an assistant professorship at San Diego State University at $6,200 for nine months. Big money for me!

1962 was a great time to get into college teaching. SDSU's enrollment was growing by about 1,000 students a year, so tenure was almost automatic and advancement came fairly easy. I became

Associate Professor in 1968 and full professor in 1971. Much of this was due to the terrific growth in our Recreation Major program. From a program with one half-time faculty position and perhaps 20 majors, it grew to 10 full-time faculty members and around 700 majors by the mid-seventies.

Most of my summers were spent working at various summer camps. One of the best was Camp Kooch-I-Ching, in International Falls, Minnesota. I worked there in exchange for tuition for my three sons, Erik, Craig and Chris. As a canoe trip leader, I paddled a thousand or more miles in Ontario's wilderness.

I was very involved in the American Camping Association, serving as president of the San Diego Section, as vice-president and education chair of the Southern California Section, and on the Board of the American Camping Foundation.

It had long been a dream for me to have my own summer camp. In 1979 I was able to purchase a campground in Willow Creek, California; I was my plan to start a camp there. As the campground didn't provide sufficient income to meet loan payments, I purchased a few "rubber ducky" rafts and started a raft rental business. The business did not earn much, but when I took six of my Explorer Scouts from San Diego on a five-day river trip, it went so well that I began offering whitewater tours for other youth groups. Thus, Trinity River Rafting Center was born! It became so successful and remunerative that when SDSU faculty members were offered a chance to retire early and keep teaching one semester a year, I grabbed it!

A New Marriage and A Camp of My Own

In 1983, my marriage ended. June and I had grown apart. In 1984, while working on the committee for the national conference of the American Camping Association I met Lyda Dicus at a Conference square dance. When Lyda told me that she was planning to go river rafting that summer I invited her to go with my group. She agreed, and we were married in 1986 on our beloved river. After our wedding on a beautiful sand bar, Lyda and I happily took off in our canoe. As I paddled I found the canoe to be unresponsive and sluggish; at the end of the trip I found that my staff had tied about

20 beer cans to the rear of the canoe: we were dragging a sea anchor!

For one semester, I commuted from Marin County to SDSU to teach. I soon decided that the time had come to take full-time retirement and get into another career. Since no one in the state was specializing in the sale of children's camps, I thought that might be a good business for me. It was! I have sold an average of one camp a year since getting certified as a broker in 1985. The business is called California Camp Realty.

In 1986 I learned of a camp for sale in El Dorado National Forest. I showed it to a number of prospective buyers at the asking price of $200,000. No one was interested. A few months later, the seller (University of California, Davis) lowered the price to $95,000. It was too good a bargain to pass up, so I called a few friends and we formed a partnership to buy the camp; our offer of $80,000 was accepted. Earlier in the year, I had brokered the sale of a camp called Mountain Camp. I called the camp's former owners and asked if they would sell their mailing list to us, and allow us to call our camp Mountain Camp II. Since they had no plans to stay in the business, they sold us the list for $6,000.

I hired most of the 1987 staff from among those who had worked at the old camp and proceeded to attract 275 campers the first summer. Within two years the camp had a large waiting list. After seven years running the camp, we decided that it was no longer necessary to work that hard. We donated the camp to the American Camping Association in the form of a Charitable Remainder Unitrust, which provides Lyda and me a life-time income.

At about this time, I became involved in the California Alpine Club. I was appointed outings chair in 1995, elected vice-president in 1996 and president in 1997. After two years as president, I left that office and went back to outings chair. In addition to running anywhere from three to eleven trips for the club each year, Lyda and I started an Elderhostel Program for the club, a family camp, and other programs. Alpine Club trips that I organized took the two of us to Ireland, Cornwall, Belize, Hawaii, the Ozarks, Utah's Green River, the Upper Missouri and all over the High Sierra.

On Happiness and the Hereafter

In 1997, Lyda and I moved to Rossmoor where I soon became involved in lawn bowling, bridge and tennis. In 2001, I organized a lawn bowling tour to England and Scotland; in 2003 I took a group of 30 bowlers to New Zealand. In 2005, we traveled to British Columbia, in 2006 to Arizona, and in 2007 led a tour to Southern California. And in 2013 back to Victoria and Vancouver.

Since we made our move to wonderful Rossmoor, and since reaching my seventies. I have given increasing thought to philosophical matters. I think Abraham Maslow had it about right when he said that only after a person's basic needs of food and shelter have been met, can she or he move on to the higher pursuits of self-actualization and esteem. In order to have a happy life, one has to feel that his/her life has meaning. To me this means giving back to others, and leading a balanced life. To this end, I devote a significant part of my time to service, another portion to physical activity, another to intellectual matters, and finally an allotment to fun and social activities. Maintaining that balance is relatively easy to do in our retirement years, far more difficult when one needs to manage a career and raise a family. Another secret to happiness is spending time with people important to you and whose company you cherish.

Strong relationships are based on shared values in things that matter: religion, politics, leisure activities, and money. Important too are tolerance, empathy and understanding. I like to say that people should not be allowed to marry until they have backpacked, camped, canoed and played bridge with their prospective spouse. I firmly believe in living together before marriage. One needs to see his future partner in the worst situation, not just in dating scenarios where we are all at our best.

One must be open to change. Though not all change is for the best, acceptance of and adapting to change are essential for sustaining happiness in life. My son had to talk me into getting a computer so that we could communicate by email. Now I spend half of my time in front of it! Having said that, we need to be careful to avoid spending too much time staring at our screens—we need to commit even more time to nature, sports and active life.

I don't believe in heaven or hell. Most religion is in my view based on wishful thinking and denial. I believe that when I die it will be the end, except perhaps for the memories of me in the hearts and minds of those who survive me. I have tried to live my life in a way that takes the world to a better place because of my having been there.

My Involvement in Peace Movements

In recent years I have gotten deeply involved in peace work – writing countless anti-war letters to the editors of local newspapers, and columns for the *"Rossmoor News,"* our local newspaper. I am wholly and passionately against the wars our country has fought in recent decades: Vietnam, Iraq and Afghanistan. I have for about ten years been very active as a member of the Board of the Mount Diablo Peace and Justice Center, and served for a time as President. I still serve as Chair of the Center's Advocacy Committee, with responsibility for planning and facilitating such events as protests and demonstrations. One of the things in which I take some pride is founding the Crosses of Lafayette. On a hillside visible from a major highway, and to BART passengers, we have placed a wooden cross for each of the thousands of American soldiers killed in the Iraq and Afghanistan Wars.

For the last few years, I have been treasurer and a board member of the Democratic World Federalists. DWF is a civil society organization based in San Francisco with supporters worldwide. Our goal is to end war and maintain peace, guarantee human rights, promote a just world community, and cope with environmental degradation and the squandering of natural resources. This can best be achieved through establishing a democratic federal world government. Rather than using force to solve international conflicts, political and judicial structures and procedures would be used. Member governments would still be in charge of domestic affairs at the country level, world courts with enforceable judgments would be able to try perpetrators of international and world-level crimes.

The model for World Federalism is the United States of America. Just as the original 13 colonies gave up foreign policy sovereignty, the colonies retained control over domestic affairs within their states. The terribly destructive Civil War, fought primarily to deny cessation to the south, is an example of the possible consequences of unrestricted sovereignty of our colonies. Had the colonies retained complete sovereignty, there would over the years certainly have been conflict and possibly numerous wars between them.

War is not the answer to resolution of issues – between states and nations – or between individuals and families. Since the advent of weapons of mass destruction, it has become evident that we must find our way to peaceful resolution of issues that divide us; we now have the means to destroy cities, kill thousands, possibly millions, and perhaps most of us in war. Not only are wars not productive of lasting peace, they are counterproductive: the dollar cost of our recent and ongoing wars, and of our insanely large "Defense" arsenal, have surely done great and lasting damage to the U.S. The cost in lost lives and lost limbs and lost minds is equally damaging.

I am painfully aware of the difficulties we face in bringing about some kind of an international government with the power and authority to maintain peace among its member nations. While it would be easy to accept wars among nations as inevitable, I think all of us should do what we can to move the world in a direction where peace among nations is maintained. Just as our fifty States maintain peace through federation, we should now move toward acceptance of a global federation in which member nations relinquish authority over matters of war and peace.

I do think that the world will one day find a way to peaceful resolution of issues. I only hope that it doesn't take a third world war—with nations destroyed and billions dead before the people of the world realize that an enforceable global law is necessary for the survival of humanity and perhaps life on earth.

****

Thoughts About Aging

As I write this, I am in my mid-eighties - as qualified as anyone to ruminate about aging. So, here goes!

Mark Twain had it right: Old age really does beat the alternative. Life in our senior years is not only good – it is in many ways better than life at 20 or 40. Here's a poem that says it well:

What thou lovest well remains.
The rest is dross.
What thou lovest well shall not be reft from thee.
What thou lovest well is thy true heritage.

Ezra Pound, who wrote those words, was right. In the end, what remains best and most important is love and those that we hold dearest. What I love well is, first and foremost, my family: my wonderful wife and my great kids and grandchildren. I love too my friends – and our Rossmoor Eden. In fact, since retirement, some 20 years ago, I have come to love everyone that is good to me! As Ezra said, "the rest is dross."

As I ponder thoughts about aging and dying, I conclude that though we age, we never really feel old. Every day, whether one is 21 or 45 or 65 or 80 or more, every new day is a gift. Every day is one more day that can be seen, as the cliché would have it, as the first day of the rest of your life. For each of us there is always something that we have not quite gotten to. A letter than needs writing, a book that needs reading, a friend that heeds to be touched, a gourmet meal that needs to be created, a child or mate or sibling that needs to be told "I love you." So, tomorrow is not a day older: It is a day on which we might get to do one or more of the things that remains on our list of stuff that needs to be done ("bucket list!"). These homilies are even more true and far more important for the aged than for the young. The press of deeds yet to be undertaken is the very thing that keeps us young!

That last sentence warrants amplification and emphasis: **In our senior years, staying involved is the key to happiness and fulfillment.** The conventional wisdom that tells us to spend our senior years watching the world pass by, as we gently snooze on our front-porch rocking chair, may be folksy good humor, but it's bad advice! Withdrawal from the twists and turns of an active life, and willful avoidance of the challenge of dealing with new ideas, can take seniors down a dreary road to lackluster days and mind-numbing tedium.

In the life span of those who tell their stories in these pages, our world has achieved unprecedented technological and scientific developments. But in those same long years we have still not learned to peaceably resolve international conflicts, poverty remains a problem, kids today are less well educated than before, and crime and drugs and obesity plague us as never before. Progress in the physical sciences during the last eight or nine decades has been nothing less than dazzling. Progress in the social sciences has been disappointing, even abysmal.

The life stories in this book provide some degree of evidence that involvement and action are the keys to vitality and happiness in senior years. For some of the men, golf and tennis on a regular and dedicated basis are important. One became a serious playwright in his 80's, and now in his 90's has achieved great success. Another undertook to become a trustee and benefactor of his university. Yet another leads tours of fellow retirees to museums worldwide. Several undertake political involvement in serious ways, including the writing of newspaper columns.

One other characteristic of the seniors who appear in this book is the desire to cultivate relationships with others. Each of them has close personal relationships and deep friendships. Most are members of discussion groups. Most dance! Many tell good jokes – some not so good ones too! All are or have been in good marriages. All are close to children and grandchildren.

Let me close this by quoting the great pitcher, Satchel Paige, who once asked: "How old would you be if you didn't know how old you was?" And here's one more from that great sage, Anonymous: "Age is a question of mind over matter. If you don't mind, it doesn't matter!"

****

Ronald Walter Benjamin Wyatt

Born and raised in Australia, Ron Wyatt spent five years as a communications officer in the Merchant Marine; half of that time was during WW II, and half in post-war service. Following his five years at sea, Ron found his way to Canadian Universities and then to the US where he attended the University of California, Berkeley, graduating with a Masters in Public Health. Ron's long career has been in hospital and regional administration, rising to become a Vice President of the Kaiser Foundation's Health Plan and Hospitals.

The Early Years

Born in 1925, and raised in a suburb of Melbourne, Australia, I was the only son in a family of four children. My father had lost his left arm in battle during the First World War. Classified as a "limbless veteran," his modest wage from work as a clerk was supplemented by an even more modest veteran's pension. My family was nonetheless poor, deprived both economically and emotionally during the years of my childhood.

Trapping rabbits in the nearby countryside afforded a sometime supplement to our otherwise mostly meatless diet; selling rabbit furs to local furriers yielded a small but important additional income for my family. As a boy, my rabbit-hunting forays were often facilitated and guided by a favorite uncle who was in many ways my most important father figure. He brought a treasured Cocker Spaniel into my life, and further enriched my childhood years by introducing me into what I deemed to be the manly arts, such as carpentry, plumbing, and electricity, and by taking me into the world of sports, including tennis, Australian-rules football, bike racing, swimming and cricket.

During those days, Australian school-kids took tests and made school choices that would commit them at the age of 12 to one of two tracks: the manual arts or academia. My father saw fit to put me into the first track. At the age of 14, I left school and went to work at various dead-end jobs, one of which was as an usher in our local theatre. I worked too for a time as assistant to a brick mason, a job that gave me a lasting interest in and modest talent for bricklaying. To this day I enjoy building things of brick: garden walls, walkways, barbecue pits, mail-boxes and other such.

World War II began in Europe in 1939. As part of the British Empire, patriotic fervor swept Australia. It became a tradition for Melbourne old ladies to press white roses into the hands of un-uniformed young men; those not in military service were deemed to be cowardly malingerers. Though I was in my mid-teens, I looked older, and more than once had a white rose thrust on me. The pressure of wartime zeal, and the urge to get out into the world, led me to view with increasing interest the merchant marine as the surest and most readily achievable route to personal freedom and to a more exciting life.

My Years At Sea

At the age of 17, eager to find a way out of my mundane existence, I enrolled in a twelve-month course at the Marconi School of Wireless, in Melbourne, planning thereby to qualify myself to enter the merchant marine as a radio/communications specialist. In April 1943, soon after graduation from the radio school, at the age of 18 plus one day, I was hired as Radio Officer by the Union Pacific Steamship Company. Assigned to the SS Kini, we departed in early April on a four-week roundtrip – to Tasmania and back, carrying a cargo of copper plates. Though the Kini was part of a twelve-ship wartime convoy, escorted by Australian destroyers, our convoy suffered attack by a Japanese submarine. My ship escaped unharmed, but the last ship in our convoy was hit by a torpedo; we watched as it sank almost immediately after the explosion. Depth bombs dropped on the sub by our destroyer-escort damaged the hull of our ship. Though we were able to limp back to port, the Kini needed repair. The crew was redeployed to various other ships; I was assigned to the SS Waitaki, on which I sailed in South Pacific waters for three uneventful months.

Wellington, New Zealand was one of our ports of call. Wanting to see wartime action and excitement, and to see more of the world, I visited the Norwegian Consulate in Wellington, seeking assignment as radio officer on a Norwegian ship. On December 24, 1943, I sailed on the Norwegian diesel tanker Basilea, from Middleton, the port city of Christchurch, New Zealand, en route to San Francisco. As it turned out, I was to sail on the Basilea for the next two years. The Basilea and other Norwegian transport ships were assigned by the London-based Norwegian government-in-exile, to serve the allied war effort under command of the Allied Pacific Fleet. We sailed alone, not as part of a convoy.

On a typical voyage, the Basilea carried some five million gallons of aviation fuel from Vallejo, California to various ports in Northeastern Australia, and later to Port Morseby (New Guinea). On each crossing, we also carried twelve P-47 fighter planes, strapped to the deck. The planes were being taken to an American Air Base in Australia. An overwhelming stench of oil and gas permeated the ship. On our return trips to California, we carried only ballast.

Interestingly, the two weeks following discharge of our volatile cargo was the time of greatest tension. The vapor in empty tanks was in fact more explosive than the liquid fuels. Thus, for the first two weeks after discharging our cargo, we crew members would sleep on deck, fully clothed in survival gear - ready to abandon ship in the event of explosion or fire. The ship was outfitted with a wind-catcher (called "vinfanger," in Norwegian) that funneled air into the empty tanks in a continuing effort to reduce the density of fuel vapors. It took about two weeks before we felt safe enough to sleep below deck.

As the war ended, Norwegian ships were released by the Allied Command, and restored to their Norwegian owners to resume peacetime commercial service. In December 1945, I signed off the Basilea while we were docked in New Jersey, then spending Christmas holidays with my sister and brother-in-law in New Hampshire. My sister had met and married an American marine during his wartime posting to Australia for rest and recuperation, following his service in Guadalcanal.

During the almost five years (1943-48) in Norwegian ships, I grew close to my Norwegian shipmates, developing a fondness for things Norwegian that has stayed with me to this day. Because Norwegian was the only language spoken, I quickly learned enough of the language to get by. The fact that I was the only native English speaker on the ship led to a second job for me: I became the ship's Medical Officer! To deal with such routine maladies as broken bones and cuts and other minor ailments, the ship's small library held a few medical books, all in English. There were in fact several accidents in which crew members were badly injured, and where I needed to do my best to patch things up until we reached the next port to obtain professional medical care.

In January 1946, some months after the end of WW II, I signed on in Boston to yet another Norwegian ship, the S.T. Adna, as radio officer. The Adna, too, was a tanker. On most crossings we carried crude oil from various ports: Las Piedras (Venezuela), Tampico (Mexico) and Curacao (Dutch West Indies), generally to a refinery in Tenerife in the Canary Islands. I stayed on the Adna for some two years, until early 1948, when I signed off while in Kristiansand, Norway - leaving the maritime life to return to Australia, via another visit to the United States.

The Stowaways

The Canary Islands, our frequent port of call, were at the time ruled by Generalissimo Francisco Franco, Spain's ruthless dictator. To escape conditions there, citizens would from time to time attempt to bribe the seamen (from the Adna and other ships) to stow them on ship. It was routine, therefore, just before departure from port, for an officer and the Bos'n to search the ship for stowaways who when found were sent back to shore. On one occasion, two stowaways escaped detection, appearing on deck after we were far enough out at sea to avoid turnaround. Our captain, a very short and thin man, was livid. "My choice," he said to the assembled officers, "is to shoot one of the two, and demand that the survivor identify the crewman who had stowed him aboard." He then took his never-before-used pistol out of the safe, and we officers returned as a group to the mid-ship deck where the two stowaways had been left standing.

By this time many of the crew had assembled to watch the drama unfold. Aware that I knew some Spanish, the captain turned to me: "Gnisten" (Norwegian for sparks!), he shouted, "I want you to tell these stowaways that unless they point out the crew member or members who helped them stowaway, one of them will be shot and thrown overboard." I started down the stairs to relay the captain's message, but paused as I noted the accumulation of a yellow puddle at the feet of one of the stowaways. Realizing that the moment had arrived to intervene I returned to the captain and other officers, and suggested to them an alternate plan: "Let us require both stowaways to work from sunrise to sunset on the toughest jobs the Bos'n can find; if they don't do a good job we can place them in the ship's brig." After a slight delay, the first mate spoke in support of my plan, and one by one the other officers agreed. To his eternal credit, the captain gave me a big hug as a large tear rolled down his weather-beaten cheek. Needless to say, the two stowaways, who turned out to be eminent journalists, became good friends of mine, rewarding me with a copy of Miguel Cervantes' "Don Quijote de la Mancha," a tome I still treasure. Upon our arrival in Venezuela, the two took out and donned suits and ties that had been stored in their kit bags; they were met and welcomed by two Venezuelan officials.

Schooling and a Major Turn in My Life

On my 1948 return to Melbourne, I was 23 years old. Because there had been little opportunity during the wartime years to spend money, and because we received war-zone pay, my earnings had accumulated, and I found myself with sufficient funds to launch a new life. Taking a clerking job at the paper mill in Melbourne, I was soon offered entry into the company's executive training program, and did that for a time. I was determined, however, to get a wider education, and applied for entry to Melbourne University. Returning veterans that had not completed high school were required to take intelligence tests and tests in English to qualify for university entry. I took both. For the English test, I was asked to write about my impressions of the university qualification process. Because I thought it was badly managed, by incompetent people, I said that in my essay. Perhaps not surprisingly, those who rated my writings decided that I was not ready for university; though I passed the IQ Test, my "failure" of the English Test blocked my entry there.

Following rejection by the Australian academic screeners, I paid a visit (in 1949) to the Canadian Consulate in Melbourne, telling them that I was interested in higher education and in seeking their advice on how I might get that in Canada. The consulate person I met with had graduated from the University of Western Ontario - School of Business, located in London, Ontario, Canada. He suggested I might try for admittance there. That was enough for me! I travelled soon thereafter (as a paying passenger on merchant ships) to Canada (via Great Britain) and went to that school seeking admission. Before departing England en route to Canada, I worked for six weeks at Selfridge's in London.

It is worth noting that my failure to pass the English test in Melbourne is the seminal event of my life. Had I passed the test, I would have gone to Melbourne University, would have stayed for the rest of my life in Australia, and would probably have continued to work for the local paper mill. I would not have met Lona. Our seven children would not have been conceived, and my fortunate professional life with Kaiser would not have happened. The road untraveled is an open question for all of us, and I of course cannot know what my "other" life might have been. I know only that the life that I did come to, here in America, with Lona, enriched beyond all expectations by my work at Kaiser, has been a life of fulfillment and happiness.

Upon arriving in Canada, I went directly to the Western Ontario School of Business in London, and there met academic rejection once again. Because I had not attended high school, I was deemed by the admissions office to be unready for the university. Luckily, the school's Dean of Admissions, overhearing the negative conversation in his outer office, came out to interrupt. His advice to me was straightforward: go to our local high school for evening classes, five nights a week for six months, and take courses in

English and in Canadian history and government. If you get passing grades in those courses, he said, come back here and you will be accepted.

I did exactly as he suggested - went to school every evening, and spent my days working in a hosiery factory. I passed the courses, and was accepted as a freshman in September 1951. All incoming students were required to take an extensive course in English; I took pride in getting the number-one ranking in that class, receiving the W.W. Tamlyn Prize in English Literature. Winning that prize was of special importance to me because it served to give the lie to the failing grade in English that I had been given on entry tests taken two years before at Melbourne University. The prize included an award of $200 Canadian, big money to me at that time!

As I immersed myself in the first year at the university in London, something wholly unexpected and endlessly wonderful happened - raising my life to a level I had not expected to attain; I met Lona Olson, the woman I was destined soon to marry. Our meeting took place at the local Mormon Church, at which we were both members. I had been raised in the Mormon tradition during my childhood in Melbourne. Lona, 23 at the time, was a girl from Utah, serving her two years in Canada as a Mormon Missionary. At the time, Mormon young women were not encouraged to go on missions; they were expected instead to stay at home, get married and breed Mormons. Missions and conversions were left to the Elders and to old-maids. At 23, Lona was considered by mission authorities to have passed her prime, and because so many 19-year-old males were drafted to fight in the Korean War, Lona was deemed both needed and qualified for assignment as a missionary.

After my freshman year at Western Ontario School of Business, in London, I switched schools, taking my sophomore year (starting in September 1952) at the University of British Columbia, in Vancouver. For my junior and senior years, I went to the University of California, Berkeley, earning, in 1955, a Bachelor of Science Degree in Public Health, and, thereupon, entering Berkeley's three-year graduate program in hospital administration. That program began with a one-year internship, a second year taking classes at Berkeley, and a third year as an

Administrative Resident. I did the internship and the residency at hospitals in San Diego, graduating from Berkeley in 1958 with a Masters in Hospital Administration.

My Professional Life

I should begin this discussion of my professional life by noting that on entering my college years it had been my ambition to study medicine, and to become a physician. But, because I was already 26 at the time I started my university schooling, and because I would have had to start with basic courses in chemistry and biology, the road to an MD seemed too long. I decided instead to major in Hospital Administration – providing an alternative route to a life in health care. That proved to be the right decision in every way!

Following completion of graduate studies at Berkeley, I was hired, in 1959, as one of the two Assistant Administrators at Merritt Hospital in Oakland, California. I was assigned responsibility for three of the hospital's departments: Dietary, Business Office, and Employee Relations. Though I learned a great deal during my stay at Merritt, that hospital's continuing pressure on occupancy levels led to what seemed to me to be an undue focus on keeping our beds full – possibly at some expense to emphasis on successful outcomes for our patients.

After five years at Merritt, I was offered the position of Administrator of a new Kaiser hospital, in Panorama City, California, located in the San Fernando Valley. I held the Panorama City assignment for four years, after which I was promoted to become Hospital Administrator of the Kaiser Hospital in Oakland. After holding that job for four years, I was appointed Regional Administrator for the eleven Kaiser hospitals in Northern California. A year later, I was promoted to become Regional Manager of Kaiser operations in Ohio. After five years in that job, living in Shaker Heights, Ohio, I was transferred to Hawaii as Kaiser's Regional Manager and Vice President of Hospitals and Health Plans. I stayed in that position for fourteen years, until my 1989 retirement from Kaiser, at the age of 65.

Marriage and Family

In May 1952, Lona had left the Mormon mission to return to her home in Utah. I got a job in Windsor, Ontario, at the Ford Motor Car assembly line, planning to save money (I was flat broke) and to then follow Lona to Utah where we could get to know one another; we had never been on a date, and had never been alone together (mission rules). During my first week at Ford, my co-workers on the assembly line went on strike. Now jobless, I took off immediately for Utah to find Lona. When I knocked on the farmhouse door, asking to see his daughter, George F. Olson, the head of the Olson family in Fairview, Utah (population 800), looked askance at me. What was this Aussie bloke who couldn't speak proper English doing on his front porch? George F. Olson was conservative in his religion, but liberal in his acceptance of people and in his politics. He was head of the Sanpete County Democratic Party for years, possibly the only male Democrat in Fairview. Mr. Olson was a school teacher/farmer, poor in worldly things but rich in wisdom and sizing up a man. He sized me up and accepted me as his future son-in-law. Lona and I headed off to Mesa, Arizona to meet her six siblings, all of whom were living there. With their blessing but never having had a real courtship, we were married on June 23, 1952. Our love continues to grow, even now after 61 years of marriage.

We have one son and six daughters. Education is deemed of special importance to Mormon families. George F. Olson took pride in the education of his seven children; six of them graduated from college, five during the depression years. Lona attended Utah's Brigham Young University for one year, transferring then to UCLA from which she graduated in Theatre Arts in 1949. Lona later attended Hayward State College, from which she received her teaching credentials, working for a time as a substitute teacher. With that heritage, Lona and I took pride in the education of our children, especially the girls. I never wanted our daughters to be beholden to a man because she couldn't make it on her own. Each of our seven has an advanced college degree:

- Constance Lynn has a law degree and has practiced family law for 35 years in El Dorado Hills, California; she has a son, now in law school.

- Nina has a BS and an MBA from San Francisco State. She adopted and has raised two special needs children, who are now adults.
- Ronald, our son, holds an MD degree from the University of Utah, and is an orthopedic surgeon at Kaiser, Walnut Creek. He is this year serving as President of the Alameda and Contra Costa County Medical Association. He has two sons.
- Julia has a CPA and is a partner in Tricadia Capital, LLC in New York City. She has one son, now a student at St. Andrews in Scotland.
- Kathryn has an advanced degree in psychology from the University of Berlin. She has a son and a daughter, both now at university in Germany.
- Kimberly has a Masters Degree in Sociology, and has two daughters, both school teachers.
- Trina Louise, a CPA, holds an MBA from New York University. She is CFO of Prana Studios, a film company in Los Angeles. She has a daughter and a son

My Senior Years

Upon retirement, Lona and I had a house built for us in Carmel Valley, in which we planned to live out our remaining years. After twelve good years in Carmel Valley, we learned about new houses being constructed here in Rossmoor. After just one look, we bought the house on Shadowhawk Way, and have lived here for the last 13 years. The endless beauty of this community is surpassed only by the quality of life afforded by Rossmoor's many amenities and the friendships with so many of like age and background.

I believe that the secret to a happy life begins with acceptance of what you have. Too many spend their lives looking for and fantasizing about something different from or better than what they already have. I am inclined to minimalism and modesty – and admire directness, simplicity and plainness. Both Lona and I have had our share of health issues, but on the whole we remain in good health. I have run a number of marathon races, and Lona and I together have run two of them – not to win, but for the pleasure of involvement.

We two have in our senior years turned away from the Mormon religion. During the early decades of our marriage, we had been stalwart and active members of the church. Indeed, I served for some years as a Bishop of the Church – and as a Counselor to the Church's State President. Our disaffection from Mormonism was not the result of changes in church doctrine; it resulted from changes in ourselves. We had for example long accepted, without thinking too much about it, the Church's crusade against homosexuality, and accepted too its insistence that homosexuality was a choice, that people could be "turned" into heterosexuality simply by choosing to do so through psychotherapy. It finally became clear to us, and I think to the majority of Americans, that just as we, as heterosexuals, could not choose to become homosexual, the opposite "turning" would be just as impossible. We were troubled too by the Mormon insistence that the husband was indisputable head of the family, that his word was law for his wife and children. Lona and I believe that marriage is a partnership where decisions are made jointly, and that wives are equal in every way to their husbands in the raising of children and all other aspects of family life.

Thoughts About Our World

I am a strong liberal, politically and philosophically. Political differences may have been a factor in my alienation from the church. Most Mormons are Republicans, strongly conservative in their political beliefs. Mitt Romney, a Mormon, stated those beliefs during the 2012 presidential campaign in his infamous 47% diatribe: "There are 47% with him (the President), who are dependent upon government, who believe that they are victims, who believe that government has a responsibility to care for them, who believe that they are entitled to health care, to food, to housing, to you name it. That that's an entitlement... These are people who pay no income tax. Forty-seven percent of Americans pay no income tax. So our message of low taxes doesn't connect. And he'll be out there talking about tax cuts for the rich. I mean that's what they sell every four years."

I take exception with all that Romney said. There certainly are deadbeats among those with low incomes, but there are just as many among those with high incomes. For every "welfare queen" there is a wealthy person that hides his wealth in the Cayman

Islands or finds other ways to shelter income from taxation. Most of the poor or otherwise disadvantaged who get government help with food, housing and health care, or who get unemployment compensation, are out every day looking for any job that will pay them enough to free themselves from the bondage of government help.

Conservatives have an aversion to paying higher taxes. In the inanity of conservative lore, the wealthy are held to be "job creators," and, conservatives add, taxing them lessens job creation and drags down the economy. The honest and self-evident truth is, however, that the rich do not invest to create jobs – they invest to make money. Indeed, in pursuit of higher returns, they are always ready to lay-off American workers when profits can be further increased by the introduction of greater efficiency and by the use of less-costly off-shore manufacture. Romney and his Bain Capital are famously a case in point. As to entrepreneurs, companies like Microsoft, Google, Facebook, Hewlett Packard and Apple came out of dorm rooms and garages; little or no investment was needed at the start. Their founders were motivated by genius and enthusiasm – giving no thought at all to tax rates. Those who later invested in them did so to make an IPO killing, not to create jobs – nor did these late-coming investors give much thought to tax rates. Warren Buffet tells us that an investor in the 35% bracket would not be turned away from investing in a new enterprise if his rate went up to 38% - or to 45%; he is looking for hot prospects, not low tax rates.

In the final analysis, of course, job creators are those who buy goods and services; appreciation of that point tells us that there is merit in some degree of redistribution of wealth. When more people have money, more goods and services will be sold, businesses will expand, and jobs will be created. Redistribution of wealth that results from progressive tax policies serves that same purpose. Unemployment benefits, and even food stamps and subsidized housing help to fuel the economy, just as does investment in infrastructure, science and education.

Conservative Americans fume against "European-style" socialism. They ignore the benefits that accrue from higher tax rates and from more government involvement in such things as health care and education. Health care in Europe (single payer, government managed) is generally about 8-9 % of GDP. We in America spend about 17% of our GDP on health care – with far worse outcomes in the quality and reach of services. Germany, for example, pays for some weeks in a spa for recovery from health traumas. The same is true in France and Norway and Sweden and Denmark. It is said that one of the reasons Finnish students score at the top of international (OECD) tests is that teachers in Finland earn salaries at the top range of professional workers. Our teachers earn less than many factory workers, and low performance in OECD tests by American kids is in part linked to that unhappy fact. Top-notch child-care and pre-school education is free for working parents in most of the European social democracies. Education through the PhD level is available at little or no cost to qualified students.

Our country has been on a war footing ever since 1950, when we went to war in Korea. Eisenhower's warning about the dangers of the military-industrial complex was prescient. Because factories that build tanks and military aircraft provide jobs, Congress is all too ready to vote for ever-higher military budgets to preserve and to expand jobs in their districts and states. Though the Pentagon has in recent times insisted that we have more than enough tanks and of certain kinds of aircraft, Congress has voted to spend and build more just to keep the factories humming – all in the (tongue in cheek) name of national security. Our country would be far better off spending those resources on infrastructure and education. The conflicts in Vietnam, Iraq and Afghanistan are now widely viewed as having been counter-productive. Though they cost trillions of dollars and killed and maimed so many people, we are clearly less well off than if these wars had not been fought. And yet we have many, mostly Republicans, who urge war in Iran and Syria, and who taunt Obama for his diplomatic "surrender" to Iran and his readiness to forgo military action in Syria. When will we learn?

****

Robert Allen "Bobby" Frankel

Every community has one person beloved by all. In Rossmoor, where live all those profiled in this book, Bobby Frankel is that person. He is a humorist – lots of jokes, yes – but more importantly interventions - always timed perfectly to lighten the mood, to bring smiles and to draw the group closer together. Bobby often makes fun of his short stature, but to his many friends, this man is always one of the tallest among us.

The Beginning

The date is April 1923. The place is San Francisco, California. The occasion is my birth, Robert Allen Frankel, the only child of Edna and Nate Frankel.

My father and his siblings and parents all emigrated from Russia. Born in 1898., my father was 13 years old when he arrived in the US; he lived, during the family's early years, in New York City. My mother was born in 1903, in Cleveland, Ohio; her parents, shown here, had recently emigrated from Poland. She had two brothers who helped their father's neighborhood horse and wagon milk delivery business. When Mom was a teenager, the family, having heard about the wonders of California, moved to San Francisco. In San Francisco Mom played the piano for silent movies in a small nickelodeon theater that had been started by her father. My father and his family ended up in San Francisco and Oakland because my father's brother was living there.

I never knew my father's parents, both of whom died when I was one year old. I knew my maternal grandparents well, and actually lived with them for three years during the depression. We lived on a small chicken farm in Mayfield, CA, a few miles south of Palo Alto. Those were happy years for me because the little farm provided me the chance to interact with animals. At the age of 12, my mother, father and I returned from Mayfield to San Francisco and lived in an apartment in the Marina district—just a few blocks from the Palace of Fine Arts. This was the time when I attended grammar, junior high, and high school. My high school was Galileo, a schooling that provided me with some lifelong friends and a good education. I was pretty much a B student. I enjoyed high school and was class president in my senior year.

During my teen years, two big things were happening in our city: the Golden Gate Bridge was under construction, and the 1939 San Francisco Worlds Fair was being held on Treasure Island. To commemorate these two events, each of San Francisco's eight high schools was assigned to write and perform a play that would depict some aspect of the history of California. Galileo High, my school, did its part by staging a play to portray the life of Joseph B. Strauss, who was the chief engineer of the Golden Gate bridge project; I played the role of Mr. Strauss' in the performance. This event was performed in the San Francisco Opera House, before a live audience, and recorded for radio. It was special fun for me and for my family to listen to the broadcast when it was aired.

Another acting experience came from involvement, during my teen years, at a drama school called the Theatre Arts Colony. We performed a play by William Saroyan, entitled "Something About A Soldier." I auditioned for and won the role of a 12-year old son – I will never forget the thrill of the applause that greeted my performance!

How I Won the War!

After graduating from high school I went to work at Western Pipe and Steel Shipyards, helping to construct Liberty Ships – destined to play a big role in WWII. In 1942, at the age of 19, I enlisted in the Army Air Corps, and did my basic training at the Stockton Air Base. I was scheduled at first to work as a mechanic on the maintenance line at the base, but while waiting to go to mechanics school I was assigned to help at the unit's bakery. Because I enjoyed that work, I applied to become the squadron's baker – and won that assignment. I served one year in Stockton, and was then transferred to Mather Field in Sacramento, again serving as a baker. After one year in Sacramento, I was sent overseas, in 1944, and transported in a 100-ship convoy to Naples, Italy. From Naples I was shipped to Bari, Italy, on the Adriatic Coast, where I worked in the officer's mess as the baker in a small unit. During my year of service in that camp, I had a number of exciting experiences, none of which included combat – other than fighting a field stove – which I found to be a formidable foe!

When the war ended, I was brought back to Naples to a huge replacement center. The center processed service men that were on their way home to the US. Because I had been overseas for only about a year, and had not seen battle, I had fewer "points" than many, and was therefore one of the last to be shipped home. I was to remain in that camp for more than a year before being returned to the states. Those of us being readied for the trip back to the states were not able to leave the camp before boarding the ship or the flight home.

Three buddies and I provided entertainment for the many soldiers awaiting shipment by setting up and manning crap tables that we made out of large wooden planks covered with army blankets. We provided cigarettes, beer and overhead lighting, along with the tables. Our crap tables were heavily attended by all ranks. My partners and I managed the tables, and took a percent of the play – which over the course of time gave us a stash of currency in the thousands of dollars. There were strict rules governing how much money you could send home, about $300 to $500, depending on your rank. If you had money in excess of what was allowed, it took some clever maneuvering to try and get it home. I managed to get $15,000 home – which was a small part of what I had accumulated.

I left the rest with a couple of "friends," and never saw it again. Getting money home in large amounts was unheard of, and how I eventually managed to get my $15,000 home will go with me to the grave. I could have made another $20,000 had I been willing to marry an Italian girl and bring her home. Many Italian families were willing to make arrangements of that kind. Wisely, I did not take advantage of that opportunity. In October 1946, I boarded ship, in Naples, for the voyage back to the states; I was discharged with the rank of Sergeant, and returned to civilian life, again in San Francisco.

Back Home

After a few weeks of frivolous entertainment, it was time to think about a job and to go about earning a living. My first experience was working for a furrier, selling furs. This occupation was not to my liking, and my next attempt was to sell ladies dresses to small retail outlets in small towns in California. That occupation was not long-lived. It was during this time that I had met a realtor who convinced me that I should apply for a salesman's license and join his company. Real estate sales were booming, partly because of the FHA and VA loans. I enjoyed the work and did fairly well. However, the company I was working for was using shady practices that I could not condone. Conscience driven, I decided to leave. Of course this meant that I needed to acquire another marketable skill.

My father had spent his entire career as a window trimmer, and was quite successful. He offered me an opportunity to learn his skill, designing window displays for San Francisco retailers. I found that I had a talent for it, and did it for ten years. My more ingenious and clever window displays came to be written about in a national trade magazine. One of my most popular windows was when I dressed a male manikin as a matador, standing in a ring of sand, in position to gore the bull. There was a large sign reading "Louis Roth clothes are the finest clothes a man can wear – NO BULL." In another instance, the store wanted to highlight a new series of high priced men's shirts by emphasizing that there was something exceptional about them. So I dressed a lovely female model in one of the shirts, cinched a belt around her waist and had the tails of the shirt hang below. She sat in a comfortable chair and beside her the sign read " Jack Davis offers something exceptionally nice in a man's shirt." There was a small stand with a telephone on it next to the model. The phone line was connected to the outside of the window so people could talk to her about these beautiful shirts – or whatever else they might want to discuss!

"Party Props" is Born

Because people who knew of my line of work were frequently asking me about decorating for parties, it occurred to me that there should be a store that specialized in party decorations. At a dinner party one evening, during casual conversation, I mentioned my idea. One of the guests thought that it was a good thought and offered to become my partner, and to finance the project. This was 1950 – and Party Props was born – a store devoted entirely to ideas and supplies for parties of all kinds. For a time, I continued my window-trimming work while setting up Party Props, and worked 16 hours a day. After a rocky beginning, Party Props, located in the Stonestown shopping center, became the first party goods store in America, and grew to be a great success.

Party Props was the inspiration for other creative ideas. One of my favorite came from grandmothers, aunts and mothers with the question, "Why don't we women have something to pass out announcing the birth of new grandchildren – like the men-folk are able to pass out cigars?" I woke up one evening with the idea of using the word "announcement" to be spelled "announcemint". We had a local candy-maker make and box a pink-wrapped candy "announcemint" for the girls and a blue-wrapped "announcemint" for the boys. At the same time we added "engagemints" and "treatmints".

While I was running Party Props, opportunities became available to create theme parties in San Francisco hotels for some Fortune 500 businesses. One time, while decorating for Chevron company business breakfast, the theme of which was "get out there and sell," I told the head of the breakfast meeting that I could had an idea that he could use for his meeting; "Have some people," I suggested, "turn all the chairs in the room, and tape a one dollar bill to the bottom of the seat. When everyone is seated for the meeting, you could announce the importance of sales and ask them to stand, turn the chairs over and remove the item that you see. When this is done and they return to their seats, you can explain that 'if you want to make a buck, get off your ass!'"

Another idea that was useful at corporate meetings was to silk-screen a message on a pillow-case that would state the message the corporation wanted to get across. Trivial stuff, now that I think about it – but it worked!

Hotel Lobby Shops

While Party Pops was growing, it was being managed by a woman I had hired, leaving me free to develop other options. I came up with an idea to build hotel lobby shops; that idea was triggered by the opportunity given to me to acquire the four-foot deep front of a San Francisco cable car. I thought that the cable-car front would serve well as a little hotel-lobby souvenir shop; I took the idea to the Hilton Hotel management. They agreed, and leased space to me at which to place it. The cable-car front was big enough for the shop's attendant to sit in, and to deal with customers. The idea worked better than I expected, and eventually I had twelve display cases at different places in the Hilton Lobby. All of this led to a string of other lobby shops: a new career was born! While at the Hilton Hotel, I was also commissioned to design and build a wine-garden restaurant in the lobby; that too was very well received.

When the new Hyatt Regency Hotel in San Francisco was being built, I had the opportunity to acquire space in that lobby – where I designed and built a jewelry store bearing my own name. I was now operating stores in four locations in the San Francisco area and the Hyatt Regency made five. During this time the management in the San Francisco Hilton offered me the opportunity to take over the gift store in the lobby of the Los Angeles Hilton, which I did. A short time after acquiring that location, the Hilton organization offered me the opportunity to build a store in the Beverly Hilton. Eventually I was operating nine locations divided among four major hotels: the San Francisco Hilton, the San Francisco Hyatt Regency, and the Hilton Hotels in Los Angeles and Beverly Hills.

There were some interesting characters in the hotel business in those days. One of the most colorful was Henry Lewin, vice President of the Western Hilton chain. Mr. Lewin and I became friends, and he backed all of my operations. He was one of the brightest hotel executives in the US, and was not reluctant to let you know it. He dressed like a peacock in fancy tailored clothes, smoked big cigars and ruled with an iron hand. As for his ego, even though a Jew, he felt that he could have been a general in Hitler's army. It was through my association with Mr. Lewin that I met and played tennis at the Hilton with Bill Cosby and Tony Bennett.

Eventually I sold all the retail stores and opened an office and small store in a building on Market Street in San Francisco, just to have a place to go and keep myself occupied. I had an inventory of jewelry and gifts and called this little store "Gift Galaxy". Everything I sold was at discount and my business survived from word of mouth advertising. During this time my previous managing partner in the Los Angeles Hilton suggested we open a shoe store in the San Francisco Hilton Hotel. It was a good location and my previous experience in the Hiltons made it easy to acquire the space. Up to this point, I had not made any serious mistakes in my business life. But that was soon to change. We opened a Bally Shoe Store that I managed for a short time. We financed its operation with our money and a bank loan that my partner and I co-signed.

Big Loss

It was during this period that an opportunity to buy a vacation house in Carmel became available. My wife and I went down to see it and bought it that same day, with the plan to retire there. I was 56 years old. A few months later we decided to move to Carmel permanently. I explained to my partner that I intended to move to Carmel permanently, and he agreed to take over management of the Bally shoe store. I had no qualms about turning over the store to him because our previous partnership had been successful, and I had no reason to distrust him. We agreed that he should pay me my original investment and he would take over the bank loan. With that agreement, we moved to Carmel. Approximately six months after leaving San Francisco, I received a letter from the bank that the loan payments were not being made. I was surprised to learn that my partner had started using heroin. Due to his addiction, we lost the store and I had to pay the loan and pay off the lease in the Hilton. This was a great financial loss, and put me in a position where I needed to start something again to create an income.

One of my tennis friends had retired from a printing-broker business – selling printed business forms to retail establishments. I told him I liked to sell, and offered to work for him to expand the customer base for his business. He had terrific business-form suppliers in Oregon – very competitive with any in our area. He was an excellent tutor, and soon the business became successful. Another friend, who was in the advertising specialty business, said that I should merge my two sales lines, and sell advertising specialties along with the printed forms. I did that, and soon found myself with a new $400,000 per year business. I spent 20 enjoyable years running that business in Carmel.

My residence in Carmel was a two story home, and climbing the stairs was getting to be a problem for my wife, so we decided to retire from Carmel, and to seek a single story residence in the Bay Area. Our search finally led us to Rossmoor, which turned out to be a marvelous move. However, after a couple of years, my wife became ill with Alzheimer's disease, and needed to be placed in a nearby care facility. I sold our place, and found a smaller residence – still in Rossmoor. Just a year or so later, this residence burned to the ground in a fire that destroyed the whole twelve-unit building, and all of my possessions. When the fire happened, Rossmoor management helped the displaced residents deal with insurance matters, and find new living facilities. Their first concern was to replace whatever medications were needed. They went around the table asking us what medications we needed and I replied "my Viagra" which provided some badly needed humor for the occasion. Good friends put me up temporarily, until I found another residence. I have lived in Rossmoor for the last 14 years.

Personal Life

When in 1946 I came home from the service, I remained single for only 6 months. My first girlfriend's mother did not approve of the relationship, so my girlfriend ran away from home to her aunt's house, calling me from there. Out of empathy more than love, I picked her up and we drove to Reno and got married. This was an impulsive decision. The marriage lasted only about two years, and there were no children.

My true love, from the time I was 13 years old, was still the person I wanted to be with. However she was married at the time and had two children. Eventually we decided we wanted to be together. So she divorced her husband and we got married. I raised her 2 children and we had one of our own. This marriage lasted 20 years, but eventually she became erratic and we divorced. We raised our son Todd, who was a wonderful child and has had a successful career in the automobile business. He lives in Oregon with his wife. His marriage has provided me with three adult grandchildren, each of whom has graduated from college and done very well. One of my grandsons has given me one great granddaughter with another child on the way.

My next marriage was to the woman who had managed Party Props for me. She was divorced and had three children. She was a marvelous person and eventually we married. Unfortunately, the end of this marriage was one of the saddest things that happened to me in my life. We were only married a bit more than two years when she died of breast cancer. The children returned to their biological father. Now a bachelor again, I bounced around in various relationships for several years until I met Mindy who was a very attractive lady. The single life was never for me and I married again, for the fourth time. This was the wife with whom I shared the years in Carmel Valley and the few short years in Rossmoor. When Mindy had to go to a care center, her family wanted us to become divorced for financial and personal reasons and I agreed. Since then I have stayed single but have enjoyed a long standing loving relationship with my current companion, Jane, a wonderful person in every way.

Rossmoor has provided me with wonderful friends and social activities. For years I played tennis as a member of the tennis club – which has been the source of most of my friendships to this day. Next, I started lawn bowling and enjoyed that for several years. I have at various times been a member of the Philosophy Club, and the chess club. I am a founding member of a club called ROMEO, an acronym for Retired Old Men Eating Out; we meet every other Tuesday for lunch. I did volunteer work in the Rossmoor library and at Jon Muir Hospital. I have always been a collector of Netsukes (small ivory carvings), time-pieces, wood carvings, and assorted artifacts; unfortunately, all of this was lost in the fire. Currently, at the age of 91, I enjoy the company of my friends, walking a mile or so every day with my partner, Jane, and watching movies and educational DVDs on TV. In the last few years I have taken many international vacations with my Jane, including trips to Italy, Bali and Malaysia, Canada, the Mediterranean, Central Europe, and the British Isles. Before I die, I can tell myself that I have had a great life, known some wonderful people, enjoyed loving and being loved, and have very few regrets.

****

Persistence and Our Portable World

We all know that any worthwhile endeavor takes determination, hard work and persistence. When we fail, it is the latter quality, persistence, that too often seems to be the missing ingredient. Victor Borge, the late Danish comedian/pianist, liked to tell the story of his grandfather, who developed a soft-drink called "One-Up." When it failed in the marketplace, he developed "Two-Up." When that failed, he developed Three and Four and Five-Up, all of which failed. At "Six-Up," Borge wryly tells us, Grandfather Borge stopped trying, thereby depriving Grandson Victor of the "Seven-Up" fortune that would have been his inheritance had his grandfather tried just one more time!

Borge, in humorously lamenting his grandfather's lost fortune, was emphasizing the need to persist. We know that Thomas Edison, in developing the electric light bulb, experimented with dozens of filament materials before finding that a carbonized sewing thread and an improved vacuum inside the globe provided a reliable and long-lasting source of light.

And here, in a 1910 speech called *Citizenship in a Republic,* is Theodore Roosevelt on the importance of persistence: "It is not the critic who counts; not the man who points out how the strong man stumbles, or where the doer of deeds could have done them better. The credit belongs to the man who is actually in the arena, whose face is marred by dust and sweat and blood, who strives valiantly; who errs, who comes short again and again; because there is no effort without error and shortcoming."

Winston Churchill put it this way: Success is not final; failure is not fatal. It is the courage to continue that counts.

Persistence might be called the hallmark-characteristic of the sixteen men who tell their life stories in *November Song,* the distinguishing trait that took each of them from humble beginnings to lives of achievement. Each of them, with unending persistence, has left a legacy of accomplishments in his corner of the world.

I found the little gem that follows, on Google. The author is unknown. I felt the words, about the lasting presence of what is in our minds and our hearts, were meant to be in this book!

My world is portable. So is yours. For each of us, our portable life consists of our capabilities, things we have learned, our memories, our plans, those we love, and our accomplishments. All of that is with me, and with you, wherever we are, whatever the state of our health and wealth. The circumstances of our lives can be fluid, and not always in our control. Events can take us from well to ill, from rich to poor, from success to failure, from joy to tragedy. But the portable aspects of our lives remain both the armor that shields us from utter catastrophe and the platform on which we can build ever-better lives, or rebuild from the inevitable setbacks that from time to time visit even successful lives. The lesson here is that we need constantly to reinforce the portable stuff: capabilities, learning, memories, plans, love, and accomplishments.

****

Arthur Charles Dreshfield

After earning a PhD in Chemical Engineering. Art had a 40-year career in the pulp and paper industry. He now plays bridge regularly, albeit with less intensity and success than he had with papermaking science and technology. He also struggles around the golf course regularly, enjoying the game but ruing that his scientific background is of absolutely no help in keeping his ball out of the sand traps and water hazards that abound on the Rossmoor courses.

The Early Years

Born in Kalamazoo, Michigan, I was the older of two sons. My father was an industrial chemist holding a steady job during the depression, so we were relatively prosperous. When I was seven, Dad was transferred to Wilmington, Delaware, and we lived there for four years. My father was an avid bridge player. While a student at Columbia, he became friends with Oswald Jacoby, one of the early greats in bridge. They often played together (usually for money) during their years at Columbia.

My parents divorced when I was eleven, and in September of 1941 my brother Bob and I moved with our mother to an apartment in

Brookline, Mass., a suburb of Boston, and the town she where she had grown up.

My father later remarried and had two more sons. My half-brothers Bill and Phil are 20+ years younger than me. We four brothers have remained in reasonably close contact considering our geographic separation. We see one another whenever it fits our travel plans, and have been able to arrange family reunions every few years.

The Pearl Harbor attack happened a few months after we moved to Brookline, and World War II had a substantial impact on life in America. Rationing and shortages of various foods changed eating habits. Gasoline was rationed; our "C" ration was three gallons per week, too little to merit keeping our car. In coastal Massachusetts, night time blackouts were required and enforced. I was a volunteer plane-spotter, spending a couple of hours a week on our roof and phoning in any time I saw a plane I didn't recognize. (I only saw one once, and it wasn't a threat.) Collections of many things for the war effort were common, including newspapers, coat hangers, and toothpaste tubes. I spent one summer on a bean farm in Maine, along with other high-school students, in a program created to substitute for men who had been called into service.

Mother started working part-time for the Boston chapter of the National Council of Jewish Women, an organization whose primary purpose was sponsorship of social and educational programs. She rose to become its executive secretary. With the post-WWII exodus of Jewish Holocaust survivors from Germany, the organization became heavily involved in helping these immigrants settle into new lives in Boston.

When I was in high school, just after WWII had ended, we had many interactions with the survivors. Most didn't want to discuss or dwell on their Holocaust experiences. On several occasions, I went with mother to meet them at the pier when their boat docked, or at Boston's South Station when they arrived by train from New York. Some spent their first night or two in America in a bed at our house until mother got them settled elsewhere. My brother and I would sleep on a couch or on the floor.

That experience and subsequent revelations about the Holocaust have had an important influence on shaping my geo-political views. My great-grandparents on both sides were predominately German Jews who came to America in the late 1800s. Most American Jews today feel fully accepted in this country, and many are prosperous and successful. But that same situation prevailed in Germany – until Hitler came along. Though there is no hint today that such widespread virulent and barbarous anti-Semitism could develop in America, the holocaust is a reminder that it is not a total impossibility. So I am a strong supporter of Israel and its right to exist, even though I am well aware of the tensions about its aggressive internal and defense policies. Israel is psychologically important to Jews around the world as a place to which they might flee if necessary. Since Israel is America's most reliable ally and the only democracy in the Middle East, this has never created any conflict of interest for us.

Education

I grew up with a strong interest in science, and had a record of good grades at Brookline High School. I considered going to three nearby universities with good engineering programs, MIT, Worcester Poly and Rensselaer Poly. However, I chose the University of Illinois because Dad was a resident of that state, and the cost for a child of a resident was much lower than the cost at those other schools. U of I had and still has a highly regarded Chemical Engineering department. I graduated in 1951 with a BS Degree in Chemical Engineering.

For graduate study, I chose the Institute of Paper Chemistry in Appleton, Wisconsin.. It was a small and highly specialized graduate school, associated with Lawrence College, that sought to educate "scientific generalists" who would be qualified candidates for technical leadership and management positions. I received an MS in 1953 and a PhD in Chemical Engineering in 1956. My research and dissertation were on the arcane subject of "Moisture Migration in Porous Media During Drying," which had to do with the drying of newly made paper, an important process in the paper-making business.

I had signed up for the advanced ROTC program at Illinois, and was at ROTC summer camp at Aberdeen Proving Grounds in

Maryland in June 1950 when the North Korean army swarmed across the Yalu River and the Korean War started. I would normally have been called up for active duty upon graduation, but was deferred because I had been accepted to graduate school in what was deemed to be a critical field. I remained in the Army Reserves for some 15 years, and was honorably discharged in 1966, as a 1st Lieutenant, never having seen active duty.

Marriage and Children

In September 1956, soon after grad school, I went to Brookline to visit my mother. During that visit, I met Ardeth Miller (Ardy), who lived with her parents in nearby Newton. Though I was living in Philadelphia, we managed over the next seven months to conduct a long-distance courtship, and were married in April 1957.

Ardy was born in Boston and grew up in the suburbs there. She graduated from high school in 1949, and from the University of Massachusetts in 1953 with a BA in Economics. She had worked for the National Security Agency in Washington, then for Raytheon in Waltham, Mass., and was working for the RAND Corporation in Cambridge when we met. She was a computer programmer on the DEW Line development, an air defense system in the Cold War era. RAND was a partner in a consortium that included MIT, IBM, and the Air Force. They programmed in octal in those days, and used punch cards to program the computer. Each card held about one-millionth as much information as a low-end flash drive of today.

Ardy and I have three sons. Kenneth was born in 1958, Richard in 1959, and Gerald in 1962. All three are college graduates, married and leading good lives. We have three grandchildren. Two are recent college graduates and the youngest is in high school. Anne, Richard and Sue's daughter, is the only one living in the Bay Area at the moment.

When our sons were in high school, Ardy went back to work – part time at first, and then full time for the last 10+ years before she retired. Her last two positions were in Duluth, first as Executive Director of the vibrant YWCA there, and then as Associate Director of United Way. She also served on the boards of several non-profit organizations; the largest being the 400-bed St. Mary's hospital. After moving back to the Bay Area, she became a very active supporter of the San Francisco Symphony, was on their Volunteer Council in various capacities for over 10 years, and was recognized as a Volunteer of the Year during that time. She still serves on some SFS committees.

We've enjoyed a wide range of recreational activities. These included square-dancing, golf, tennis, bridge, swimming, sailing, travelling and reading. Our interests and perspectives have changed as we've aged: we've gained knowledge, insights, and perhaps some wisdom.

My Life in the World of Paper

My first job out of grad school was with the Philadelphia-based research labs of Scott Paper Company. Hired as a Research Engineer, my assigned tasks were to evaluate papermaking equipment and processes, and to develop ways to make paper better and at lower cost.

In 1957, after two years with Scott and shortly after our marriage, Ardy and I moved from Philadelphia to Walnut Creek, California, joining Fibreboard Paper Products Company – the company with whom I was to be associated in various capacities for 15 years, in their Antioch, Ca. Research and Development (R&D) lab. I began there as a group leader responsible for improving the company's pulping and bleaching technology, became Research Director in 1963, and Director of Product Development in 1968.

In 1972, I joined the Potlatch Corporation, with whom I would be associated for 23 years – initially as a Division Director of Development and subsequently as a Division Manager of Research, Engineering and Environmental compliance, working from the company's San Francisco office. In 1980, I was transferred to Cloquet, Minnesota to become the company's Director of Fiber Research and Development, the position I held until I retired in 1994 at age 65.

We enjoyed much about living and working in Minnesota, and had many good friends there, but decided we'd be better off returning to the Bay Area after retiring. That's when we moved to Rossmoor, a decision we've never regretted.

For the next ten years, I did part-time consulting related to pulp and paper technological and economic concerns. In the last three, I served on a program sponsored by the US Department of Energy and administered by Georgia Tech to foster energy conservation in the pulp and paper industry.

Secrets to a Happy Life

You need to begin by distinguishing long-term happiness from moments of joy. Real lasting happiness is a by-product of how you live your life. The Declaration of Independence speaks of "life, liberty and the *pursuit* of happiness," a profound distinction. Pursuit of happiness is a realistic and meaningful opportunity for everyone. I've come to believe that successful pursuit requires that you have:
- something worthwhile to do,
- some one or something to love, and
- something to look forward to.

Activities that lead to happiness can be something useful, something educational, or something recreational. A job, philanthropic work, community service, a sport, a hobby, a project, reading, writing, singing, sewing, gardening; anything that gives you pleasure, a sense of accomplishment, and that you feel is worth doing.

For some 15+ years I've served as a volunteer docent on the former (FDR's) presidential yacht *Potomac*. I started because it gave me a chance to enjoy cruising on San Francisco Bay, but got the greatest satisfaction from helping visitors have a better experience. I enjoyed doing the cruise narrations and the one-on-one contacts with visitors. With rare exception we benefit from having some involvement with others; we are, after all, social beings. It is essential too to take a moment now and then to appreciate beauty in its many forms, or to celebrate a milestone or an accomplishment, however large or small.

Regarding love, I use it in the broadest sense here – ala "love thy neighbor." In its simplest terms, I think it means trying to help others have a better life, to share common interests and goals, and to being a good friend, which in turn leads to having good friends. Practicing the Golden Rule is a simple if not always easy way to go about this – particularly if you add the complementary Jewish version: *Do not do unto others that which is hateful to you.*

Enjoying your work is another very valuable aspect of a happy life. For professional careers, the philosophy for success is really quite similar: treat others well and help them succeed. This maxim applies to superiors, peers, subordinates, coworkers, suppliers, customers, neighbors, government officials, and others you interact with. I found Steven Covey's *Seven Habits of Highly Effective People* and other writings of his to be pertinent and helpful.

Ardy and I both enjoy classical music, and have had season tickets to the San Francisco Symphony for the last 15+ years. We also hold season tickets to the San Francisco Ballet, and to the Center Repertory Theatre, and California Symphony at Walnut Creek's Lesher Center; we also attend and enjoy performances by various other musical and dramatic groups and performers in the area and when we travel.

A focus on what you have, rather than what you don't have will also help immeasurably. A positive attitude, a sense of humor, and enthusiasm are usually contagious and help create happiness.

Thoughts About Technology

Technology means different things to different people. Although many equate it today to smart-phones, computers and the internet, it is much broader than that. I'll define it as the combination of knowledge, skills, tools, materials and equipment that enable people to achieve a desired result. The ability to develop, improve, and use new technology is a key distinction between we humans and other living beings.

Technology in and of itself is amoral. Whether it is good or bad depends on how, where, and how widely it is used. All new technology will have some unforeseen impacts and consequences. Many will be beneficial, but some will be troublesome. Many technologies found to be useful for peaceful purposes were initially developed and applied for military applications. Examples abound: the most obvious are computers, the web, space satellite-enabled communications, GPS, radar, jet aircraft, prosthetics, and so much more.

Technology has evolved since the dawn of civilization, and will continue to evolve, probably at an increasing rate. Power generation is a fine example. For many millennia, the only sources of power were from human effort, animals, wind and water. The technology to produce power from *external combustion* first emerged about 350 years ago with the advent of the steam engine. It quickly provided orders-of-magnitude increases over wind, water, and animal power sources, and has enabled game-changing improvements in construction, manufacturing, transportation and many quality-of-life factors.

The technology to produce power from *internal combustion* was invented just over 200 years ago. Widespread use quickly followed the discovery of oil about 150 years ago. It has revolutionized land, sea, and air travel for peaceful and military purposes. It has improved the nature of urban and rural life in many ways, and has largely succeeded the steam engine. But it has also increased congestion, injuries, and air pollution. It is dependent on non-renewable resources, and is arguably a significant factor in oceanic acidification and global warming, and their worrisome impacts on climate and all forms of life.

The technology to produce power from *nuclear fission* is only about 60 years old. Whether it has long term viability is still in question following the Fukushima meltdown and disposal of long-life radioactive waste.

Similar stories of benefits and unforeseen consequences can be told about chemical technology, nuclear technology, farming technology, medical and genetic technology, and computer and internet technology. It is worth noting that the impacts of successive technologies have grown from local to regional to global, while the socio-political ways of dealing with them have barely changed.

I have no doubt that future new technologies will have the same patterns. Some applications will be beneficial – but some will not. A bit of relevant wisdom is that people must learn to prevent or avoid what they cannot manage, and learn to manage what they cannot avoid or prevent.

I don't pretend to foresee what the most significant new technologies will be. Having said that, it's pretty obvious that digital computer technology, the internet, and related subjects such as robotics will continue to be among them. Facebook and other social networking technologies, and their ability to connect people are becoming increasingly significant factors in geopolitics; that influence is certain to grow, both in good ways and bad. There is a crying need for power generation from renewable non-polluting sources, and for ways to store large quantities of power. If necessity is the mother of invention, some exciting new technologies should be forthcoming in this area. I believe (thanks to insights from my grandson David) that nanotechnology will also have a tremendous impact in many critical areas. It seems inevitable that new understandings and capabilities in the field of genetics will create some fantastic opportunities, and difficult moral issues.

Concerns About the Future

I am concerned about dangerously increasing dependence and interdependence on very large networks and systems. The electric grid and the internet are prime examples. Modern society cannot function if either of these is disrupted – and the potential impacts have grown from local to regional, continental, and even planet-wide. Our world is so utterly linked to and dependent on digital technology that we have become vulnerable to disruption by accident or malevolence.

I am concerned too about the possibility of new world-wide plagues. Ongoing overuse of antibiotics may well result in the emergence of deadly antibiotic-resistant bacteria. Global travel and commerce can rapidly spread any local outbreak. On a more general basis, I am concerned that we don't adequately understand the exquisitely complex and delicate interrelationships of the global and local ecosystems, so will continue to unwittingly alter them, usually for the worse. A current example is the unexplained decimation of the honey-bee population.

I am concerned about the increasingly dysfunctional governmental paralysis in our country. Every issue, especially the most important or urgent one, gets treated by both parties as a wedge opportunity to gain short term partisan advantage and to please their activist extremist supporters. A close Supreme Court decision (Citizens vs. United) has effectively eliminated campaign-funding limits by corporations, unions, and other special interests. As a result, we are more and more getting the best laws and politicians that money can buy.

I am concerned about the increasing concentration of wealth and income in the hands of the very wealthy, and the decline of the middle class. This pattern is typical of third-world countries, and is a threat to the social fabric that binds our nation.

On a very fundamental level, civilized existence requires that every individual's freedom to act unilaterally must be balanced against the needs and desires of other individuals and groups. The evolutionary traits (physical, mental, and emotional) that enabled our ancestors to survive and prosper in more primitive situations are inadequate and often counterproductive for the current situation. I am concerned that we will not be able to change this sufficiently to avoid man-made catastrophes.

Thoughts About War, Disputes, and Competing

Humans have fought wars since the beginning of recorded history. They seem to be a very counterproductive consequence of our basic instincts and needs. We are instinctively competitive, acquisitive, and territorial. We compete for material stuff (essential or not), territory, mates, power and recognition. We also are members of various groups – some by choice – some not. They may be geographic, ethnic, religious, racial, tribal, political, commercial, social or ideological. Some groupings are essential (or useful) for survival; others aren't.

Arguably, the most basic and important goals of society and civilization are to organize human affairs in a way that balances each individual's needs and desires with those of the other individuals and of the group as a whole. And to enable a balance of the goals of one group with those of other affected groups, and the balance of current impacts with future ones.

Groups of any significant size require some organization and leadership. In many cases (especially political ones), the attributes that enable a person to best their competition and thereby become the leader (elected or otherwise) are not conducive to maximizing the common good, or to optimizing a balance between short term and long term impacts. Although there are noteworthy exceptions, many who rise to top political positions are highly competitive, manipulative, and motivated by power and self-interest. Some are ruthless and vicious. All politics, as Tip O'Neill famously noted, is ultimately local; the problem is that good current local politics can be – and often is – at odds with broader longer-term interests.

Mob psychology is another factor than cannot be ignored. Groups of people will do all sorts of hateful or destructive things that individuals would not do, even if they could. Mob psychology is particularly ominous when the opposition has been demonized or dehumanized and brought to be viewed as a threat. A common enemy is a very strong bond. Hate is a very strong emotion – often stronger than love. Emotion will often overwhelm good judgment. And scapegoats are very useful substitutes for positive productive action.

So where does this leave us as a civilized society when there will inevitably be competition, conflicts, corruption, and troublemakers for the foreseeable future? I've found it helpful to sort conflict resolution into five approaches: accommodate, avoid, compete, compromise, and collaborate. This is applicable to everything from trivial disputes between individuals to world-wide geopolitical competition between nations. They are not mutually exclusive in any particular situation.

War is the ultimate form of inter-group competition. It results from the failure of the other four approaches to provide a less destructive resolution to whatever the dispute was over. It is usually fomented by a minority of extremist activists who overwhelm the moderate live-and-let live majority, and is abetted by short-sighted, self-serving politicians and bureaucrats.

Technology has increased the ease of killing and destroying, and made it potentially available to anyone and everyone, and to groups of any size all over the world. And the threat has evolved to increasingly diverse forms. Wars, once limited to nation vs. nation have devolved to *sub-national conflicts* such as Sunni versus Shiite, Muslim versus Jew; to *asymmetric combat* where small uncoordinated groups challenge the establishment; and to situations where it is very difficult to determine *who is a friend and who is a foe*, or *who is a combatant and who is not*, or *whom to negotiate with* to arrange an end to the combat; and *how to deal with brain-washed terrorists* who truly believe the finest thing they can do with their life is to kill and maim a lot of their enemies and terrorize many others as possible in a final suicidal act.

I see no easy or simple answer to preventing these situations. In the absence of an extra-terrestrial threat or enemy that could unite everyone on earth, it behooves everyone to think constructively (but not worry futilely) about what can be done to channel competition into constructive and socially acceptable forms; to solve intergroup disputes by some combination of non-destructive approaches; and to minimize their magnitude and impact. Just do everything in your power to help make things and others move in the right direction. And then go on with the gift of life, liberty, and the pursuit of happiness that you have been given.

Thoughts about Religion, God, and the Hereafter

I am a Jewish agnostic. I see no evidence that there is any sort of sentient being that planned or is controlling the universe, or is giving individuals, groups of individuals, or the human race any particular attention or primacy. I also doubt that we individuals have a soul that will continue to exist after our physical death.

Having said this, I see no reason to challenge those who believe otherwise. For starters, it is impossible to conclusively prove any negative. And more basically, I think our brains and senses are far too limited to ever truly and completely understand the universe. This is not meant to demean the scientific insights that have been made about the universe, about living and non-living matter, and about human affairs. They help explain a lot of observed phenomena and devise important technologies.

But here are some examples of unanswered questions:
- Is the universe we observe the only one that exists?

- Are there more than three dimensions; (or four if you recognize time as a dimension)? How many? What are they like?
- If our universe started from the Big Bang, what was there beforehand? If it is not infinite, what is beyond its boundaries?

I never spent time dwelling on these questions. Like life and death, they are what they are, and they likely will never be fully understood by humans. But they remind me to be humble and tolerant: neither my beliefs nor opposing ones can be conclusively proven or disproven. It is important that the separation of church and state be maintained! We should not forget this has been the exception, not the rule, around the world and over time.

In terms of my personal hopes, I would like to continue living as long as I have sufficient mental and physical capabilities to be independent and not be a physical, financial or emotional burden on any of my family or friends. When I no longer can do that and there is no reasonable hope for recovering, I'd like a swift painless ending. For sure, I'd prefer hospice to some drawn-out efforts to prolong my days. I think our country has a long way to go to deal properly with end-of-life issues.

An Ethical Will

Temple Isaiah in Lafayette, Ca., and Temple Israel in Duluth, Minnesota both played significant positive roles in our lives, mainly in social and non-liturgical areas. We were members of a Havurah at each. A Havurah is a synagogue- sponsored social group blending features of an extended family, a friendship circle, and a study group. Ardy and I had a role in founding one of the earliest ones some 50+ years ago in the 1960s. Our Havurahs have done lots of things and covered a variety of subjects, ranging from ethical issues, to Jewish professional athletes, to the Last Supper.

We once tasked ourselves to put on a single sheet of paper a set of notions to pass on to our heirs about our ethics and ideas about life. Ardy and I wrote the nine-point document that follows in 2000, some 13 years ago, and still subscribe to it today. There shouldn't be anything new or surprising in it to our friends and family. We hope our behavior, and to a lesser degree our words, have conveyed our thoughts, feelings, beliefs and values. Here it is:

1. Life is a gift and a blessing, and it's finite. Accept it, and take maximum advantage of it. Enjoy and appreciate your accomplishments and good fortune, large and small. Look at the bright side of things.
2. Life is too important to be taken seriously. Keep your sense of humor, see the humor in most everyday situations.
3. Stay in touch with family and friends. Love and friendship are indeed the most important and valuable aspects of humanity and a full life.
4. Ignore the small slights and irritations. Forget them if you can. If not, forgive them and mean it.
5. Don't let material things come between you and your family or friends. Whatever you have is enough for you to be happy, and there will always be something more you think you'd like. And giving is much more rewarding that getting or having.
6. Give time and help as well as money and things.
7. Some sadness, pain and tragedy are inevitable. Don't let them upset your life any more than is necessary or natural. And don't spread sadness or pain to others. Spreading joy and helping others is the best cure for your sadness and theirs.
8. Appreciate the larger social groups that you have some connection to. Your coworkers, neighbors, fellow townsmen, countrymen, coreligionists, et. Al. Build bridges, not dividers.
9. For all its imperfections, the USA is a great place to live. Do your share to keep it that way and improve it.

No one will ever understand the basic nature of life or truth, or know if there's a god or a cosmic meaning to life. Think about these questions, study them, talk about them, and get the views of others. But don't be disappointed or worried that you don't find the answers.
Signed by Art and Ardy.

****

Andrew Moorhead "Duke" Robinson

Duke Robinson, a retired Presbyterian Minister, journeyed from traditional Christian beliefs to Christian humanism, taking his flock along on the journey. In his exceptionally rich and accomplished retirement years, Duke has founded and led discussion groups, theatre groups and writer's groups. He has written and published four books, and has been active in the search for ways to resolve conflicts without violence.

The Early Years

In January 1933, I am born in – of all places – Philadelphia's *Women's* Hospital. As a kid, I can't stand the thought of my buddies knowing this. Our large household includes my father and mother, my father's mother, Anna, my mother's half-brother, Uncle Wharton, my three older sisters: May, Diz and Ella, and me, the spoiled boy. I am not an afterthought, or a mistake, but the son for which my parents–at least my dad–kept trying. We live in Havertown, a western suburb of Philadelphia. Our three-story, corner home sports a front and back porch, separate dining and living rooms, six bedrooms and ... one bathroom. The most common question in our house is, "How long are you going to be in there?"

One dreary day in October 1943, at seventy-five and still working, despite not feeling well, Anna goes to work at Philadelphia's Women's Prison where she's a beloved matron. Later that morning, she takes the trolley home, gets into bed and an hour later dies quietly. I love Anna, and I feel so sad when this happens. I have never been so close to death before, and it hurts. I never knew my paternal grandfather, Alexander. My dad told me only that he was *a drunkard*.

My wild and wonderful Uncle Wharton is a hunchback, standing just four feet tall, the result of suffering a broken back when a child. He works as an accountant at the Baldwin Locomotive Works where they make *real* trains. He is a fisherman, stamp collector, calligrapher, and the only Episcopalian in our home. He helps me realize there are good people who don't believe exactly what my parents believe.

Family legend has it, that when I am two, my father stands on a ladder painting second story window frames above the back yard while I play on the lawn below. Accidentally (he later assures me), he knocks over a near-full can of paint, which hits the grass and splatters bright yellow paint all over me. The trade name for the DuPont Company, which makes the paint, is *DUCO*. My family jokingly calls me *Duco* for a few weeks. When they buy me a Cocker Spaniel, whose pedigree is Duchess, they think it cute to call me Duke. Sometime later I find out that Andrew means "manly and brave," I end up happy to go by Duke. It's with me today as both a nickname and professional name.

My father serves in the food service of the army during World War I, and then works his way up to be advertising manager for The American Stores, an eastern chain of supermarkets based in Philadelphia. He holds that position until he retires in 1955. My mother, during my childhood, is a stay-at-home mom, but later opens a neighborhood store, The Dress Shop, where she sells dresses of her own creation and does alterations.

I come to see the Robinson-Presbyterian worldview as uncompromising: a supernatural God created everything, remains in charge of it all, and has a good plan for your life; the Bible is God's Word; we all are God's wayward children and bad sinners; heaven and hell are eternally real; Jesus, God's Son, loves us; and every week we must go to Sunday school – the most boring place in the world. Bad people, that is, everyone who doesn't believe like we do, go to the everlasting fires of hell when they die. (I'm not sure which is worse, Sunday school or hell, though hell does sound pretty bad).

In the summer after sixth grade, my parents send me for a week to a boys' camp in the Pocono Mountains 75 miles north of Philadelphia. They hope the evangelist, Percy Crawford, who runs the camp and preaches daily at the boys, will *scare the hell out of me.* Their plan works. The man is a master manipulator of young, undeveloped minds and raw emotions.

I already know I am a terrible sinner, but for the first time I am knocked out by the compelling notion that though Jesus knows this about me too, he was willing to die for me. It is the beginning of my seeing that unconditional love is what can give us joy and make us fully human. It changes how I feel about God, other people and myself. No, I don't become religious or fully express God's love, but I now *want* to treat everyone respectfully, and I have an experiential framework for thinking about such love—I have been *born again.*

I start to attend the local Presbyterian Church, where my school chums go. My father doesn't like it, but he can see my attitude toward Sunday School has changed. It still doesn't thrill me, but the new pastor's daughters are good looking, church services are lively, the youth have lots of sports activities, and, did I say? – the new pastor's daughters are good looking. This church takes over for my parents and deepens my supernatural worldview. Through my impressionable teen years, it indoctrinates me by testimonies, ritual and endless Bible teaching. I buy the whole package. At that age, when people tell you something that changes you for what you think is the better, it's natural to trust them about other matters, especially when nearly everyone around you sees things the same way.

In the summer before the 8th grade, the church holds its annual Sunday School picnic at a local park. Our pastor's daughters tell me that a girlfriend of theirs, who is "a star athlete and beautiful," and is a member of the church that their father served previously ... plans to be at the picnic. I want to meet her. I do, and I discover what the fuss is all about. I sense God's plan already. I go home that afternoon, *in love*. That night, lying in bed, I tell God that, if he one day will make Barbara Hargreaves my wife, I will do whatever he wants. (I know, I know, I'm just 12.)

Four summers later, having not seen Barbara, a mutual friend arranges for me to be able to take her to another church youth outing. I have a great time, that is, until she tells me she will soon leave for nurses training near Chicago, half way around the world. In the fall, I hear she's going with some hotshot, sophomore class president at nearby Wheaton College, a Christian school where youth from our church have gone. I begin to suspect God doesn't answer prayer.

In my senior year at Haverford High School, rather than sticking to my studies, I focus on drama, playing basketball and one of the minister's daughters. My grades do not impress, but I manage to graduate in 1950. During our state basketball playoffs in March of that year, my mother falls and breaks her hip. Doctors put a pin in it, but ten days later, a day after she says she's begun to feel like her old self, a blood clot lodges in her heart, and she dies quickly and quietly. I've elsewhere written that it was probably the worst day of my life. I remember wondering what possible good God could make of this. I still wonder.

God, Formal Education and More of Barbara

Through a big-time *fluke*, a rather long list of unbelievable coincidences and an unwitting cast of characters, all in relation to our high school's last basketball game of our regular season, I am admitted to Wheaton College. During my freshman year, I keep pinching myself. The school is noted for academic rigor–*Time Magazine* once referred to it as the "Harvard of evangelical colleges." It's also known for its serious if petty piety. Neither academics nor piety mark my style, though I do think the Bible may be on to something, and I find Jesus fascinating. But it's there I begin having trouble with fanciful doctrines (a Bible without errors or contradictions, Jesus being born without sperm donor, Jesus flying into outer space and coming back to earth some day, and the pathetic doctrine of hell, come to mind). Despite this unease, I enjoy the early 1950's sheltered milieu of Wheaton, playing basketball and wondering what I will do with my life. (Actually, I was assuming God would take care of that.)

In the fall of my junior year, I am suddenly cut from the basketball team, which strikes me as a major mistake by God. The new coach has recruited bigger and faster players than me. Four years later they lead Wheaton to the small college national championship, which made memory of the *cut* a little easier to bear. Two immediate developments, however, help me handle my painful reality quite quickly. First, I now can study. I sense this is probably good. I choose philosophy as my major and settle down academically. It's philosophy that teaches me to think (until then I'd done very little thinking). It also helps me to evaluate the trite fundamentalism taught at the school. Strangely, it's also at this time that I hear a quiet but convincing call to go to seminary, though I have no idea what I'll do with such an education. But it gives me a sense of direction, so it must be God's will.

Second, I bump into Sheila Hargreaves, Barbara's older sister, a Wheaton senior. She asks, *Guess who's graduated from nursing school and is joining your class for the second semester.* I pause, look a little cockeyed at her, and respond, *It isn't your sister Barbara, is it?* She nods and beams (she likes me and knows I like Barbara). I beam back and think, *Aha!* A month later, when Barbara sets foot on campus, I start right after her. Yes, I might have done so while playing basketball, but I now have more time, and being with her is a lot better than fast breaks and jump shots. (Okay, God apparently knew what he was doing, after all.) I fight off several other suitors and chase her until she catches me.

During high school and college summers, I work at a Bible Conference Center in Maryland. For my last summer, 1953, I sell the center's girl's camp director (a phys-ed professor at Wheaton) on hiring Barbara as the camp nurse. Brilliant move. With the camp just 200 yards from the center, I get important time with the nurse. Late one moonlit night, in mid-August, while we're sitting alone in the dark on the large screened-in veranda of the center's lodge, I tell her I'd like us to get married the next summer before I leave for Fuller Seminary in Pasadena. She says she does too. So that settles that, and that's all there is to the evening. At least that's all I'm going to talk about here.

On August 14, 1954, Barbara and I marry at her family's home church. We spend a week honeymooning in a cottage on the beach at Ocean City, New Jersey. We then pack up everything we own and spend our second honeymoon week driving cross-country from Philadelphia to Pasadena. Even I, who abhor long drives, enjoy this second half of our honeymoon, sleeping with Barbara Robinson in a different motel every night. For what more could I ask? God runs everything. God is doing all right.

Two Seminaries, Two Churches and Children

Fuller, a nondenominational seminary, stands a too-short step away from the narrow Wheaton worldview; and I'm increasingly disturbed by such theology. I'm also impressed with one professor whose class on Kierkegaard, the Christian existentialist, expands my vision. Because of my roots and the impressive Presbyterian form of government (Presbyterians shaped our national constitution based on "elected representation"), after two years at Fuller, I transfer to the Louisville Presbyterian Theological Seminary in Kentucky. That's where Barbara gives birth to our daughter, Margaret Anne ("Pegge" then, later, "Margo") on Easter Sunday morning, 1957. I graduate the end of the next February with a Masters in Theology, and we move to Orlando, Florida, and a three-year ministry in education and youth at the Park Lake Presbyterian Church. Our first son, Andrew Moorhead Robinson, III (Rob) is born in Orlando in September of 1958.

In November of 1960, through another set of fascinating, unpredictable coincidences, I accept a similar call to the conservative Walnut Creek Presbyterian Church in the East Bay Area of Northern California. I increasingly am seeing supernatural religion as fantasy. It's a step back theologically, but it's the fourth largest church school in our denomination, with 150 high school kids on Sunday mornings; and I like working with them. Most church adults strike me as simply wanting their prejudices confirmed. The students are thinking and eager to learn. I am satisfied with my work. Son Stephen Barclay is born in Kaiser hospital there in February 1961. We like Walnut Creek, but I am feeling vocationally boxed-in. From two experiences with senior pastors of large churches, I've learned a lot about the kind of pastor I don't want to be.

In November of 1963, we leave Walnut Creek for me to be pastor of a New Church Development project in El Sobrante ("The Leftover") on the edge of Richmond, CA, about a half hour from where we've been living. We move the week John F. Kennedy is assassinated. We are the St. Matthews Presbyterian Church, renting space from St. Phillip's Episcopal Church, on the main thoroughfare, The San Pablo Dam Road. The small sanctuary handles the 30 who show for my first Sunday, the very morning Jack Ruby shoots Lee Harvey Oswald, the alleged assassin of our president.

We are two ill-suited congregations in an area that is supposed to grow dramatically, but in 2014 still hasn't. Texan and Oklahoman folk, who migrated here for work in the Kaiser shipyards during World War II, brought a narrow Bible-thumping fundamentalism with them, and it's everywhere. At St. Matthews, we offer the area an alternative church experience. Our most distinctive offering is *Forum Theater*. In the movie house that also sits on the main drag, one-night-a-month we show a provocative film, domestic or foreign, followed by small group discussion next to the theater, in a community room over a bar and cleaners. We average 100 in the theater and 50 for discussion. We become known as *The Church on the Dam Road that shows dirty pictures.*

Forum Theater runs until the summer of 1966, when five things happen at the same time: the movie house gets sold; the Presbyterian Church in neighboring San Pablo dies; St. Matthew's leaves St. Phillip's to rent from Temple Beth Hillel, a Reform synagogue nearer San Pablo; we change our name to Covenant Presbyterian Church; and a handful of San Pablo members merge into our congregation. We continue Forum Theater at the synagogue, using 16-millimeter film projection.

In the next couple of years, the rabbi, a nearby priest and I create the West Contra Costa Open Housing Committee to stop racial redlining in our area. We also start the Greater Richmond Interfaith Project (G.R.I.P.), which hires a community organizer to help mobilize the poor. In 2014, it still serves that area. Of course, these efforts do not endear me to a lot of local folk, and people stay away from our little church-in-a-synagogue in droves.

It's also an important time for child rearing. Barbara, who is not working outside the home, cements our strong sense of family. When we move to Richmond, Pegge is six, and helps with mothering her brothers, Rob five and Steve almost three. Stuart Thomas is born in December 1965, at Alta Bates Hospital in Berkeley, during the night. I come home early in the morning and wake Rob and Steve to announce their little brother. We go right to Pegge's room while she's asleep, bang on her door and together shout, "Pegge! Pegge! We love you! But now the score is four to two!"

In the synagogue, we gear Sunday celebrations to bring out the best in us, using dance, music, literature, and film we think will help. Clergy friends hear about our goings on, and tell me that you can do that in a little, rinky-dink congregation housed in a Jewish temple, but you can't do that in a "real" Presbyterian Church. I suspect they are right. I love what I do, but I begin to think of community college teaching in the humanities. Two friends on nearby faculties tell me that, if I'm interested, they have enough pull to get me hired. I'm flattered, but the ego spark does not build a *fire in my belly*.

In the fall of 1967, the pastor-seeking committee of the *real* Montclair Presbyterian Church in Oakland asks to interview *me* (the traditional process). So, I decide to interview *them*. I want to be certain that wherever I go next it will be a good fit for the church, for my family and for me.

The Montclair Church Family

Montclair is the lovely, heavily-wooded hill area of Oakland. But the church stands fractured and has been in membership free-fall for five years, declining from 750 to 450 members, with the 450 figure a bit inflated. It averages 125 at the Sunday worship hour. I see it as a challenge. The Church does not have the fundamentalist mindset of the Walnut Creek congregation, but it includes a residue of John Birch Society types. At the same time, it sits in the shadow of the University of California, Berkeley, and exhibits a more sophisticated culture than Richmond and San Pablo. Actually, I'm licking my chops.

I want to *do* church differently than it's generally done. I have instincts and insights but few if any positive role models. I am passionate about helping create authentic human community and realize I must first be *a person* not just *the professional*. So I don't use Rev. or Dr. and never refer to them as "my church." I want us all to be in touch with reality, do our own thinking, take responsibility for our lives, and be able to be both graciously supportive and appropriately honest with one another in community that's both broad and deep. To these ends, I make moves in my first year that I feel are right but don't realize how right they are. Change happens much more quickly than I could have predicted.

Sunday mornings become celebratory, participatory, planned but also spontaneous, and natural (no *churchese* spoken here). Someone once said, "Watered-down grape juice is a fairly apt symbol for the Protestant church." So, for communion, rather than tiny cut cubes of white bread, we use torn-off chunks of whole grain breads that members bake and, instead of juice, we tap bottles of wine they bring from home. Within two years, we run 225 on Sunday mornings; and it's not just because of the wine.

Music lifts the spirit of our celebrations. Our choir sings the likes of Bach and Vivaldi, sometimes with a chamber orchestra. But it, and we, also sing folk, jazz, rock, Broadway, and pop, any music that helps us celebrate the glories of human life. In 1972, a Dixieland band emerges, which, more that forty years later still plays on Easter, other special Sundays and at festivals.

We begin to think of ourselves as "extended family," a live *organism*, not simply an *organization*. For diversity, we build a staff of part-time, professional associates with specialties such as theology, psychology, drama, music, administration, peacemaking, rather than call a full-time, generalist, associate pastor, as most churches do.

I sell our official board (Session) on treating its committees not as lackeys running around beneath it, but as satellites alongside it under their own power. It delegates authority to its committees, encourages them to be creative, and trusts them to do their best. A fresh breeze of freedom and appropriate pride blows through the church. Several members birth a Creative Resources Committee. Each year for many years, it holds a festive Epiphany Yule Feast with costumes, slack rope-walkers, jugglers, rowdy dancing, and fantastic food and wassail (it's still going on in 2014), and also a colorful, magical Mardi Gras. People tell us we throw the best parties in the East Bay.

Adult education evolves into diversified, small, highly participatory groups shaped by people's needs and interests. During any semester, it may engage a seminary professor to lead Bible study, but it regularly features such diverse groups as Drama Discussion, Cinema Conversation, Training in Nonviolence, Writing Your Own Theology, Study the City, and Pottery-making.

Prayer as miracle-working fades. Some members believe in praying for others. One Sunday, when I announce that a member, John Williams, is recovering from surgery in the nearby veterans' hospital, I ask members *not* to pray for him ... until they've sent him a card with a note. They get it. And John gets so many cards the nurses string them up and down a long hallway wall outside his room and staff and patients come from all over to see them.

When I visit, a nurse tells me they haven't been able to wipe the smile off John's face, and she credits the cards as much as his surgeons for his good recovery.

We are not just having fun. The Vietnam War triggers a Ploughshares Committee. It hires buses and takes 225 people to the largest peace march ever in San Francisco. In 1972, we give sanctuary to a conscientious-objector sailor who has orders to report to the aircraft carrier Oriskany for duty off shore of Vietnam, and with the help of KPIX, we orchestrate his honorable discharge. Later in the 1980s, we provide sanctuary for Central American refugees fleeing torture and "disappearance."

While in ministry 38 years (28 at Montclair), I do more than 400 weddings. I marry my four kids (some more than once) and a lot of nephews and nieces. In the mid-1970s, I get a call from a Montclair family asking me to marry their daughter to Frank Oz. Oz is right-hand-man to Jim Henson, the genius behind The Muppets, and is the creator of Miss Piggy. I claim special status: as far as I know, I am the only minister in Western civilization that can honestly say, "I married *Miss Piggy*."

On a Sunday in October of 1991, a firestorm sweeps out of the Berkeley hills into Oakland like a blowtorch on wheels. It destroys more than 3,000 homes and kills 28 residents trapped in canyons. Barbara and I must evacuate. That night, in the home of friends a couple of miles south, we hear a radio report that tells us our house on Merriewood Hill and the church buildings below us are gone. We are sick at heart. Later that night we find the reporter was mistaken, and the fire missed us by 300 yards.

The church family rises to the occasion. By 9:00 am Monday morning, several members have gotten into the church office. They put a map on the wall and begin linking members who've not been burned out with those who have been. In the Family Room, they begin to set up a clothing bank to serve the community. They organize potluck suppers for members and nonmembers alike every night that week.

That next Sunday morning we celebrate *Fire Survival and Supportive Family*. I immediately invite the thirty-some member-families, including two of our staff associates, who lost their homes, to gather in the center aisle. I then ask everyone to stand, to turn toward the survivors, and to place their hands on the shoulders of those in front of them so everyone in the room is touching, and an 11-year-old girl from a family that lost everything but their lives sings *Bridge Over Troubled Waters*. After the song, we sit down and I invite survivors to come forward and speak about their experience. The hour is given to listening to, crying and, yes, laughing with, embracing, and applauding those who speak. CNN and NBC tape the hour from the balcony. A church family traveling in Spain sees us on television. Families and friends of members across the country witness excerpts that night on CNN news and the next morning on the Today show. Our church buildings become the Oakland hills fire recovery center, with neighborhood groups meeting there day and night for months.

The Loma Prieta earthquake shook us in October 1989; the firestorm touched us in October of 1991, and in October of 1993 I undergo radical prostate surgery for cancer—I don't know about anyone else, but for the next several odd-numbered years, I keep my October eye open for a plague of locusts.

From the first decade at Montclair, members are urging me to write down the things I talk about in my extemporaneous Sunday morning commentaries (read sermons). And I invariably reply, "I'm a talker not a writer; the last thing I'll ever do is write a book." It turns out I was right about that — it is in my *last* years serving Montclair that,, late at night and on days off, I write my first book.

In the mid-1970s I spent my three-month sabbatical in the Lake Tahoe summer home of dear friends, socked-in with an Apple IIe computer and a dozen books on how to write. In 1978, fed by my experiences on a two-week trip with 30 church members to Palestine/Israel (and a week in London) for my doctoral dissertation project I write a screenplay: *Savior*. Over the next twelve years, I keep dropping notes, articles, and excerpts from my Sunday commentaries in a big desk drawer. On my 1992 sabbatical, I sort them out and, having observed well-meaning people like myself in community, begin writing *TOO NICE FOR YOUR OWN GOOD*. With the help of an amazing agent who engineers an auction with major publishing houses, Warner Books buys it in 1995 and publishes it in 1997. I'm pleased to say that it's still selling briskly.

In the early 1990s, I write four editorials and deliver them on the KPIX series, "On My Mind." One of them wins a Northern California Emmy for the station. It begins to sit *on my mind* that writing is something to pursue further. I am beginning to see myself as a writer as well as a talker.

For most of the time in Montclair, Barbara finds her own vocations. In 1970, Stuart starts school, and shortly thereafter she takes Public Health training in San Francisco and goes to work as a nurse for the Oakland Public Schools. She spends 26 years traipsing all over the city's toughest sections in a *ministry* of teaching good health, testing and giving shots. For 22 years, she also leads the Oakland chapter of Amnesty International, which she founded. She turns 65 on June 9, 1996, and retires. I am just 63, but am spent and ready to end the great ride I have had with the Montclair church family. In June, we both shut down our primary careers.

At a wonderful courtyard retirement party that follows my last Sunday morning, the church family presents me with a book that members have written and published. Three years before, they had marked my 25 years there with a classy Saturday night dinner party, featuring great food and drink, testimonials and wild storytelling. (By now, I genuinely am feeling that, unlike Woody Allen, I won't mind missing *my own memorial service by a few days.*) We spend the next four years in our Montclair home spending more time with each other and doing many things we'd not been able to do through our years attentive to work and children.

Real Retirement – and a New Life

In 2000, we move to Walnut Creek's Rossmoor, beautifully described in the *November Song* Prologue. We feel fortunate to be in a lovely place and enjoy the good lives we're able to lead. We play golf and tennis and go regularly to local theater together with good friends. We stand for five years almost every Friday afternoon with other Grandparents for Peace members outside Rossmoor's gate, protesting the war in Iraq. Barbara commutes monthly to her Oakland Amnesty International group, and I begin writing again. Life is good.

For four years I work on a tri-part book on basic human contraries: *Sex and Love; Secular and Spiritual;* and *Living and Dying*. I also pull out my dissertation project and translate the screenplay, *Savior*, into novel form. I do nothing with either of these works. In 2004, I supervise the creation, production and promotion of a tennis club 2005 calendar, "Tennis Women of Rossmoor: Off Court, Off Color, Out of Control...and having fun."

Between contributions and sales we raise $53,000 for Breast Cancer Action of San Francisco.

In July of 2008, still enjoying retirement immensely, we are stunned to find that a malignant, non-smoker's tumor in Barbara's lung has metastasized to her brain. After radiation treatments, and two terrible chemo sessions, she decides she wants to live whatever time she has left without the chemicals. After fifty-four years of marriage, and three months of precious times together while she's under hospice care, on October 26, she dies, peacefully, surrounded by her loving, grieving family.

The next June, while coming out of my grief and chairing the committee to establish the Drama Association of Rossmoor, we find that a MRSA ("mersa"), a nasty staph infection resistant to antibiotics, has abscessed on the base of my spine. After weeks of ineffective infusions of heavy antibiotics, two major back surgeries, six months in a body cast and a year of different antibiotics, I am finally cleared for good health. About the time I am first hospitalized, I have begun to develop a relationship with Claire Blue, a woman I've known and liked for eight years, and who played tennis with Barbara every week for five years before she became ill. My illness bonds us much faster than either of us had foreseen. If it hadn't been for her, I'm not sure I would have gotten through that very hard year. She becomes the woman I love and who loves me.

In 2010, having been through a difficult two years, I go back to the book I was writing years earlier to rework the section *Living and Dying*, and publish in December 2011 my second nonfiction book, *CREATE YOUR BEST LIFE – How to Live Fully Knowing One Day You Will Die.* In two postscripts in this book, I tell in detail Barbara's story and my story with Claire.

In 2012, I pick up my converted screenplay, entitle it *SAVIOR: An Old Notion in a New Novel; of Unthinkable Absurdity*, and publish it that September. Right after that I chair the committee to launch The Published Writers of Rossmoor, in which I today am still very much involved.

As I write this chapter in *November Song*, I have completed the manuscript for *A MIDDLE WAY: The Secular/Spiritual Road to Wholeness*. The book is a pull-no-punches poke at dogmatic, supernatural religion and narrow-minded *scientism*. It reveals why and how far I've moved away from the supernatural worldview of my childhood. It may make some readers faint, throw-up or scream. By the time you finish reading this book, it should be available on Amazon.com and through bookstores everywhere.

My four children seem stabilized and generally happy while suffering the normal struggles of work and parenting. (I have nine wonderful grandchildren and one really great, great grandson).

Claire and I, with medical issues that regularly beset us, have had to give up tennis and play little golf, but we continue to participate in various clubs, *do* theater and some light travel. In our later years, we continue living together in a setting and relationship we both love. And, finally, I see myself, now, as a writer as well as a talker.

****

I wrote this "87%" essay some years ago for my earlier book, "InSight and OutRage." It concerns the life of writer John Updike, a life that by any measure was successful and well-lived. Yet, Updike rated his life as only 87% successful. Why so low? What are the implications of Updike's tough standards for the sixteen well lived lives reported here in "November Song?"

The 87% Life: A Report Card

Writer John Updike, who died recently at age 76, had over the years appeared many times as a guest on the Charlie Rose PBS-TV interview show. To memorialize Updike and his very extensive and widely acclaimed body of work, Charlie replayed excerpts from a number of Updike's appearances. In one of the excerpts, Charlie asked Updike whether he had achieved the goals he had set for himself. Updike pondered the question, and finally rated himself as 87% successful! Charlie then asked what had caused the remaining 13% to slip away, to which Updike said something about timidity and unwillingness to risk new directions.

So, let's pick up where Rose and Updike left off. Most of us would rate our "life score" at something less than 100%. For me, perhaps for you too, 87% seems like a good number. I will resist the chance to psychoanalyze myself on these pages, but let's look in general at some of the possibilities for our self-diagnosed failure to fully grasp the brass ring. As with Updike, timidity, fear of failure, perhaps some lack of conviction in the rightness of the direction of our lives, these may be some of the things that might have kept you and me and probably most people from taking professional and personal chances that might have closed the 13% gap.

Yet, I would argue that no one could have done much better than Updike did. He mastered, perhaps better than any contemporary American writer, the art of writing novels and essays that portrayed the people and mores of his time. Considering his prodigious output, the many prizes and honors and his very large income, Updike, was clearly too harsh in his self-appraisal. The same can probably be said for most of us: we demand too much of ourselves.

Updike lost a bit of what might have been a consequential part of his life by not pausing to enjoy his success, or by not basking sufficiently in the good life that he had earned and deserved. Instead, he pushed himself relentlessly to ever-greater achievements. For Updike, the joy of success was the opportunity that his success provided for him to add ever-more luster to his reputation as a preeminent man of American letters. At the time of his death, age 76, Updike was still writing, still seeking acclaim and still refusing to rest on his laurels.

The reason for Updike's relentless striving became clear in yet another taped Rose excerpt in which Updike ruminated about what drove him. Born in 1932, Updike's early years were times of economic deprivation. His father, he said, was long unemployed, and the family was always at the edge of poverty. All of that of course created the anxieties and uncertainties that marked Updike's personality. His psyche, he confessed to Charlie Rose, was burdened by the never-ending concern that his life of success and wealth could end at any time. To maintain and fortify his success, he felt pressured to keep on working; only in that way might he close the 13% gap! To add weight to this insight, Charlie Rose, also a child of depression years, also the son of a man unemployed and underemployed for many of those years, confessed to having inherited exactly that same burden of economic insecurity and the same 13 % achievement gap. Same for me, and probably for others whose early years were spent in economic uncertainty.

In yet another taped excerpt, Updike noted that as a young person he had often thought about dying, and had been troubled by the prospect of its inevitability. Though he still thought often about death, he was now, in his older years, far less troubled by its prospect, having come to peace and to complete acceptance about its inevitability. He saw this as somewhat of a paradox. I took special note of Updike's observation about death because it is true for me too, and I think for most of my aged brethren. None of us wants to die -- we seek to delay its inevitability to the best of our ability. But, in the end, as we get older, we accept with equanimity the notion that death is the inescapable price of birth. As Updike indecorously put it in *Rabbit is Rich,* "The great thing about the dead, they make space."

Let me close by profiling you and me and each of us. Our lives have been and are: joy and pain, success and failure, warmth and chill, love and hate, wisdom and stupidity, responsibility and irresponsibility, faith and doubt, greed and generosity, acceptance and rejection, diligence and sloth, messy and orderly, tragedy and comedy, patience and stubbornness. Depending on where you weigh yourself on these and comparable attributes, you might take your final report card up from 87% to 91, or drop it to 83. I will not tell you my score!

****

Joseph Emanuel Potozkin

Ethnic neighborhoods in the Bronx are part of American folklore. Stickball in the streets, kids hanging around the candy store, walkup apartments, with life often at the edge of poverty but always full of joy and strong families. Joe Potozkin grew up here, graduating from the same high school later attended by Colin Powell. Joe served in the Navy during World War II as a signalman aboard a troopship, and made his mark by winning the Pacific Theater's Welterweight Boxing Championship. The GI Bill took Joe to CCNY, where he earned BA and MA degrees in Education, which led to a lifelong career as Middle School teacher in Brooklyn.

A Bronx Childhood

I was born in Harlem, in 1926. Soon after that, we moved to the Bronx, which is where I grew up in a neighborhood of mixed ethnic groups. In those early days we moved fairly often because you got one-month free rent! We finally settled into a fourth floor walkup in a large apartment house where I spent most of my childhood years.

In growing up, I remember that most of the time, when I was eight or nine years old, we played every day in the street, at stickball or kick the can. We stayed in the street until it was time for dinner, usually around six- o'clock. After dinner it was back to the street, hanging around by the candy store. It was a good childhood. Life in our dense urban neighborhood was safe and comfortable. We children had a lot of fun, talking constantly about every topic imaginable.

My parents were both immigrants. My father had come from Russia to America at the age of 19; my mother came to this country from Poland at the age of 16. They met here as young adults, and married at a young age. My father worked as a paperhanger. In those days there was never enough work for the entire year, so he would go to work in Detroit for a few months, working there too as a paperhanger. My mother was a homemaker for most of her married life. But when my father died, in 1947, just after I came back from the Navy, my mother went to work as a seamstress, working in a clothing factory.

I had a sister who passed away about five years ago. She was two years older than me. We were close. I had a brother who died before I was born.

As a kid, I went to nearby public schools. It happens that my high school, Morris High, was attended some years later by Colin Powell – who is considerably younger than I am. I graduated from high school in January 1943, just days after turning 18. I was drafted just a few months later into the wartime military,

The Navy

Since this is to be the story of my life, I must tell you about something that has been on my conscience ever since that time. On the day that I reported for my draft physical examination, upon passing the physical, I entered a place at which there were two tables, one manned by an Army recruiter and the other by a Navy recruiter. To my surprise, I was asked which service I preferred. Guessing that the Navy might be a bit less dangerous, I said that I preferred the Navy.

Shortly thereafter, when I reported for induction, I was placed into another long line that would lead to my induction into the Navy. Once again, there were two recruitment desks, one for the Navy and the other for the Marine Corps. While waiting in that line, I noted that every fifth person in the "Navy" line was tagged to serve in the Marine Corps. After realizing that, I counted swiftly, and determined that I was 45th in line. To get a number that was not a multiple of five, I stepped out of line and went back a couple of places saying that I wanted to stand with my buddies. So it was that I became a sailor and not a Marine. In the seventy-odd years since, I have been troubled by the fact that the person standing behind me, who became 45th in line when I stepped out, went off to the Marine Corps in my place. I can only hope that he survived the war – a war in which Marine Corps casualties were especially high.

My two years in the Navy were spent as a signalman on the USS Shelby, an Attack Transport, essentially a troop ship. We saw considerable action as we carried troops to various battlefield destinations in the Pacific. While we were in the waters off Okinawa, we went to our battle stations seventeen times in two days.

I must tell you that while in the Pacific Theatre, I shot at many Americans and many Americans shot at me! Everyone knows that the Japanese had Kamikaze aircraft; few know that they also had Kamikaze boats, small boats that would ram into our large ships and explode. We too had small boats in the water. When it was dark, we couldn't distinguish our boats from the Japanese. So we worked out a system of light signals. As the ship's signalman, I used a flashlight to make a big "O." Our ships would signal back "OXO"; if we made an "X," our boats would signal back "XOX." When our signal failed to get a response, we assumed that the approaching boat was Japanese and we would shoot at them. Half the time the guys in the American boats were sleeping, and would not have seen our "O" or "X." Our shooting at them woke them up, and they would shoot right back at us, aiming at the big light that I was operating. One time they missed my head by six inches.

I took up competitive boxing aboard ship, and ended up winning the Navy's Pacific Theatre welterweight boxing championship when the finals were held at Pearl Harbor.

Until recently, our ship's crew had met for a reunion every year since the war. Each year we would meet in different places, one year in Corpus Christie, Texas, another in Charleston, South Carolina, and so forth. It stopped just two years ago because so many of us had died. I was only 18 when I entered the Navy in 1943, so I was one of the younger ones; I am almost 88 now, one of the few left.

I want to add a thought about World War II. It was a time when the whole country was supportive of the war effort; everyone played a role. Young men were all subject to the draft. For civilians, much of the food was rationed, gasoline was rationed, and people bought war bonds. None of that unity of spirit has been with us for wars since then. The Second World War was thought by all of us to be a just war; we knew who the enemy was: we had been attacked. My parents were air raid wardens, a job they took seriously. Schoolchildren took air raid shelter drills.

City College of New York and Shonny

Prior to being drafted into the wartime Navy, I had no thoughts about university level education. That was just not something that seemed within reach for me or for others in my neighborhood. But the war, and the postwar availability of the GI Bill changed that mindset for myself and for countless other returning veterans. So, soon after release from the Navy, I enrolled at the City College of New York. My goal at the onset, since I was good at sports, was to become a coach, so I took courses that led to a degree in education, with a minor in physical education. I went on to a Masters degree in education, also at CCNY.

I had hoped to play basketball at CCNY, but that didn't work out. I was, however, on the boxing team, undefeated during the entire four years at CCNY. During those years, I once had the opportunity to fight Sugar Ray Robinson; we sparred for three rounds. Sugar Ray told me that he was impressed, and encouraged me to become a professional boxer. My mother would never have allowed that! Instead, I became a schoolteacher.

I met my wife, Shondell, while I was a student at CCNY. Shonny, which is what we call her, is a few years younger than I am. Though we had lived in the same neighborhood, and had seen one another over the years, we traveled in different groups, so never became acquainted. One day, as I was leaving CCNY after class, I was about to get onto a bus and I saw the beautiful Shonny standing in line waiting to get onto the next bus. I left my bus and went over to talk with her. She told me that she had just come from CCNY where she had taken the entrance exam. Our conversation ended in a date, and we have been together ever since! It was 1949 when we found each other; we married in 1953. We waited those four years because I wanted first to complete my education and get a job. I did get my Master's Degree in 1951, but did not get my teaching job until 1953.

I should add that, as it turned out, Shonny went to Hunter College, not CCNY. She graduated in 1953, and became a Reading Teacher in New City, New York.

As a schoolteacher, I had summers off, so I worked every summer as a counselor at a camp in Spring Valley, a town some sixty miles outside New York City. After some years there I became Director of the camp, which was a camp for underprivileged kids. The camp was financed by a group of wealthy people who as children had attended it. They bought the camp in 1939 and supported it with private funds. Sophie Tucker was one of those sponsors; Ted Lewis was another. The Director that preceded me became Chancellor of Schools for New York City.

Shonny and I were together every summer at the camp, and we both became fond of Spring Valley. We decided in 1968 to buy a house there. Shonny got a teaching job in Spring Valley, and for the remaining years of my teaching career in New York, I commuted every day, a commute that took some 90 minutes on a good day.

Shonny is an artist. She is essentially self-trained, but during the summers that I spent at the camp in Spring Valley, Shonny attended the nearby Woodstock School of Art. She paints mostly in acrylics, and her special interest is abstract art. She never sells her work, though she has given a few paintings to our children and to friends. Our second bedroom has been made into a studio for her work. She once won a Best in Show Award, at the Las Vegas Art Museum, winning a $500 prize.

Shonny has for many years been afflicted with Lyme disease, which comes from being bitten by a Lyme tick. Though she can be completely healthy for a time, that Lyme affliction can weaken her to the point that she requires extended rest.

Our Great Children

Our daughter, Amy, was born in 1956. Our son, Jerome, was born in 1962. Amy went to the State College of New York, where she majored in theatre arts; She went on to Brandeis for a Masters Degree. Amy became an actress, working for many years at theatres across America, including the Shakespeare Theatre in Oregon. Along the way, she saw an advertisement for Casting Director at the Berkeley Repertory Theatre, a job she ultimately got. Amy has been there for many years, and loves that job. Some years ago, Amy married, but that marriage ended in divorce. They had no children.

Jerome went to the University of Pennsylvania for his undergraduate work and then on to NYU medical school, where he became a Dermatologist. He was awarded a fellowship in Mohs surgery at the University of San Francisco. Mohs surgery is a method where Basel Cell cancers are removed in layers, a method far less intrusive than deep surgery. Following his graduation from USF, his professor offered Jerome a position in his practice in Burlingame. After a couple of years there, Jerome opened his own Dermatology office in Danville.

Jerome married a fellow doctor, Monica Brar, who had come to the U.S. from India at the age of three. Monica was an ObGyn, with an office in Walnut Creek. After some time, Monica went back to school for training in Dermatology, and she now works together with Jerome in a new and larger office, still in Danville. We could not hope for a better daughter-in-law.

Jerome and Monica have two sons, now 9 and 11 years old. Shonny and I baby-sit for them every Saturday night so that our son and his wife can go out. We love doing that; it keeps us close to our grandsons. When the boys were younger, before they went to school, I took them every morning to places all over the area. I did this every day, usually from nine to noon, despite the fact that my son and daughter-in-law had hired a Nanny. At noon I would return them to their Nanny. On our morning journeys about town, the boy's favorite places to visit were the Barnes and Noble bookstore children's area, Sharper Image, where they would play with the robots and other such, and Nordstrom, where we would ride the escalators up and down to their delight.

Teaching

Let me speak a bit about my teaching experiences. The school at which I taught, a Middle School in Brooklyn, was known as a special service school, serving minority kids. I was, at the beginning, the school's basketball coach. I was able to establish close and even warm relationships with the youngsters; I liked them and listened to them. They responded by respecting my efforts to teach them. After being a gym teacher for my first year at the school, I became a math and science teacher. In those days, teachers were moved around to different specialties. I was at various times offered classes in Music and English, but chose to stay with Math and Science. I was even asked on one occasion to teach French. When I told the principal that I had never studied that language, he said that it was necessary only to stay one day ahead of the kids.

After being asked to take the math and science class in the coming semester, I spent the summer at my camp learning as much as I could about the math and science curriculum to prepare myself for the coming school year! I feel strongly that teachers cannot hope to succeed in any teaching assignment without being well versed in the subject.

Teaching inner city kids, those who too often come from difficult family and neighborhood situations, is of course a central problem in secondary education. My view is that there are no formulas, no methodologies that can solve the problem. The answer is to find teachers who can win the affection and respect of these children. Only then will the kids embrace the subject being taught, and only then will they be willing and even eager to learn. Too many teachers are afraid of these youngsters, do not like them, and are unable to reach them in ways that foster learning. Children are very perceptive; they know whether you care about them. If they sense otherwise, they reject any efforts aimed at teaching.

After eight years of teaching, I became the Dean of Discipline; shortly after that I became Assistant Principal, and then Principal.

All this was in the same school. I found that I didn't like being Principal, primarily because I missed direct interaction with the kids. Many of our teachers were inept, unable to teach the inner city kids. It was my task as Principal to impose discipline on the teachers, and to fire some of them. I found that difficult both because of union rules and because I knew most of them so well, and as their friend it was hard for me to punish those with whom I had for so long been a colleague. So, after some time I asked to be relieved of that job and went back to being Assistant Principal, the job from which I retired at age 65 after 36 years in education.

Good neighborhoods in America generally have good schools, and high aptitude students. Our problems with elementary and secondary education are primarily in inner city areas. Families there don't read to the kids. Their youngsters come to school not knowing letters and numbers and colors. Our focus needs to be on getting parents involved. But, there the problem is too often the lack of family structure. The father is not present, the mother is working, often two shifts. She is tired and not especially motivated to read to or even to talk to her children. There is too often no family expectation of scholarly success. These kids don't have the vision of college. They have no computers or iPads in the house – and no experience in using them. So the answer is more than better schools and better teachers, we need better jobs, better neighborhoods.

Though I loved my teaching job, and took great pride in it, I was ready for retirement at age 65. One of the happiest days of my life was the day of my retirement party. What pleased me especially that day was that people who came to the party included the ladies from the school cafeteria, the custodial workers, the security guards, and the teacher aides. The party was held at the Fort Hamilton Officers Club, and the cost was $49 per person, which in 1988 was a lot.

Someone made a DVD recording of my retirement party; I watched it just recently. My wife spoke, and my kids flew in from California to take part. It had been said by other speakers at the party that retirement is the happiest day of one's life, to which my son said, "Every day is the happiest day of my life, because I have a father like that." Just listening to these speeches on my DVD, so many years after the event, brings back wonderful memories that are on a par with my wedding day and the days on which my children and grandchildren were born.

Life Today

For me, living here in Rossmoor, life is like summer camp all year around! At age 87 I still play tennis, use the pools whenever I want to, and take walks around the golf course. *[Editors Note: Joe is to this day one of Rossmoor's star tennis players!].* In retirement here, every day is Sunday. You learn to enjoy every day – because the days are fleeting. I enjoy my children and my grandchildren. Shonny and I have no interest in traveling; we love it here. We might go to Napa or to Carmel, but no further. We live in Eden.

For me, being happy comes from interacting with family and friends. I am completely satisfied with my life in this Rossmoor Eden. I can't think of anything that would top this.

One of the things that troubles me, in my otherwise perfect life, is America's endless involvement in war. Some in Congress are pressing for US involvement in Syria. Doing that could lead to entanglement. Most Americans want no further US military involvement in the Middle East, yet we elect politicians who press for such involvement. By electing such people to Congress we continue to keep our country on a war footing. How can intelligent people vote against their own interest? We have also elected people into Congress who believe that rape cannot lead to pregnancy because rape "shuts that function down." How can intelligent people vote for such stupid politicians?

I recently saw a rerun of the movie "All is Quiet on the Western Front," which is about World War I, a war fought a century ago. When I think about the lunacy of soldiers running toward each other with bayonets in that war, I realize that we have learned nothing about how to resolve issues without violence.

As I think about my long life, I have great pride in helping to form my children, both of whom are good people and so accomplished and successful. As for my own accomplishments, one in which I take pride is my induction into the Softball Hall of Fame. This was a big event, as only three people are inducted each year. The ceremony took place in 1993, in Nyack, New York. I was for many years a pitcher in a Spring Valley Softball League. We played in tournaments against teams from other cities. My deep involvement with softball began when I came out of the Navy, and continued through my adult life; in fact I was pitching softball into my seventies. Recently I got a call from the Walnut Creek "Creekers," a softball team here in our town. I told them that my softball days had come to an end, that I am now playing only tennis.

Another thing in which I take pride is my boxing career. As I told you earlier, during my time in the Navy, I won the Pacific Fleet Boxing Championship, then went on to box with my college team, and was undefeated during all those encounters.

I am almost 88. Most of us want to live on and on. There are many here in Rossmoor well over 90, and I know one person over a hundred. Most retain all their faculties, and remain involved. Some are doddering, and you would wish for them to fade away – there is little quality in their lives. Yet, even those who are over the hill, fight to stay alive. The will to live is strong, and it is that will that has sustained us in difficult circumstances.

My wife believes in reincarnation, and I don't know! I think when you die, that's it. You don't come back! Shonny thinks that she has lived before.

****

Timothy J.W. Wise

Born on Boston's south shore, Tim grew up in Cambridge, Vermont & New York City. Graduating from Harvard as a music major, he later went to night law school at Boston College. Tim had separate careers as an executive at Raytheon, criminal and civil rights trial lawyer, real estate developer, actor, and mediator. Baseball, skiing, and tennis were his sports.

Parents

Theirs was the unlikely union between a bon vivant lace curtain Boston Irishman who'd flunked out of Harvard, and the WASP, Barnard Phi Beta Kappa daughter of a prominent New York attorney. I never learned how Eddie Wise came to know the Willard Brown family – he'd dated each of my mother's two older sisters before settling on Garda, fourteen years his junior, and charmed my grandmother while informing her that he just knew he "was going to marry one of your daughters."

Both Eddie and Garda were born into families of considerable wealth, practically all of which, unfortunately, disappeared. My father was doing all right on his own, however, as an advertising copy-writer, until Black Friday and the onset of the Great Depression. It is much to their credit that a very deep love sustained them through the difficult time that followed. And I've always taken some pride, perhaps like all Leos born in the summer of 1930, in being a true "Depression Baby," since, obviously, at least a part of their reaction to the events of October 28, 1929, was to copulate.

Moving from a fairly affluent existence, into which my older brother was born, to a house with a privy outside the back door and a coal-burning furnace in the living room, must have been difficult for my parents. But the bond between them and the warmth of their love kept me from ever feeling deprived. Apparently, my big blue eyes were helpful in the baby carriage while my mother sold cosmetics.

Eventually, my father found work again and my memories of preschool years abound with visions of Eddie and Garda entertaining the many friends they'd acquired in the small town of Hingham. She starred in pageants, kept a flower and vegetable garden, and campaigned for Roosevelt as she had for Al Smith. They were inundated each year with Christmas cards.

My father taught me to waltz, stretching my hands high and gently placing my tiny shoes on his stockinged feet. Years later, I would see hints of moisture in the eyes of a woman I'd never met before, as she told me she had once danced with him. He taught me chess. We played tennis on a tiny court scratched in the sand at low tide, hitting the ball with our hands – he'd played on the eastern grass court circuit; in fact, he proposed to Garda by telegram from a tournament in Florida.

Having the "Irish Malady" well before there was an AA, he dealt with it in his own way. He discovered that, after his all too frequent passing out, his very attractive wife had to fight off the lecherous attentions of invited guest males. He immediately swore off hard liquor, confining himself to Ballantine Ale. I remember the aroma emanating from tall green bottles left around the house.

He took me for a walk when I was eight, holding my hand, bending down, and talking in a way I wasn't used to. Soon after that he entered the Naval Hospital far removed from Hingham. My mother commuted from Hingham to her newly found job in Boston, and then to the hospital. This became untenable and we moved to an apartment in inner city Cambridge. I vividly recall being in his room on the last night of his life. His speech impeded by the tumor in his brain, his "Gaw bess our Timmy" echoes in mine to this day. Completely unprepared for his death, I became ill and was unable to attend the funeral.

My mother provided lovingly for her two boys and developed a career that took her to New York, where she worked with Eleanor Roosevelt on education and on a welfare program. At age 62, she obtained her Ph.D. As a consultant at Banks Street College, she was instrumental in the creation of the Head Start program. She had remarried and was known professionally as Garda W. Bowman, the name under which her work on early education was published, as well as her articles in the *Harvard Business Review* on women executives and on Adlerian concepts of aging in *The Grove Press*. She was the recipient of New York State's first Human Rights Award. She also left voluminous poetry, which it has been my hope to have published. She lived to be 94. A tough act to follow.

Schooling, Athletics and an Event

Public schools in Hingham and culture shock in Cambridge were followed by boarding schools, on scholarship, after my mother moved to New York City. Attending the Putney School in Vermont had a profound influence on my life. My love for music found full expression. I'd sung from an early age, despite my parents and brother being tone deaf, yet now I was immersed in Bach. On top of a lovely hill, boys and girls working the farm, skiing like mad, and enjoying 80-minute classes while never knowing our grades, we all prepared for the country's top colleges. I played first base from the 8th grade on, learned to ski, was on the state champion team as a senior, and played tennis on the side.

Strangely, I let baseball push tennis aside, though I probably had greater natural ability on the courts. When my mother once visited me at a summer camp, she watched me in an informal match. In tears afterward she said, "Your serve is exactly like your father's." I'd never seen him play. At Harvard, the tennis coaches wanted me to join the team, yet I stuck to baseball, even when it seemed I might not make the team. I sprained my ankle as a sophomore and was cut. The coach let me work out when I recovered and noticed I had good control as a batting practice pitcher. He gave me a uniform and I traveled with the team in that capacity. When the first baseman got sick I went in against Yale and got three hits, driving in five runs. By my senior year I became the third baseman, even winning MVP, and, after college, played shortstop on a championship team in the Cape Cod League. Yet, I've always felt that I wasted a chance to develop in tennis.

I also wasted very much of my Harvard education, I'm ashamed to say. I attended class as little as possible, concentrating instead on baseball, my duties as captain of the ski team, and starring in Hasty Pudding Shows. I was in the process of recovering from the bouts with alcohol that had caused my suspension for a year, yet my squandering of the academic opportunities my mother was paying for was inexcusable. As always, she showered me with nothing but love and understanding, nevertheless.

During the year away from college, in addition to getting sober, I took voice lessons with a wonderful Viennese maestro. It became my intention, majoring in music and having studied German extensively at Putney, to follow up on Hasty Pudding theatricals with a career on Broadway, doing *lieder* recitals for art. Having failed a course, I had to attend summer school. I'd just secured a church soloist position and walked happily along the streets of Cambridge, past a playground where a baseball game was in progress. One of the players was a guy I knew from summer baseball. He called out my name and asked me to join in – which I willingly did, but soon wished I hadn't. My larynx was injured in a collision, and I found myself needing artificial respiration. That ended my church job, along with any chance I might have had to make a career out of my voice. Even so, I took part in community theatre musicals and even sang solos with classical choruses.

My final stint of education came later – night law school at Boston College, which was made more interesting by the many talks I had with Dean Father Robert Drinan about my having left the Catholic church before confirmation. He beneficently granted me a "continuance without a finding," which, I was learning in Criminal Law classes, permitted young offenders to have no record if they behaved. He also offered me a full scholarship if I would switch to days. I declined, my first child having just been born.

As for tennis...I played until my arthritic hands prevented holding a racquet, and I've had my moments. At age 60, I managed twice to take sets off my stepson, who'd had a tennis scholarship in college. There were tournaments over the years, yet never any hardware; my ground-strokes never caught up to my serve. C'est la vie.

Janine and Raytheon

It is hard to write about my first marriage, which ended in bitter divorce. My alcoholism certainly played a role, as it did in the irreparable separation from two of my three daughters. My eldest has pointed out that it may have been more my egocentricity.

I've worked to overcome both and have now been totally sober since age 51, more than 32 years. And, I was so very lucky to never have an accident during my drinking years, never injured anyone, never become belligerent. The "Irish Malady" however, which I had come by honestly, made itself known early on. My "Auntie Mame," Agatha by name, was a spirited, flamboyant creature, an actress on Broadway, who had been married to a sculptor, and been tragically maimed in an automobile accident. I often visited her in her New York apartment. When I was thirteen or so, she let me taste her martini. Soon thereafter I was mixing them for her. Appearing older than my age, I was served in bars during school vacations. By the time I'd found a home amidst the aroma of "Bally" on tap in Jim Cronin's of Harvard Square, and been sent home from college, doctors said I was a case of gin away from cirrhosis.

Sober in my final years at college, I remained so through my Bohemian existence in Greenwich Village and into my marriage with Janine Cauhape. We met as teachers at Grace Church School, walking in the afternoons to my cold water flat. We played piano four hands until she took over. The daughter of a French violist, a principal with the Boston Symphony, she was truly gifted. Her right hand was the envy of many concert pianists. She didn't become one, though she had a teenage recital with the orchestra, because she never disciplined her left.

We were completely infatuated and very attracted physically, though always stopping short of intercourse. At the end of the school year, we went separately to Cape Cod, she to her family in South Chatham and I to Orleans where I was director of athletics for a boy's camp. We had resolved to be married and I'd given up with finality any thought of a career in the arts. I was to start in the fall with Monsanto as a sales trainee, in large part because my brother was already established with the company. When I spent the last few days of August at South Chatham, some disturbing differences surfaced between Janine and me as to our views on life. I felt fully committed and resolved to continue with our plans. I left to drive to St. Louis, neglecting to fully wipe the early morning mist from my windshield. On the way out of the long driveway, I scraped the right side of my car against a tree. It seems symbolic to me now, in that I was taking a "wrong turn" in entering the marriage and the business world.

Our lovemaking was joyous and we had many happy times in the early years. We could have had a fabulous affair. And we did produce three remarkable creatures. For whom Janine was a wonderful mother. The things that divided us would eventually hold sway, however, as I was living someone else's life, it seemed, and she became increasingly discontented.

Undaunted by Monsanto's dismissal of me as a misfit, we drove east with Janine pregnant and me looking for work. Our first daughter, Natasha, (named after my mother-in-law) was born, and I started night law school and began my career at Raytheon, all in the same week, in September 1957.

Hired as an administrative assistant, then put into their advanced management program, I became a trouble-shooter, the first incumbent in every position I held thereafter. These included business manager/controller for R&D of the Hawk missile system; liaison with DOD to resolve a worldwide spare parts crisis; stateside manager of a huge program installing Hawk batteries in Saudi Arabia, along with building an Air Force Academy and hospital at Jedda; and manager of Japan Hawk, licensing their production of Hawk (for defensive purposes only, of course). I'd become a gun-runner, the last thing a Putney/Harvard musician could have envisioned.

Early on, my relationship with my father-in-law blossomed, to the extent that he thought it would be a great idea if I joined him in sampling his homemade absinthe. I had been sober for more than eight years. Within two months, I was too hung-over on New Year's Day to hang my new license plates on my car.

Though I never missed work, my drinking increased gradually over the years, as Janine and I drifted apart, and I smoked four packs a day. When her sister was tragically killed, I was not really there for her. Our family doctor was, however, as she recovered from the shock, and they formed an alliance of which I was unaware until they married shortly after our divorce. My pleasure in doing community-theater was not shared by Janine, I think. And in my growing disenchantment with my work, she was not there for me. I wanted very badly to leave Raytheon, and, through my mother, met the President of Rockland Community College in New York. He wanted to enhance their facilities and extra-curricula programs, and sought funding from the state in order to offer me a job as special vice president. On the phone with my mother, I excitedly described my plan to sell our house and make the move. "Over my dead body" came Janine's voice from another room. We separated not long thereafter.

I transferred to another Raytheon location, my mission being to use their huge technical publications organization as a building block for entry into the emerging education business. As I encountered the duplicity in top management's attitude towards a minority-training program, part of the 1,000-person organization I had inherited, my unhappiness became desperation. Had I stayed on, perhaps I might have drunk myself to death. As it was, together with leaving the company, I stopped on my own. I had significant separation pay, yet after some months, my income being seriously curtailed, the court ordered a reduction in my child support payments. Janine never forgave me for that, as she saw to their needs until I put the older two through college.

The Law and Hope

On my final day at Raytheon, I was heading to my car when my secretary came into the hall telling me there was a phone call, "...something about a play." I'd vaguely planned to bicycle in Ireland or some such, to clear my head. The call was to ask me to step in for the lead in a community production of "Funny Girl." I did, going straight to a rehearsal that evening. Asked during a break what I did for a living, I first replied, "Nothing, at the moment...." Then, "But I am a lawyer." Through Harvard connections I was introduced to a wonderfully cantankerous, activist lawyer. "I can't pay you anything, but you can use the desk in our library and be helpful whenever possible." Thus began my second career.

I acquired a few divorce clients, did pro bono criminal defense, and expanded into real estate law. Needing steady employment, I moved to the public defender's office, running an experimental neighborhood office in Lowell. The most interesting part of that assignment was convincing the crusty old District Court judges that co-defendants needed separate counsel to preclude conflict of interest. I organized a panel in the local bar to bring this about.

From there, at the behest of a Harvard friend, I went to the Massachusetts Attorney General's office, where I represented the State Commissioner of Education in the school desegregation case that achieved national prominence. We were the only such office to be on the side of the plaintiff. I appeared regularly in Judge Garrity's court, worked with federal marshals and local police to quell riots, and, much to my surprise, argued the case for desegregation in the First Circuit Court of Appeals, one step below the Supreme Court.

Hope Costin, actress, poetess, and wonderful person, came into my life. She was 25 years younger, the same age difference, we happily noted, that separated Sean O'Casey and his wife. We met playing the leads in his "Juno and the Paycock" in a Wellesley College production during her senior year, and later appeared together in Boston lunchtime theater. At this critical period of my life, I could not have asked for greater support or deeper love. Our years together, through marriage, abortion, and addiction, were some of my most meaningful. Hope dealt with her own eating disorder and alcoholism and helped me initiate the final stages of my recovery.

She stood by me through a difficult time, professionally and personally. I was troubled in that, being fully adult and blessed with stage presence, I gave an appearance in court far beyond my experience as a lawyer. As gratified as I'd been by the work I'd been exposed to, I had misgivings about continuing in the profession. I emerged, however, as chief of the Criminal Trials

Section, and was catapulted into heading the prosecution of the largest ring of arson cases ever assembled. I spent months interviewing our primary witness, the "torch," at a secret location in Boston Harbor protected by machine-gun bearing troupers. I was personally handling the conspiracy case that was to be our coup de grace. Under great pressure in a very public setting, I panicked during my opening of the trial. I managed to stall and tread water until we recessed for the day.

I spoke with the Attorney general that night. He and I had become friends, partly due to my giving him tennis lessons. I wanted out, feeling I'd not do justice to our work as I was in over my head. "I knew you were a defendant's guy at heart, just like me," he said. The trial, taken over by others, resulted in conviction, and he graciously accepted my resignation.

Lawyering for seven years had taken its toll. I'd started drinking again and felt lost. When my mother visited, she and Hope accompanied me to a care facility. I entered a large room permeated by the dysfunction of the assembled patients. I turned, abruptly, and left, ready to proceed with life.

I learned that, as an accredited attorney, I was entitled to take out a real estate broker's license. I did so, opening an office from my home and prospering. We moved into one of Cambridge's large, brick and ivied apartment buildings near Radcliffe. I became associated with an office doing large-scale condominium conversions, entering into some beneficial partnerships. It occurred to me that my own building was a prime candidate and I convinced my landlord of that fact. Selling my 40-odd co-tenants on the idea of buying their units produced significant income.

Hope, in the meantime had become sober, attending AA meetings. I felt crowded, I guess, announcing I was going on a trip to examine real estate opportunities in North Carolina. Actually, I purchased a large pickup, equipped it for camping, and headed off, stopping at the first bar I passed in Connecticut. I drank, slept it off, and drove, making my way south to Florida. I vividly recall coming to my senses, in my underwear, in the moonlight on a desert, a pint of Jack Daniels in my hand, baying at the moon. I drove north, stopping in North Carolina at a motel with a six-pack in tow. In the wee hours, I awoke, opened a beer and then threw it out the back door. I drove 16 hours straight to Hope's AA meeting and burst in, announcing, "I'm Tim. I'm an alcoholic."

I've been sober since then. It has happily become my way of life, yet it wasn't easy at first. In the Christmas holidays, with my marriage ending and withdrawal tensions extreme (I'd also stopped smoking), I was alone in my condo. I felt I had three choices, suicide, a drink, or a cigarette. I went out for a pack of Marlboros.

Acting

Amicably divorced, reasonably flush, and sober, I indulged myself by pursuing my long lost dream. The theatre was after all in my blood. It was really Hope who had set it in motion, though. I had accompanied her when she auditioned for "Sea Gull." The director didn't use Hope but did cast me as Dr. Dorn.

Once again it was during rehearsals that I struck upon a path towards a career. A member of the cast told me about her acting teacher, and I made the contact. Adding some intense training to my fairly impressive resume from many plays and musicals in community theaters, I was marketable in Boston. I managed to gain entry to the unions with some bit parts. I contacted a big time agent in New York who had been stage manager for the Hasty Pudding shows I'd done at Harvard. He took me on and we had some modest success. Though he advised against it, I decided to go to Hollywood.

AA meetings were sort of fun there, because of the recognizable faces. I now had agents on both coasts and did enough work to collect unemployment. That was a big hurdle to cross – 97% of Screen Actor's Guild members don't work at all! I even earned almost enough to break even one year. The end came, however, with the crash of 1987. The modest portfolio garnered in real estate was extinguished. It had been an ill-advised venture from the start. Too many men my own age were there ahead of me, and struggling, as my Hasty Pudding friend had cautioned me. I returned to New York, downcast.

It had been a good run, though. Highlights included appearances on the likes of the TV program "Dallas," and in movies of the week and miniseries with stars like Robert Mitchum, Cliff Robertson, and Martin Sheen. Still, the work I had done in theater, both professional and amateur, was the most gratifying. When I played Victor in Miller's "The Price," on stage from the opening to the end in a small North Shore theater, I felt as if the audience was going to come up and pull the buttons off my policeman's uniform in the curtain call. During an intense dialogue, my mother and Hope being in the audience, a woman was heard to say, "I feel as though I'm eavesdropping." The memory of a standing ovation after "Man of La Mancha" in a Maine summer theater still causes goose bumps. And, after performing in "Love Letters" here at Rossmoor, I was deeply touched by the tears in the eyes of the audience as they filed out of the theater.

June, Mediation and Retirement

And then there was June, the love of my life. We've spent the last 25 years together, after a separation of almost a half-century. We are first cousins. At ages 10 and 11, we were two of those little ones who just pair off in an intimacy that seems instinctual. When I took the train to visit, we spent countless hours with the stuffed animals in her room. She recalls tearfully presenting me with one of her favorites in the station as I departed.

About fifty years later, after I'd returned from Hollywood with my tail between my legs, we met at a family gathering at my brother's house. Seeing her as she arrived, my heart seemed to skip a beat. We sat together, absorbed in each other, as though no time had elapsed. She was visiting from California. Was she married? No, widowed. And I? Divorced. We arranged to meet privately before she returned to the West Coast.

We were alone, sitting across from each other. I said it felt like an interview. June suggested I join her on the couch. I did, remarking that it felt odd, our being cousins. June said, "Why don't we just forget it?" We kissed, joyfully, passionately. We walked hand in hand along a snow-covered Park Avenue into Grand Central for her train to her sister's, parting once again on a platform. Two days later, talking long distance, it was settled that I would visit her in California. She showed me around her townhouse, a picture of her grandparents on the wall of her bedroom - my grandparents! We made love in front of her fireplace. I met her sons; we took a trip to Sea Ranch and played tennis; everything meshed. There was nothing we couldn't and didn't talk about. Feeling as though miraculously restored, I returned east to gather my things and have been here ever since.

In our new situation, what I needed was employment. Ever resourceful, June found an ad in the paper. A San Francisco "mediation company" was hiring. I knew what the word meant, yes, but how was it something one did? I was hired, just as the company, American Intermediation Services, was being acquired by Judicate. The retiring founder of AIS asked me to support her doing negotiations. They ended with me as president of AIS, a short-lived assignment, as the entity ceased operations. I'd been able to learn about the process and parlayed that into work with another company.

Fully trained and by now developing a following, I established my own "Wise Mediations." I did well over 900 mediations before retiring at age 70, forming an association with my peers that was the most gratifying work experience of my life. We fancied ourselves "master mediators," working around the country and, in one instance, traveling to London to introduce the process. My pals used to kid me that I was "doing it for the hugs." Maybe I was, but the pay was damn good, and sparing people the anguish of trial deeply rewarding.

June and I were married 20 years ago, in 1994. Our love continues to grow, as does our support of each other through every obstacle and the joy we share, in the littlest things, or with major achievements. We cherish our "November" days at Rossmoor. And I cherish the enrichment of my life that has come from the love I share with Peter and Kevin, my stepsons, and granddaughters Rebecca and Adrienne, and the reclaiming of a relationship with my daughter Natasha and her children, William, and Alixe.

Philosophies and Such

I prefer not to be categorized. The term atheist is inherently objectionable to me because it is a negative – a denial. I have no belief in a deity, yet I am more than willing to accept that others do. "Agnostic" sounds hollow for me -- I think we are coming to know more and more about the cosmos, especially as we learn more about what we don't know. "Humanist" would perhaps most closely describe the way I feel about myself, though I make absolutely no claim to scholarship.

I was baptized a Catholic, and never missed a Sunday, battling snow storms if need be, while constantly at war with my inner conflicts. At age 12, I stopped going to mass and refused to be confirmed. I was able to enjoy the midday meal on Sunday for the first time in my life. I had not, at that tender age, formulated a set of beliefs to replace my religion; I just knew that I could not, in honesty, utter the first words of the Apostle's Creed: "I believe in the Holy Catholic Church and all that it teaches."

I have formulated over time a firm conviction that the only way our existence makes sense is that it takes place in the course of infinite time and space. Creationist doctrine is lost on me because I part company with the bible after "In the beginning..." because it negates a continuum. I am equally disinclined to accept scientific theory as to a "beginning" or outer limit. To me the questions that persist are "...yes, and before that ... and beyond that?" It is inconceivable to me that, in nature, there has ever been only one of anything.

My mother organized the community councils utilized to implement New York State's ground-breaking laws against discrimination. She and my stepfather were prime movers in the formation of the Liberal Party. I've never had the slightest hesitation to follow in that tradition, even when active in the very bowels of the establishment.

The greatest sorrow for me has been my failure as a parent for my girls. I take pride in believing that, with all my faults, I've had a positive influence on many lives, directly and indirectly. However, that shortcoming will accompany me to my last breath. Perhaps I could have lived my life differently, without alcohol, pursuing tennis, dedicated to music and theater. Yet, if living two-thirds of my life as I did was what it took to bring me to this one-third with June, I wouldn't change a thing.

****

More Thoughts About Aging: Stray and Otherwise

Writers are admonished to write about things that they know, about events from their own experience, and about thoughts relevant to their own lives. OK, then. There is little in this world of mine that I am more deeply involved with than the aging process. The fact that I get older every day intrudes itself into my psyche every time I go to the grocery store for bread and cheese, and, even with my wife's shopping list in hand, find myself wandering the aisles trying to remember why I'm there. Or when I emerge from the store with no idea where I parked just 20 minutes before.

Can there be any doubt that post-retirement years are among the best of our lives? As a younger man, I would pass the local tennis club every day on the way to work, envying the players who, unlike me, didn't have to spend their day in an office.

At my current age, 85, it's time to get serious about what to do with life. By 2049, I'll be 120 years old and there won't be time left to win a seat in the Senate, play the impossibly difficult (for me, at least!) second movement of the Moonlight Sonata, break 45 on the nine-hole golf course, or write a best-selling novel.

It is a sobering thought that when Mozart (who died at 35) was my age he had been dead for 50 years.

Growing old is what happens while you wait for life to begin.

The young have aspirations that never come to pass; the old have reminiscences of what never happened.

From Somerset Maugham: "When I was young I was amazed at Plutarch's statement that the elder Cato began at the age of eighty to learn Greek. I am amazed no longer. Old age is ready to undertake tasks that youth shirked because they would take too long."

Though there is some truth to the cliché that wisdom grows with age, it is not an unalloyed blessing. As George Burns once put it:

"By the time you're eighty years old you've learned everything. You only have to remember it."

"Just remember, when you're over the hill you pick up speed." Charles Schultz

Many of us are living longer: reaching our 80's and 90's is getting to be fairly standard. Here's some longevity data for animals: mice live for only two years; bats live for 30 years, squirrels for 25, elephants for 70, horses 50, and tigers reach 25. Eagles can make it to 55. Queen ants live to 15 years, and Giant Tortoises to 150.

"Grow old along with me! The best is yet to be: The last of life, for which the first was made." Robert Browning

I always believed in the adage that old age is 15 years older than you are. That was certainly the case when I was 30, or 40 or 60. Now, however, at 85, I am confronted by the reality that 100 looms just ahead. I no longer take comfort in the notion that old age is 15 years older than I am. At 85, old age has clearly arrived for me! I have no wish to be younger. Life at this age, as I have said again and again, is as good as it has ever been – in some ways better. My only wish is that I could live on at 85 for a very long time.

We who have lived our long lives in this age of television and automobiles and computers have experienced greater wealth than emperors of earlier centuries. Napoleon. Tsar Peter, George Washington and Cleopatra would have envied our cars and the flights we can take to far off places. They might have envied even more our indoor plumbing and central heating and our life-extending access to antibiotics.

From Eric Hoffer: "Old age equalizes -- we are aware that what is happening to us has happened to untold numbers from the beginning of time. When we are young we act as if we were the first young people in the world."

From Golda Mier: "Old age is like flying through a storm. Once you're aboard, there's nothing you can do."

****

John Caleb Gosling

John grew up in unusual but altogether pleasant circumstances. Raised with two siblings and with numerous nearby cousins, John was introduced by his father to hunting and fishing, a way of life that continued into adulthood. His graduation from the Merchant Marine Academy in Vallejo led to a lifelong and successful career in marine engineering. With marriage and three children, John ventured into motorcycles and a much used family airplane. His early retirement years centered on travels across America in a motor home.

The Early Years

The year of my birth was 1936. I was born and raised in the Napa County, California poorhouse. My father ran the poorhouse; that was his job. It was known formally as the Napa County Infirmary. The poorhouse was a big place, consisting of five or six buildings and a big barn. This was before the days of welfare. And so, if you lived in Napa County, and the County Supervisor declared you to be indigent, you would end up being sent to my father's place.

The poorhouse had separate wards for men and women. There were about 200 people resident there. My family lived in a separate house on the grounds. There was a central kitchen and dining hall. The people were all elderly, all were single, and they were all indigent. Some of them were not quite right in the head; some were alcoholics. There were no counselors for these people; this was before the age of professional counseling. The poorhouse was located in the center of acres of farmland; residents were expected to work on the farm insofar as they were capable.

There were five or six nurses on the staff; my father and other members of the staff were employees of Napa County. My father was a political appointee to that position. The families of both my parents were lifetime residents of the county. My grandparents, on both sides, had been farmers in the Berryessa Valley; their schooling had ended in the eighth grade, which was standard during those years. Though my parents both graduated from high school, and my father did spend a year at the University of California, higher education was not for them. Their lives were in the main dedicated to work and to raising a family.

My father's passion was hunting and fishing, and it remained so for the rest of his life. He brought me into that world, and for many years of my early adulthood I, too, was an avid hunter and fisher. My brother and my uncles and cousins did the same; it was the center of our family's time together. Annual deer hunting and trout fishing was a big thing for all of us. I have pictures of my grandfather with a dead deer on his horse.

I have a sister, Janice, some ten years older than I am, who graduated from the College of the Pacific. My brother, George, about six years older, graduated from Berkeley. Both became schoolteachers.

Growing up, I was surrounded by an extended family. Lots of aunts and uncles and cousins. I lived an idyllic childhood – though you don't know that at the time. For much of my life, I had no friends who were not relatives. Indeed, I have more non-family friends here in Rossmoor than I ever had before we came to this community.

We still, to this day, remain a close family. All of us, together with our children and with descendents of other Berryessa Valley families, gather every Memorial Day at the cemetery at which my parents and grandparents are buried. Altogether, about 40 of us assemble for a big picnic. While there, we sit on the headstones.

Merchant Marine Academy

I kind of drifted through high school. In those days, California schools had what they called a 6-4-4 plan. Grades 1-6, grades 7-10, followed by grades 11-14, with the latter being grades 11 and 12 followed by two years of what we today know as Junior College. So, after high school I spent one year in grade 13, knowing all the while that I needed something more than that. So, during the last year, I applied to the Merchant Marine Academy in Vallejo, and signed up for Navy ROTC to get some of my tuition paid for.

The Academy is essentially a vocational school; students wear uniforms. It is part of the California university system. The Academy was, and is, a three-year school, but students attend twelve months a year, so it affords the equivalent of a four-year program. Upon graduation, I was commissioned as an Ensign; my ROTC obligation required me, upon graduation, to serve two years of Navy active duty.

The Academy offered two curricula: Deck Officer or Engineering Officer. I signed up for the latter, and marine engineering, in various offshoots, became my lifelong profession. Training at the Academy was good; it had its own ship, an old Navy transport, on which we students spent about three months each year on trans-ocean voyages to develop and apply skills learned in the classroom. The whole student body and teaching staff would be on the ship at the same time. We sailed to various places in South and Central America, spending most of our time in the engine room learning how to make the ship go.

Going to the Academy was not part of any kind of life plan. It was for me a series of open doors. I had no special affection for the seaman's life or for boats or for engineering. But it all came together in ways that have afforded me a satisfying and rich professional life. I graduated in 1958, and immediately entered onto the obligatory two years of active duty in the Navy. Based for the whole two years in Long Beach, California, I was assigned as engineering officer for a fleet of twelve small minesweepers. All twelve came to shore every night, having spent the days sweeping the ocean between Long Beach and Catalina Island. I was responsible for the maintenance and repair of the twelve boats along with the correct operation of their engine rooms. Once a year, each boat was dry-docked in one of the local private shipyards. I also looked after that.

Career in Marine Engineering

When I left the Navy in 1960, never having had sea duty, I thought I should spend some time at sea. So I joined the engineers union (MEBA). One could not go to sea with first joining the union. I went to the union hall looking for a job, and got one on the President Fillmore. I sailed on that freighter for a year or so on what was called the "jungle run." We went to Guam, Manila, Jakarta, Bangkok, and finally Hong Kong.

I then worked for three years for a small shipyard in San Francisco, learning every day. The yard was humming with activity - maintaining ships of all types. Working there was a wonderful education, the best job I could have had because what I learned there became the basis for much of what followed. The people who worked in that shipyard were educated only in the school of hard knocks. None of them had ever seen a university classroom, but their innate skills and inborn intelligence and essential wisdom and their dedication to hard work gave me great and lasting respect for working-level people, and taught me much of what I needed to perform at the highest level of excellence as a marine engineer. There were some 300 craftsmen, such as welders, sheet metal workers and electricians. They were divided into two shifts, day shift and night shift. I ended up running the night shift.

Much of my work at the shipyard was in support of Matson, a leader in Pacific Ocean transport; ultimately that led to my getting an offer from Matson to join them as Port Engineer. When I joined Matson, cargo was moved, package-by-package, onto and off of the ships. Longshoremen by the hundreds were employed to do this work, and strikes and work stoppages were a common and disruptive part of our way of life. Labor costs were high. The volume of shipped goods was increasing by leaps and bounds, and it was clear that we needed to move to the use of large shipping containers.

But everything needed to handle containerization had not yet been invented. Containers had to be designed, the transports to carry them to and from the ships needed to be outfitted, the cranes needed to move containers onto and off of the ship needed to be designed and built. And the decks and holds of our ships needed to be reengineered to facilitate this new way of moving cargo. As Port Engineer, I was deeply involved with that evolution, and over the years took on increasing responsibilities, and ultimately became Matson's Vice President for Engineering, a position I held until retirement.

Marriage and Children

About a year after I left the Navy, my brother's wife, then a student at Sacramento State University, called to tell me that she was bringing her roommate to our family Thanksgiving dinner. Joan, her roommate, came from the State of Washington, too far away for her to travel just for Thanksgiving dinner. That roommate was Joan, and I was smitten at first sight.

I was 24 at the time, and Joan was a year younger. After that Thanksgiving dinner, I made regular weekend visits from San Francisco to Sacramento to be with Joan.

Less than a year later, we decided to marry, so Joan went home to plan and arrange the wedding, When I went to Washington for the wedding, I met her parents for the first time. Amazingly, they had never met the man she brought home to marry. Big shock for them. Though her parents were given no choice in the matter, I passed the test and we got married two days after I arrived.

We came back to a small apartment in San Francisco. Some twelve months after our marriage, in 1963, our son Daniel was born. After that, we rented in Marin for a few years, and finally bought a house in San Rafael.

Cathy, our eldest daughter, was born in 1965 and Sarah, our youngest, in 1968. Joan was a stay at home Mom. She had a degree in education and was certified by the state, but as it turned out she never did teach.

Daniel went to Berkeley, majoring in physics. After graduation, he went to work as an options trader but left that after some years. His first marriage, from which a son was born, did not work. The son, who lives with his mother, is now at the University of Chicago. Daniel recently married a much younger woman, and they recently had a daughter. Daniel now works as a chef.

Cathy went to UC Davis, majoring in psychology. She wound up managing an office for Manpower Corporation. Cathy is married, has two daughters. She has long lived in our former home in San Rafael. Cathy's husband has a successful career as a sales rep for Merck. They have two children, both daughters.

Sarah, our youngest, had academic problems in high school. We wound up sending her to a private girls school in Connecticut, where she became an academic superstar, graduating as valedictorian. She then attended Scripps, one of the Claremont schools, but left without graduating. But her sister, Cathy, was able to place Sarah in a temp job with IBM, where Sarah met and soon married an IBM salesman. Her husband, who has master's degrees in both computer science and business, is still with IBM, and has had a very successful career. They have two daughters and a son.

Each of our three kids, and their families, live nearby. Joan and I, together with our kids and their families, have contributed toward a one-week rental of a houseboat on Lake Shasta later this summer. We have done that before, and it is something we all look forward to. The boat has a great kitchen, beds for all. We have also rented a speedboat that we tow and use for water skiing. Some years ago Joan and I rented a small houseboat for just the two of us. Every night we beached the boat. Joan liked sleeping inside, in the cabin. I slept outside, on the deck. One night, as lay sleeping, I heard a noisy thump near me on the deck. I looked up to see a big bear only five feet away. In my terror, I shouted to shoo the bear away. He would not move. I finally threw a deck chair at the bear, at which he turned and sauntered casually away onto shore. I spent the rest of the night in the cabin!

I said earlier that I grew up with special enthusiasm for hunting. In later years, I developed three other interests that have been an important part of my adult life: airplanes, motorcycles and motorhomes, and these interests developed in generally that order. After

I was settled in at Matson I started taking flying lessons. Then I discovered the GI bill. Before it was over I had collected 5 ratings, over 1000 hours in the air and Joan and I had flown over much of the US, Canada and Mexico. Then came motorcycles, most of which I did alone; Joan was never into motorcycling. I ended up traveling by motorcycle from the Arctic Circle in Alaska to the Panama Canal, and took numerous rides into Mexico and three trips to ride in New Zealand.

After I retired, we bought a motor-home, moved our oldest daughter into our home in San Rafael, and Joan and I lived and traveled for almost five years over most of the US and Canada in the motor-home. We managed to get as far east on the North American continent as you can drive: St Johns, Newfoundland. Of course we carried the motorcycle on the back of the motor-home. The motor-home is still with us here in Rossmoor but the motorcycles and the airplane are now gone, a casualty to the common Rossmoor conditions of advancing age and tenuous balance.

Senior Years

I think most of us would agree that our senior years are in many ways the best years of our lives – assuming health and enough money to provide the comforts of life. But one of the downsides of our retirement years is a sense of irrelevancy. Where for some four decades we had been essential to the well being of our families, important to our businesses or professions, and proud of a lifetime of accomplishments in our corner of the world.

Our families counted on us for support and guidance, and our professional involvements kept us productive and held our interest for the forty or more years of work life. And then it all came to a stop. Our children became adults no longer dependent on us for sustenance, and busy workdays were replaced with open schedules where we needed to find things to do. You are no longer needed. You have plunged from essential to irrelevant

Travel, yes. Also golf and crossword puzzles and long walks. Passing wisdom to grandchildren, yes. But none of that takes the place of the pride and satisfaction that came from earning a steady income and performing work as a productive member of society.

Happiness, at our age, comes mostly from contentment; if you are not content, you will never be happy. My youngest daughter would often ask me why I never wanted to have fun. I told her that I was satisfied with contentment. Fun is here today and gone tomorrow. Acquisition of new things provides momentary joy and pleasure, but it too is here today and gone tomorrow. That search for joy and happiness is an unending and in the end unsatisfying quest. Contentment, on the other hand, is lasting. I'm not sure what being happy is. I was always a little lazy, and I always preferred to be alone. The search for happiness requires effort, and usually requires involvement with others. Contentment can best be gotten as a byproduct of indolence and privacy.

When I was younger, there was always much that I wanted to have more time for. But all of those things require energy and strength that I no longer have. So my list of things I would like to do, such as flying my plane and riding my motorbike, are no longer possible for me, given my lessened ability to do them.

Now I have the chair in the corner of my deck (where we are now seated), next to which is a table holding the book I am reading and my book full of New York Times Sunday crossword puzzles. And there is golf, and I have the birds to watch. And I have my wife to look after me. I have enough time for all of that. But given my age and my physical limitations, there is no unease or restlessness about needing more time to do other things.

As we go through life, a good relationship with your life partner is important. I think it is developed and sustained primarily by good communications. I have gotten better at that as I have gotten older. My hearing is bad, and that gets in the way. But increasingly I feel that my wife has gotten wiser as I have lost some of my wisdom, so listening and learning is not only helpful to our relationship but also important to my well-being. Mostly I get advice disguised as information. Joan has always taken lots of vitamins and minerals, and I have always pooh-poohed it. Because of my recent medical problems, she has taken a great interest in my diet and medication. Her research has led to recommendations for me to take particular vitamins and minerals, none of which I have ever bothered with. I feel certain that since I have begun that new regimen that my health has improved.

Friendships too can be maintained only by communication, only when the parties make an effort to reach out to one another. After extended periods apart, friendship wanes. Letters, email, phone calls, visits: any or all of those is needed. That applies even to your children. Relationships with adult children are essentially friendships. If not nurtured by contact, they grow cold.

It is interesting that we bring into this conversation our relationships with adult children. They are friends, yes, but they remain our children. My youngest daughter has gone back to school, part time; she called us this morning, overjoyed to tell us that she had taken and passed a test in chemistry – with and "A". Now, this daughter is in her mid-forties, and she felt the need to report with pride to her parents that she had passed a test. So, once a parent always a parent; once a child, always a child – even into one's forties. We, as parents of forty or fifty year old children worry about them and take an interest in their lives just as we did when we and they were much younger.

We are lucky when our adult children don't cause us much worry or problems. There are too many parents whose adult children cause them endless concern. And trouble.

As the World Turns

Much has changed during the course of our long lifetimes. When my father was born, in 1898, there were trains, but no automobiles, no airplanes, no refrigeration. But they still lived, happily. They were not denied anything that was available in their time. They did miss out on all that is available to us – but we in turn will be denied those things that will be developed in coming decades.

I think the biggest breakthrough during the next forty years, the biggest change, will be in education. On-line education will change things dramatically. More people will be educated, and they will learn more and learn it faster. And on-line students will not be weighed down by college costs and student loans that are so burdensome to many. The value to the nation and to the world of wider and deeper education promised by on-line methods will have profound impact.

The internet has already revolutionized education, and it has only begun. One problem that needs to be addressed is that many of the young who most need on-line education have no computers or access to the web. The answer of course is that our communities and the nation need to invest in bringing these internet tools to those who do not have them. The costs will be high, but the rewards are so great that we cannot afford not to make the investment.

One more thing: Many teachers are not competent. Those that are very good at teaching will, when they win big on-line audiences, become like rock stars, famous and highly paid. Highest quality teachers will be available to every on-line student. Some are already available, many at no cost; many more at modest cost. Those who are not the very best will be left behind. These changes will increasingly result in turmoil at our universities and in our high schools. Even elementary education is affected by the emergence of Khan Academy.

One thing that I think will not change during the next forty years, and I regret to say this, is the propensity of mankind to resort to violence. Wars have existed throughout history. All we can do is contain them. We as a nation need to avoid entanglement in conflicts that do not directly affect us. Syria is a case in point. Our experience in Iraq and Afghanistan has proven the futility, indeed the counterproductive nature, of our involvement in faraway conflicts. Conflicts in the Middle-East are spawned by long-standing religious differences. Such tribal and religious conflicts are seemingly best contained by the iron fists of despots, such as Saddam, Assad, and Mubarak. When we step in, knowing nothing of their cultures and religions and languages and geography, we can only make things worse.

As we age, we know that we are in the later years of life. There could come a time when life is no longer worth living. Incurable and painful illness could bring that about, as could loneliness or extreme poverty or the serious loss of mental capacity. But on the whole, most of us value life, and hang on even when much of the joy is gone.

As I ponder the many years of my life, there are a few accomplishments in which I take special pride. Having run a number of marathons is something in which I have pride. Marathons are among the most satisfying things I have ever done. But they were physically satisfying, not really the kind of accomplishments that merit Nobel awards. I guess I am proud of having become a Vice-President of Matson. I never thought I deserved it, but it did come about.

And, this is strange, the only person I really wished had known about my professional success is my father, and he died long before any of that came about. I don't think my wife or kids cared one way or the other about my success at Matson, but I know it would have meant a great deal to my father. So, yes, the more I think about it, my elevation to Vice President is an accomplishment that means a lot to me – but would have been much more important had my Dad been here to know about it. He had no expectations about my future, but then again neither did I. I just flowed through life, no plan, no expectations, it all just happened.

We all have expectation of longer lives than our parents and grandparents had. Much of that is because most of us remain healthy for longer years than did our parents. We tend also to remain more involved in life, more active than did our parents at this age. I think living in Rossmoor has a lot to do with that; this wonderful community offers an endless variety of activities. It also provides easy and ready access to social interaction and physical involvement. Altogether, this is a wonderful place in which to live.

When you die, it all ends. When you are gone from life, there is nothing after that. No afterlife, no reincarnation. There is nothing but the end of everything. People do like to believe in things, but believing in afterlife in any form is to me illogical.

As I ponder special moments in my life, my wife says that the nicest thing that anyone has ever said to me was when she said "I do!" And the older I get, the more I believe that is true. She gets smarter all the time. My marriage is a better deal now than it ever was. The happiest day of my life, though I did not know at the time, was the day of my wedding to Joan.

The only nagging concern, in my otherwise very good life, is how to avoid getting really sick. I hope to have some kind of reasonable ending to life. Not a painful one, or from an extended illness. The older you get, the more you think about that. We all want to die in bed from old age having gone to bed feeling just fine.

As I ponder issues before the world, things like global warming come to mind. Many are deeply concerned about that. My own view is that it is over-hyped by the media. Everything about it has become more like a religion that a science. It is politically correct to be concerned about global warming.

I like people, but I certainly do not like everybody. I have to admit that during a good part of my life, whenever I had a choice of being with people or being alone, I generally chose to be alone. If I could pick an age at which to live forever, it would be early fifties. That's when most of us are at the height of our intelligence and authority.

I read a lot. Some books and authors have been important in forming my views about life and the world. John Dos Passos and his "USA Trilogy" are at the forefront. I remember as a kid reading that and being excited about it. John Steinbeck's "The Grapes of Wrath" and Hemingway's "For Whom the Bell Tolls" are two more. Through these books I gained insight into the lives of the downtrodden and the distressed - of the little guy against the oppressor. Good against evil. In the times in which they were written, if you were a thinking person, you either became a socialist, or heaven help you, a communist! Think of the backgrounds of all those who were dragged before the House Un-American Activities Committee during the McCarthy witch-hunt.

Though my first love is history, I cannot forget philosopher Eric Hoffer and his "The True Believer". That book has had a lasting impact on me. Wherever I look today I see the "true believers" as described in his book. In both politics and religion, there are true believers everywhere. And they are still just as I remember Hoffer's description of them: narrow minded, belligerent, intolerant and always adamantly self-righteous.

****

Ralf Parton

Ralf is an artist. He was a professor of Sculpture and Chaired the Department of Fine Arts at the University of California, Stanislaus. He holds a Master of Fine Arts degree from Columbia University, and has won both national and regional awards for his paintings and sculptures. Ralf pioneered art-travel courses for the California State College System, completing more than thirty tutorial trips around the globe. Since retiring to live in Rossmoor, he has led Rossmoorians on over fifty art tours worldwide.

The Early Days

I was born in New York City, July 1932, in the Manhattan Jewish Hospital, which provided my parents with a hospital-created birth certificate. Though the document looked official, stated the name of the doctor who delivered me, and was replete with my parent's thumb-prints and my footprint, my parents never received an official birth certificate from the city. To make matters worse, the hospital certificate gave my name as "Baby" Parton; my parents were undecided on a name until some days after my mother came home with her new baby. So I went through life thinking this document was all I would ever need. And it was enough until, many years later. I applied for a passport to take my first trip abroad. I proudly proffered my so-called birth certificate, and was informed that I needed an official one from the Board of Health of the City of New York. So, I went to that office, and did get one – with the name "Baby Parton!" Luckily, my parents were both still alive, now living in Florida. They needed to go before a judge, with witnesses, to testify that they were the parents of Baby Parton, and that his name was Ralf Parton. I finally had a duly-recorded name, and was able to get the passport.

My father was born in America; my mother came to America at the age of nine, from Vienna, Austria, to be with her father who had come to America some years before. Her mother had died, a victim of the 1918 influenza epidemic that had devastated Europe.. My surname, Parton, is derived from my great-grandfather, a French Jew, who, to avoid service in the French army, migrated from Strasbourg to Russia.

I knew from the very early days of my childhood that I was destined to be an artist. My father had a small fruit and vegetable store, and I often played on the saw-dust covered floor, using a heavy black-lead pencil to draw pictures on paper bags that were used to pack customer's groceries. Customers would ask for the bags adorned with my pictures, thinking that they were cute and precocious.

From the earliest days, adults in my life were unanimous in the verdict that one day Ralf would be an artist! I went through the New York City public school system, from elementary through high school, always taking whatever art courses I could get. In high school, I was teaching art to kids a year or two behind me. During these years I was winning prizes for my artwork – including a nationwide American Automobile Association poster contest.

My Brush with Crime

As a ten-year old boy, I wanted to have a Christmas tree in our house. The problem was that I was born into a Jewish family, and my grandparents were vehemently opposed to even the idea of a "Hanukkah Bush." We were living in an apartment house across the street from Bronx Park, which houses the New York Botanical Garden. One day, a Friday near Christmas, I was strolling through the grounds where I came upon a beautiful four-foot high evergreen tree. Seeing that I was utterly alone in the park, I went to work with my Cub-Scout pen-knife, and after a half-hour of hard work I had felled the tree. So, I put the tree over my shoulder and scurried across the busy street to Gilderber Arms, the fancy name for our apartment house. Hiding the tree overnight, I got up early on Saturday morning, and after my father left for work I made pop-corn, and threaded it onto string to ornament the tree. My father came home, watched good-naturedly as I placed the last trimmings onto the tree, whereupon he asked "Ralf, what's that tag hanging off that limb." I had never noticed it. But when I reached for it, I read aloud: "This Chinese fir is a gift to the City of New York from Madame Chiang Kai-shek."

My Babe Ruth Story

I always liked to do sculptures. In my earlier years, my favorite medium was soap-bars – sculpted into dogs and horses and the like. When I was 15 or so, the city sponsored a snow-sculpture contest in Central Park. I of course entered, and built a snow-sculpture meant to depict a hobo carrying his bag of goods on a stick over his shoulder. A reporter for the New York Daily Mirror took a picture of me and my sculpture and said "Hey kid, that kind of looks like Babe Ruth," so I changed the stick into something that looked more like a bat, and put a baseball cap on the snow-man's head.

The photographer took another picture – and the next day it appeared in the paper; I won the contest, and was awarded a gold cup. That story, and the picture of my sculpture was picked up by the local movie-tone news and appeared the next weekend in movie houses across the city! I had achieved a kind of local fame. Two months later I got a letter: "Thanks kid for making me famous. The Babe." The story has a bad ending: that letter would today be worth money, but while I was away at college my mother threw the letter away - along with the gold cup.

Buffalo

Howie Goldstein, my boyhood special pal, and I, had been accepted at City College in New York. But we both wanted to get away from home to see a bit of the world. Having learned of the Albright School of Art, in Buffalo, I applied for and got a scholarship. Howie did not win a scholarship, but we went together to Albright, a three-year school then rated as one of the top three art schools in the nation. We both stayed for the full three years, and both graduated with honors. Howie went on to win a PhD, and became chair of the art department at Trenton State University. We two remained close friends over the years – and I learned just recently, from his wife, that Howie had died after a long illness.

Across the street from Albright was the Buffalo State Teachers College, and I took courses at that school too – winning a BA Degree in Art Education. During my third year at Buffalo State, I met the most beautiful girl in the incoming freshman class. Her name was Mary Jean Foley! I spent my senior year at Buffalo State courting Mary Jean. She was a native of Buffalo, and lived at home while a college student. So during the time of our courtship I needed to meet and win-over her very Irish Catholic parents - who were not at all happy with their daughter's Jewish boyfriend.

When I graduated from Buffalo State, I went to Columbia for one year, earning a Masters in Fine and Industrial Arts. In January of that year, 1955, I got a call from Mary Jean, then in her junior year at Buffalo State and still living at home, sobbing while telling me of the difficulties she was having with her parents. Though we had decided to wait for marriage until after I graduated from Columbia, that conversation led to our deciding to get married immediately – so Mary Jean quit school the next day and came to New York, where we married in January of 1955.

While a student at Columbia, I was teaching art at a Junior High School in Merrick Long Island. During my remaining time at Columbia, Mary Jean decided to convert to Judaism – her decision, not mine! She did it to please my two sets of very orthodox Jewish grandparents. She took lessons at the 92nd Street Y. As the spouse of a Columbia student, Mary Jean was also allowed to take courses at Columbia, at no cost. Those were busy times for both of us.

Camp Counselors

After my 1955 graduation from Columbia, we moved back to Buffalo, Mary Jean reentered Buffalo State, from which she graduated in 1957, and I landed my first professional job as Art Consultant to five elementary schools in Niagara Falls. We were living with Mary Jean's parents. Mid-way through that academic year, an art professor at Buffalo State went on sabbatical leave – and I was offered his position – which I happily accepted, becoming an Associate Professor at the age of 23. I stayed in that job through the remainder of the school year, and for the next full year. Looking for summer work, I learned of a job as Director of Arts and Crafts at a Fresh Air Camp outside Detroit. I took the job, and Mary Jean took a job there too as a counselor.

The camp's director, Tom Cohn, was a Professor of Psychology at the University of Michigan - where he was doing research on "gifted" children, studying their attributes and special academic needs.

After summer at the camp, Mary Jean and I returned to Buffalo. I received a call from Tom telling me of an estate property for sale near Traverse City, in northern Michigan, asking me to join with him in buying it. His plan was to turn the estate into a camp for gifted children. I turned down the offer to go in on the buying, but did agree to come to the camp the following summer to help in building the facilities and to become its Art Director.

Tom did buy the property, setting it up as a camp for high IQ kids. The estate included a 28-room mansion, a 14-room tenant farmer's house, and four-car carriage-garage with an apartment for the chauffer. It sat on a hilltop overlooking eight lakes, surrounded by 380 wooded acres, and has its own 80-acre lake. The estate, which was in remarkably good condition, had been the summer home of heirs to the Reynolds Tobacco fortune. Amazingly, Tom was able to buy the place for $50,000. It came fully furnished, including Persian rugs. To make the place ready for use as a children's camp, Tom needed to auction off the furnishings - which netted some $60,000!

In its first year, 1956, the camp had 100 kids, ranging from 5 to 16 years old, from Cincinnati, Chicago, Detroit and elsewhere in the mid-west. Because of Tom's reputation as a specialist in gifted children, many of the kids were children of academics. We had a staff of 50 adults - many were leaders in their academic fields. The night watchman had a PhD in math! Our two cooks had Masters degrees in Home Economics. The camp's doctor was a professor at the U of M Medical School.

Our Six Years Living on an Estate!

At the end of the first summer, Tom asked Mary Jean and me to stay at the camp during the coming winter; the camp's maintenance man and has wife, an older couple, would also stay to help us care for it, and for us. We both quit our Buffalo jobs and as it turned out stayed there for the next six years. Mary Jean got a teaching job at a nearby grammar school, and I spent my time painting and sculpting – and lecturing and developing an art department at Northwestern Community College in Traverse City. We lived on that estate for the next six years – teaching during the camp's summer program, but living there year-round.

Our first child, Eric, was born in 1962, and in 1963 Mary Jean and I moved to California – where I had been offered a Professorship to build and chair the art department at the newly formed California State University at Stanislaus County, in Turlock, California. Mary Jean took a job teaching at an elementary school in Turlock. Our second son, Jason, was born in Turlock in 1965. We were to stay in Turlock for 25 years, both retiring in 1988.

During my years teaching at CSUS Turlock, I pioneered travel art courses for the California Sate University system. These courses were built around three-week-long art tours for students in Europe. I designed and developed the course's itineraries, and lectured to my students as we toured art museums and galleries – with visits to artist's studios in European cities. Altogether, during my 25 years, I conducted many such art tours in Mexico and abroad, including visits to Russia, France, Spain, Italy The Netherlands and Great Britain.

Mary Jean and I moved to Rossmoor in 1990, and soon after arriving here joined the Rossmoor Art Association. For years, people at Rossmoor asked me to do art tours for them – and my answer was always "No, been there and done that!" But in 1994 I arranged the first tour for Rossmoorians – to museums in Paris, Amsterdam and Bruges. That turned out to be the first of many. Someone suggested to me that I add a tour to Africa; the idea was intriguing to me – but I wondered what I could offer there – after all, I have expertise in art and art history of only the Western world. So Mary Jean and I took an exploratory trip to Africa, and loved it. I decided that my knowledge of photography would be of some value. So we designed and set up a guided "Wildlife Safari" visit to Africa, and to my surprise we had 23 people sign up. That tour has now become one of the most popular in my list of travel tour offerings.

Our Two Sons

As I have said in earlier paragraphs, Mary Jean and I spawned two wonderful sons, Eric, now 51, and Jason, 48. Eric is an urban cowboy, who lives, works and plays in San Francisco. He is a rabid sports fan and loves Rock concerts. Jason is our country boy - he loves fishing and riding his mountain motorcycle. He lives and works in Turlock for Creative Alternatives, a non-profit foundation dealing with abused children.

Mary Jean and I often wondered at how different our sons' personalities are, considering that they had the same parents and went to the same schools. So much for the age-old question about the relative impact of environment and genetic endowment. Our one and only grandchild, Skylar, Eric's daughter, is now a beautiful 20-year old redhead, and a philosophy major at the University of San Francisco.

Ode to Mary Jean

As an art student across the street, I first saw her through the Student Union's basement windows, dancing in a chorus line. Mary Jean Foley was a beauty, a sophomore at Buffalo State College. After nearly a year of courting I married my Muse, although everyone said it would never last, but they were proved wrong. She was brought up in Buffalo, an Irish Catholic and I was a Jewish atheist from the Bronx. Mary Jean loved politics, and as students we campaigned together for Adlai Stevenson. Mary Jean was a complete woman, my lover and wife, a mother, a teacher, counselor, politician, and devoted grandmother. She loved reading books and me, dancing and me, family and me, traveling and me, and we had 57 beautiful years of great togetherness until the day she died.

We spent the last four months of her life in our home with hospice, permitting us lots of time to reflect and share memories of the many wonderful adventures we enjoyed as part of our "Abe's Irish Rose" marriage. Life had been so good for us, that she had no regrets having to leave, save for the promise of even more travels together enjoying the Arts, scenery and people on our planet. Mary Jean kept insisting that I find somebody to continue my life, "and make it a blond this time" she said. I was blessed having her as my life partner and blessed that she was able to come to the end of her life totally without pain, having enjoyed the Thanksgiving holiday the previous day with our two sons, her brother, our nephew and our granddaughter all in our Rossmoor home.

And Now, Carolyn: A Perfect Match!

After spending nearly a year alone, and at the insistence of my two sons to get out and start living again, I attended a Tennis Club Party. There she was, Carolyn Hinrichs, a very attractive silver haired woman, but I didn't approach her because I felt awkward having been out of the dating game for some 58 years.

Some weeks later I was to attend a Saturday opening of a former student's painting exhibition in Oakland. On that Saturday afternoon, with great hesitation, I called her and asked if she cared to join me, and she said, "I would be happy to." We had a great time, and after dating some two months I asked Carolyn what her original hair color had been, "blond," she said. Somehow I knew right then and there I had found the woman I wanted to share the rest of my life with. All kidding aside, Carolyn is a warm loving person, intelligent, creative, a retired teacher who is also a devoted grandmother. She is a fantastic dancer and happens to enjoy traveling the world and is also in love with me and I adore her. After some three months of togetherness we had a coming out party with our mutual friends. They all toasted us and said that we two were a perfect match. Now, a year and a half later, we heartily agree.

On Being an Artist

If I had to choose between the disciplines of science or the arts, I would certainly pick the arts. Both afford excitement, even thrills, but the arts are more fun. Both are serious adventures in the search for truth, but $E = MC$ squared does not, for me, provide the beauty of a Rembrandt, or come close to the sounds of Bach or to the words of Shakespeare. Science is just not visceral enough for me.

In the arts, there are as many different ways of expressing lemons or love as there are writers and violinists and painters. Artists have no limitations when they seek to objectify their found truths.

I admire, understand and respect the quest for knowledge, both of ourselves and of our universe. I applaud rational thinking, and wish there were more of it. But it is the artist that gives me pause to reflect on his creations, and that brings me happiness. The reason most museum visitors never achieve a visual orgasm, an art experience, is due to not seeking it. They listen to their museum radios for a cheap intellectual quickie – never initiating a visual foreplay. The verbal pap too often distances them from a natural intuitive response, and shuts their eyes, the real windows to the brain.

The art experience occurs when our eyes lovingly caress and open a path to our brain, which in turn ignites our sleeping spiritual world and floods our entire body with a warmth that forces us to gently sigh and release our breath back to nature.

My Life in the World of Academia

The one other thing I have a passionate love for, aside from Art, is teaching. The idea of sharing with students the search for truth and beauty, along with the visual language and discipline to express myself, became the major justification for my chosen profession. I always enjoyed teaching and was pleased to have had the pleasure of hearing my students applaud, following my lecture or when I shared in an intimate class discussion. I probably would never have opted to take early retirement save for my disgust with most University administrators. Their desire to maintain the status quo, a don't rock the boat attitude, finally drove me to leave University life even though one year I was the recipient of the "Most Outstanding Professor" award, resulting from a campus wide vote of all University students.

Art Departments have always lived a rather unwelcome life on a University Campus. They're messy, they dirty up their part of the grounds, and their dress is woefully un-academic. By the very nature of the studios needed for drawing, painting, print and sculpture, the faculty/student ratio is low and thereby expensive. The free-spirit atmosphere irritates the Administration's sense of the natural order of things academic.

I most always sided with the students on campus-wide issues, one of which was should the university cops carry guns. I helped the students sculpt a six-foot pistol mounted on a large dolly with appropriate signage to parade it around the Student Union and Administration Building. During the Vietnam War I counseled students on non-objective service or refuge in Canada.

When then Governor Reagan appointed a new President (a conservative Texan) for our university, he fired 50% of the Jewish faculty over a period of four years. I painted a large mural in the College Gallery portraying the President as a giant crazed bull, with a necklace of seven Stars of David strung between his teeth, and one arm with each faculty name on one of the stars, in gold leaf. Needless to say it made the papers all the way down to Los Angeles from our little Campus in the San Joaquin Valley. The rest of this story will come in another book if I ever get around to writing an autobiography.

On Atheism

I am sure that it happened while I was growing up but exactly when I can't say. Who can recall when maturity sets in? Please don't get me wrong, even as a Jewish child of five I believed in Santa Claus. Then again, what child doesn't? I know it happened sometime before I was twelve because I vividly remember arguing with my orthodox grandpa about the virtues of my preparing for bar-mitzvah, since I didn't believe in God. It hurt, and I felt terrible about having to admit this to my grandfather whom I dearly loved. It broke his heart, but years later, when I was in college, and after a long conversation – my grandpa told me that my philosophy of life had gained his deepest respect, and then with a warm smile on his face, he added "It's not too late for your bar-mitzvah."

On my block, there were six of us boys, all the same age. While playing stoop-ball, we discussed everything from girls to baseball to politics and religion. I think it was here that my curiosity overwhelmed my faith. But, by high school, I was a full-blown atheist, questioning everything in my search for truth.

When one lives the life of an artist, there are few rules and even fewer constraints. The world and the entire universe and everything in it are in play. There are no limitations on your thinking or feelings; we are free to try anything and fail. Atheism has given me that freedom to think, feel and enjoy all that this cosmos has to offer. Far removed from the anguish of a fearful hell or the cheap thrill of an awaiting heaven, atheism has given me the opportunity to extend and enrich my life through understanding and appreciating the vastness of our universe. Atheism provides me the ultimate brotherhood and oneness with all living creatures, unlike most of the limited, narrow and bigoted religious belief systems. Atheism allows me to anticipate, enjoy and welcome the possibilities of life. Atheism is the basis for understanding and appreciating the billions of years that the universe has existed. Fundamentalist religious believers have at most some 10,000 years of history that they crowd with dogma such as original sin, Noah's ark, virgin birth and redemption. Atheism allows us to recognize and admire the genius of homo-sapiens, who through his intellect and skill gives us music, poetry, literature, drama, architecture and other arts. What a wonderful animal we are.

When, some 150 million years ago we stood up and looked around some of us were scared, but we atheists, from the beginning, were curious. I find religion too restrictive, too full of wrong answers, to allow the abandonment necessary for creativity. The artist, in his studio, is God! You must be free to be yourself. The vastness, the immensity if our universe never ceases to amaze and excite my imagination, and foster a curiosity that would be cheapened by a belief system that would attempt to answer all the wonderful questions with a belief in God.

It is a life you live without a God that counts. To live a good life, you must build your own moral system. With your rational mind you are forced to develop a set of values. For the God-fearing, it's easy; they are given rules to live by – rules weighted with centuries of tradition. The atheist, having freed himself, must think his own way to a life of convictions.

Achieving A Visual Art Experience

I wrote the following words many years ago to guide my students in the need to look at art with both *heart* and *eyes* wide open. A work of art is not just depiction of an object; it is intended to create a mood and to stimulate emotional connections.

I want my eyes to seek, to find
I want my eyes to caress, to fondle
I want my eyes to tremble, to swoon
I want my eyes to feel the joy, the ecstasy, the rapture
I want my eyes to laugh, to cry, to sing
I want my eyes to praise without sound, to silently say wow!

My eyes have had that experience, that thrill,
When confronting Rembrandt's impasto helmet,
Vermeer's soft smooth exteriors,
Soutine's scrambled portraits.
Van Gogh's determined brush strokes.

My eyes have enjoyed
The energy in a Matisse contour,
The energy in a Cranach head,
The colors in Cezanne's white table clothes,
The imagination revealed in a Bosch landscape.

****

The Dessert Bucket List

I provide here three items that belong on your dessert bucket list: things you must create and taste before you leave this earth. Each of them will bring immediate happiness to your life! My guess is that most of you are already happy - but we can all use a greater measure of joy, especially when getting it is so easy. There is no money involved! No risk of failure! No need for outside help! The surge to happiness these three items bring may not be sustainable, but quick and certain results are guaranteed for the here and now!

I urge you to make and enjoy each of these three desserts! Recipes follow. Each dessert is easy to make, and so good that you and your family and guests will swoon with joy! Let's begin.

#1: Opa's Chocolate Cake
You might have guessed that "Opa" is grandpa, is me, your humble author. I bake this chocolate cake for every family birthday party. The recipe, which follows, is not mine. It comes to us from the Hershey Chocolate Company, and is (in print too small for old people to read!) provided on the back of every box of Hershey's excellent cocoa.

Batter

2 cups sugar	2 eggs
1 ¾ Cups Flour	1 cup milk
¾ cup cocoa	½ cup vegetable oil
1 ½ tsp baking powder	2 tsp vanilla extract
1 ½ tsp baking soda	1 cup boiling water
1 tsp salt	

1. Heat oven to 350 degrees. Grease and flour two 9" round pans.
2. Combine dry ingredients in large bowl.
3. Add eggs, milk, oil and vanilla.
4. Beat on medium speed 2 minutes
5. Stir in the boiling water. Batter will be thin.
6. Pour into pans. Bake 30-35 minutes – or until pick in center comes out clean. Cool completely. Then apply frosting.

Frosting
1. 1 stick (1/2 cup) butter
2. 2/3 cup cocoa
3. 3 cups powdered sugar
4. 1/3 cup milk
5. 1 tsp vanilla extract.

Melt butter, stir in cocoa. Add powdered sugar and milk, beating on medium speed to spreading consistency. Add more milk if needed. Stir in vanilla.

#2: **The Famous Neiman-Marcus Cookie Recipe Hoax**
This recipe produces the best oatmeal chocolate chip cookie ever. But the recipe comes with a story that needs to be told before I tell you the recipe. The story has been going around the globe for some fifty years, and it is completely untrue. Here is the story:

My daughter and I had just finished a salad at Neiman Marcus Café in Dallas and decided to have a small dessert. Because both of us are such cookie lovers, we decided to try the "Neiman-Marcus Cookie."

It was so good that I asked if they would give me the recipe and the waitress said with a small frown, "I'm afraid not." "Well, I said, would you let me buy the recipe?"

With a cute smile she said "yes." I asked how much, and she said, "Only two-fifty, it's a great deal!" I said, with approval, "Just add it to my tab."

Thirty days later I received my Visa statement from Neiman-Marcus, and it was $285. I looked again and I remembered I had spent $9.95 for two salads and about $20 for a scarf. As I glanced at the bottom of the statement, it said "Cookie Recipe $250."

That's outrageous! I called Neiman's Accounting Department and told them that the waitress said it was "two-fifty, which clearly does not mean two hundred and fifty dollars by any stretch of logic."

And now, to make a long story short – I paid and decided to have $250 worth of fun. I told the woman at accounting that I was going to see to it that every cookie lover in the United States with an email *account would receive this $250 recipe for free. So, folks, here it is! They really are the best ever. Here is the recipe. Enjoy!*

2 cups butter
24 ounces of chocolate chips
4 cups flour
2 cups brown sugar
2 tsp. soda
1 tsp. salt
2 cups sugar
1 8 ounce Hershey Bar (grated)
5 cups blended oatmeal
4 eggs
2 tsp. baking powder
2 tsp. vanilla
3 cups chopped nuts (your choice)

Measure oatmeal, and blend in a blender to a fine powder. Cream the butter and both sugars. Add eggs and vanilla, mix together with flour, oatmeal, salt, baking powder, and soda. Add chocolate chips, Hershey Bar, and nuts. Roll into balls, and place two inches apart on a cookie sheet.

Bake for 10 minutes at 375 degrees.
Makes 112 cookies.

3: A World-Class Smoothie

The following recipe, my own invention, is taken from my earlier book, *Rossmoor: Eden in California*. I felt compelled to include it here because it may well be the most joy-giving of all recipes! Here it is:

Happiness can be put into a bottle! Do it by making the best "smoothie" in the world. Here's the secret: into your blender, place a few strawberries, half a banana, one container of strawberry yogurt, half cup of milk, half cup or so of ice chips, and a scoop of vanilla ice cream. Pulse your blender until all is liquefied. Pour your newly made smoothie into a tumbler, pick up a good book, go out onto your deck or balcony or patio, and sit in the sun. Slowly sip the smoothie and ascend for a while into nirvana!

****

Ignazio John "Nace" Ruvolo

Nace Ruvolo, a native of New Jersey, is a graduate of Rutgers, and holds a law degree from the University of San Diego School of Law, graduating as class valedictorian. One of the Bay Area's most eminent attorneys, Nace left his partnership in a successful law firm in 1994 for appointment to a judgeship on the Contra Costa Superior Court. Two years later, in 1996, he was appointed to be an Associate Justice of the California First District Court of Appeal, Division Two. This was followed, in 2006, by an appointment as Presiding Justice of Division Four.

The Early Years

My grandparents, on both sides, emigrated from Italy to the United States in the early 1900's. Arriving with little formal education, they lived the typical immigrant life. Working hard, they found their way into the American culture, raising large families, always certain that they had made the wise choice by coming to our shores. My paternal grandparents arrived in the U.S. shortly before my father was born, settling in Elizabeth, New Jersey. My paternal grandfather worked for the Elizabeth Public Works Department his entire life, while my grandmother raised their six children. My maternal grandparents settled in Scranton, Pennsylvania, where my maternal grandfather found employment as a coal-mine inspector, while my grandmother raised their six children.

My father, Vincent, was born in 1918, in Elizabeth. My mother, Lucy, was born in 1919, in Scranton. Upon graduation from high school, my father went to work on the loading dock of an umbrella factory (Hollander & Son) in Elizabeth. He met my mother while working there through a blind date arranged by her sister, Yolanda, who also worked at the factory. My parents were married in November 1951, in Scranton, where my mother had been living. Dad was 24, Mom was 23. They returned to Elizabeth to live.

I was the third of four children in our family. My oldest sister, Paula, was born in 1942, before my father was drafted into the army, in 1943. He fought in the Pacific Theater, mostly in the Philippine Islands, earning a Bronze Star for bravery. A second sister, Angela, was born in 1944, having been conceived while Dad was home on leave. When the war ended, my father returned to Elizabeth, where I was born in 1947; my brother Peter was born in 1949.

On Dad's return from the war, the same umbrella factory reemployed him. As it turned out, he would spend his entire working life there, rising from the loading dock to General Foreman. When we kids were small, my mother did piece work at home for the umbrella factory, sewing tips onto the umbrella frames. After the four children grew older, my mother took a full-time job at the A&P Supermarket, starting as a checker and moving up to be the store's bookkeeper.

We moved to nearby Rahway, New Jersey (within commuting distance of Elizabeth) when I was very young. I went to high school in Rahway, graduating in 1965. As I look back on it, I see that I was a cut-up and an extravert – belonging to as many social and academic clubs as would have me. In my senior year I became President of the Student Council. One of my greatest regrets is that I didn't excel academically during those early years, simply because I didn't apply myself to the task. I did, however, do well enough to get into Rutgers, majoring in history, and graduating in

1969. I did reasonably well at Rutgers, but did not catch fire academically until I went to law school.

During my college years, I gradually came to the conclusion that I didn't want to spend my life in the cold weather Northeast. Though I had never been in the western part of the country, the lure of California was strong, so I applied to the University of San Diego Law School - which was as far away from New Jersey as I could get, and which was then the only ABA accredited law school south of Los Angeles.

Two weeks after graduation from Rutgers, after getting notice of acceptance from San Diego, I loaded my VW bug with everything I owned, and drove westward – first to Berkeley. I didn't know a soul on the West Coast, and went to Berkeley because my Rutgers fraternity had a chapter at Cal, and that chapter house had agreed to let me stay there during the summer prior to law school. Within three days of arriving, I had a California driver's license and had landed a job working the night shift at the old Del Monte cannery in Oakland. In short order I realized how much I enjoyed life in Northern California – so much so that I concluded that I would one day return to live in the San Francisco Bay area.

Law School

But, having committed myself to USD, I went to San Diego to begin law school, and loved it there, too! I loved everything about law school – and for the first time became fully engaged intellectually in my studies. I did well academically, became editor-in-chief of the Law Review, and graduated from Law School in 1972 as class salutatorian, becoming de-facto valedictorian (and presenting the valedictory address) when the woman who graduated first in our class declined the honor.

As I neared graduation, the preceding editor of the Law Review called to urge me not to join a law firm upon graduation, suggesting instead that I spend my immediate post-school years working in Washington for the U.S. Department of Justice (DOJ). The experience gained there, he said, would serve me well in whatever area of the law I might ultimately get into.

Department of Justice

I applied for a job with the Torts Section, Civil Division of the DOJ, and was hired into their Honors Program. So, in September 1972, I loaded up my VW once again, and drove, eastward this time, to Washington, D.C. On my first working day there, I went to the DOJ legal library to find everyone crowding around a TV watching the Watergate Hearings; someone had brought a TV set into the library conference room for that purpose.

I was with the DOJ for almost five years, working progressively under six separate Attorneys General (plus two acting). Yes, the 1970's were a tumultuous time in Washington. Because cases were tried all over the country, I found myself on the road for about 90 days each year. I was tasked with defending the government against tort cases, most involving alleged negligence on the part of the government that caused injury or death to members of the public. During those four-plus years I tried twelve cases to verdict, and won all of them.

A good example of the cases I handled was one that charged that the government was responsible for injuries sustained by a person who had slipped and fallen down the steps of a U.S. Post Office in Albany, Georgia. The victim, wife of the local Baptist mister, pretended to limp, but had been seen (and videotaped) walking normally. My job was to convince the federal judge in Macon, Georgia, who would likely be sympathetic to the local minister's wife, that her suit was baseless. In the end I was able to do that, and won for the government.

Another case resulted from the fatal stabbing of a young prisoner by a fellow inmate in the El Reno Federal Reformatory in Oklahoma. There had been a riot at the prison, and a lockdown had been imposed. Concluding that the riot had been quelled, the lockdown was ended by prison officials, and the prison population returned to normal activities. The family alleged negligence by the government, asserting that the prison riot conditions still prevailed at the time of the stabbing, and that the lockdown had ended prematurely. In that case, too, I was able to gather evidence sufficient to convince the court that the suit was without merit, and was thereby able to win the case for the government.

As time went by, I was assigned to cases with ever-greater responsibilities, with increasing financial risk to the federal government, and with wider legal implications. For example, I dealt with several that arose from mine disasters in which many mine-workers were killed, where the government was sued for failure to set and/or monitor compliance with safety regulations.

In any event, it was never my intention to stay at the DOJ for my entire career, and I longed to return to the West Coast. I took the position originally as an investment in my professional future, knowing from my editor-friend's experience that I would be given responsibility early in my career to manage complex and high-stakes civil litigation, while also gaining early trial experience. This was experience I would not have gained had I joined a private law firm right out of law school.

Bronson, Bronson and McKinnon

I had taken the California bar exam before going to Washington, so after almost five years based on the East Coast I decided to return to California to enter the private practice of law. I applied to a number of the civil litigation law firms in the San Francisco area, finally joining Bronson, Bronson and McKinnon in 1977. In 1974, I had met and married Ellen Green, a woman from Pennsylvania, who was working as a social worker for Montgomery County, Maryland, a suburban area adjacent to Washington. By 1977, Michael, our son, had been born, and my wife was pregnant with our daughter, Sarah. I drove the family station wagon to California, while Ellen flew with young Michael, and Sarah in-utero, to San Francisco. We lived a short time in Concord, and then seven years in the Montclair District of Oakland, before settling in Orinda.

My early case management and trial experience at the DOJ paid off, as I was given more clients and case responsibilities than many other young lawyers in my firm. Rather than sitting "second chair," or being a "bag carrier" for senior partners in trial, I found myself litigating and trying cases throughout the state and federal courts in Northern California myself.

As it grew, my practice focused on commercial, construction, and franchise litigation, professional liability and general torts. My clients included a very large trucking firm, industrial, commercial, and residential construction companies and subcontractors, architectural and engineering firms, law and accounting firms, and franchisees engaged in disputes with their national franchisors. I both brought suits for plaintiffs and defended civil actions in other cases.

In one case, I represented the developer/owner of the Monterey Plaza Hotel against a very large mechanics lien claim relating to the construction of the hotel. In another, I obtained a defense verdict after twelve days of hearings defending a claim brought by investors against the promoter of a research and development tax shelter. In still another case, I represented a contractor in Marin County against claims by more than thirty homeowners contending their properties were flooded because of improper levee work by my client. After a six-week trial, the case against the contractor was dismissed. In all, I tried almost a dozen cases while at Bronson, and won all but one of them. (Another ended in a hung jury, my last trial before becoming a judge.)

Moving to the Bench

Our firm was large, about 150 attorneys, and after some seventeen years there I became one of its senior partners. As I rose higher in the law firm, I had to devote more time to firm and client management, and less to the actual practice of law. To return more fully into the actual practice of law, and to find ways to "give back" - to serve the community - I was increasingly attracted to the idea of leaving the firm for service as a judge. My work at the law firm had begun to seem routine, and I longed for a new challenge that would take me back into the courtroom where I could use my legal acumen and courtroom know-how to its full extent once again. Though remuneration as a judge would be far less (about one-half) than I was earning from my law partnership, I found myself yearning for a return to the theater of the courtroom, and the intellectual challenge it presented. A judgeship seemed to offer those prospects.

In January 1994, I sought and received an appointment from California's Governor Pete Wilson to the Contra Costa County Superior Court. But nomination was only half the battle. The term for the seat to which I was appointed was set to expire in June

1994, and I would have to win the election for that office in order to keep my job, if I were challenged. Indeed, I did draw a challenger--a prominent divorce lawyer and member of the county's Republican Party Central Committee, who himself had wanted the appointment I had received. The election was to be held in June, so from February to June, I spent every available moment off the bench meeting voters. I sought endorsements from civic organizations and influential personages, such as law enforcement, local mayors and council members, county supervisors, and members of the California State Legislature, among many others. In the end, I prevailed, and won the election by more than fourteen points.

Two years later, in 1996, I was appointed by Governor Wilson to be an Associate Justice of the California First District Court of Appeal, Division Two. In 2006, I was appointed Presiding Justice of Division Four by Governor Schwarzenegger; I still hold that position at this writing, in 2014.

Life in non-partisan public service demands that one submit fully to transparent evaluations by others concerning fitness for office. In all I have won three elections: one superior court contested election in 1994, and two appellate retention elections in 1998 and 2006 (I will be on the ballot for retention again in November 2014). In addition, I have been evaluated three times for judicial office by the State Bar Judicial Nominations Evaluation Committee, twice by the Commission on Judicial Appointments, and several times by a number of bar associations. Along the way, I have been honored by receiving awards for Appellate Justice of the Year by the San Francisco Trial Lawyers Association, Trial Judge of the Year by the Alameda Contra Costa Trial Lawyers Association, and Judge of the Year by the Italian American Bar Association of Northern California.

Our court, which sits in San Francisco across the street from City Hall, hears appeals from twelve county superior courts in Northern California, including appeals from San Francisco, San Mateo, Alameda, Contra Costa, Marin, Solano, Sonoma, Napa, Lake, Mendocino, Humboldt, and Del Norte counties. We are composed of twenty justices sitting in five separate divisions of four justices each. We hear all types of cases from criminal to civil disputes. Because the California Supreme Court accepts for review only about 100 cases annually from all six appellate districts around the state, we are the court of last resort for virtually all litigants in our appellate jurisdiction.

University of Virginia LLM Program

Early in this millennium I was encouraged to apply for a special graduate law program offered by the University of Virginia School of Law to appellate judges around the country. I was accepted into the program and attended law school full time during the summer months of 2002 and 2003 with about 30 other appellate judges and justices. The classes, which covered such subjects as advanced constitutional and international law, law and economics, and legal philosophy, were taught by some of the most prominent law professors in the nation. They were absolutely stimulating. We took exams just like all law students, and we each had to research and write a master's thesis in order to earn our Master of Law (L.L.M.) degrees. I was thrilled to attend and participate in the graduation ceremony by walking "The Lawn" in Charlottesville with hundreds of other university graduates, and thus in becoming a member of the Class of 2004.

Marriage and Children

My wife, Ellen, and I divorced in 2001 (Ellen hired the lawyer who had challenged me unsuccessfully for my judgeship in June 1994, but that is another story altogether). Although we had been married for 27 years, it was not a good marriage, but as is so often the case, we stayed together for the sake of our children. Upon our divorce, I moved from our house in Orinda, buying a house for myself in Walnut Creek. I lived in that house until 2011, when I moved to Rossmoor. About a year ago I met and fell deeply in love with Barbara Whittingham. Barbara is a fellow Rossmoorian, a gifted soprano, who also had a successful career as a licensed Marriage and Family Therapist, and has worked for the Santa Clara County Mental Health and Public Health Departments. We are now engaged, and plan to marry in September 2014. Barbara also has two children, both living nearby.

My son, Michael, holds a PhD from Stanford in cell biology; his partner, Rachel, has a degree in biology. They have two children. Both work in the genetic sciences. My daughter, Sarah, and her husband Kyle, live in Concord. Sarah also earned a degree (from Cal Poly) in biology, and she teaches science in a local middle school. Her husband runs the drama program in a nearby high school. They also have two children. Given the fact that both of my children became scientists, I am desperately hoping that at least one of my grandchildren becomes a lawyer. I've got my eye on Michael's four-year-old, Lauren, who is particularly fearless and feisty.

Philosophy of Life

I am an atheist. I have never in my adult life believed in a God or in an afterlife. I share the common wonder at the universe, and the reality that our world exists. I have no explanation for how it all came about, but have no belief in a grand designer or a deity or supernatural force that brought it all into existence. That does not diminish in any way my awe at the breathtaking splendor of nature and the world, nor in my belief that it is our moral duty to accord dignity to all forms all life, including our fellow humans.

Compatible with both my lack of spiritual beliefs and my judicial philosophy, I am also a secularist. To me secularism is the principle supporting the separation of government from religious institutions and religious dogma. One manifestation of secularism is protecting citizens' rights to be free from any imposition by government of religious rules or teachings. Another manifestation of secularism is the view that public activities and decisions, especially political ones, should remain uninfluenced by religious beliefs and/or practices. Thus, it will be unsurprising to learn that one of the people I most admire who has lived in modern history **is** Thomas Jefferson.

Despite my lack of spirituality, I have a very strong moral core. I believe in the need for complete and total honesty in all things, and I strive to live my life that way. I am sure that I inherited this value from my Dad, who was the most honorable person I have ever known. I have sought to teach my children to abide by that same code of ethics.

Because morality is so central to my life, I have devoted my extracurricular professional life to promoting legal and judicial ethics, however and whenever I can. Within two years of starting private practice in San Francisco, I joined the Bar Association of San Francisco Legal Ethics Committee, and later I was appointed to the California State Bar Committee on Professional Conduct and Practice. Ultimately, I served as chair of both committees. In 1990, I founded and became the President of the Contra Costa Bar Association Section on Professional Responsibility and Practice. I am also a former member of both the American Bar association Litigation Section Committee on Professional Responsibility, and the Association of Professional Responsibility Lawyers.

My strong interest in ethics continued after I became a judge. After a year as a superior court judge, I became a member of the California Judges Association Judicial Ethics Committee, serving as its chair in 2000. In 2013 I received what I consider to be the ultimate honor in ethics, when I was unanimously appointed by the Supreme Court to serve a four-year term as the only appellate justice commissioner on the eleven-member California Commission on Judicial Performance. This body is empowered by our State's constitution to investigate complaints of misconduct brought against any judges in California, and to impose discipline as necessary to protect the public.

The code that guides my life does not translate necessarily into my being a tough judge. In varying degrees, I accept the three goals of punishment: retribution, deterrence, and rehabilitation. In the case of rehabilitation, my experience has led me to conclude that, although it is possible and may even include redemption, rehabilitation, or the permanent altering of one's moral being for the better, will not be achieved without society's investment of major resources to make it happen. And, even then, it will take decades of dedicated implementation of the programs sponsored by those resources.

People ask me "Why can't we do this? Look at what has happened with technological growth." There is no doubt that, particularly in the last fifty years or so, growth in technology has been phenomenal. Computers, satellite navigation, medical and biological breakthroughs, and the like have changed our world, usually for the better. But there has not been a corresponding improvement in the social sciences. While we can diagnose psychological and pathological conditions that lead people to commit immoral acts, social science has done little to structure, let alone implement, treatment protocols to correct these conditions.

Part of the reason for the wide gap between the explosive growth of technology and the lack of growth in the social sciences is that investment in social science has not kept pace with investment in technology. Resources for technology have been readily available because there is always the tangible promise of profit. Therefore, technology can be supported with private investment. On the other hand, funds that might improve the human condition come primarily from public sources, and can therefore be too easily delayed and denied. As a consequence, education and health and infrastructure are underfunded, understaffed, underprovided, and under-researched.

National political trends do not bode well for improving public services needed to correct our society's view of abnormal and dangerous behaviors, at least not in my remaining lifetime. There is little profit incentive for the private sector to step in, and the cross-current demands on our legislators seeking to direct how public funds are used will not yield that improvement. The courts will therefore remain the public's primary refuge from "man's inhumanity to man."

The prospects for human improvement, as least as we see it, are even bleaker globally. Our world hosts diverse cultures, religions, languages and historic experiences. This diversity necessarily results in the development of sometimes vastly different mores and values from our own. Who is to say that one culture's virtues are not another's vices? Given this diversity, can we really expect to impose a system of values uniformly throughout the world? Even if that can, and should, be done, where would mankind find the resources and united will to take up such a challenge? The answers to these questions are self-evident, and lead inexorably to the conclusion that global conformity to a unitary view of morality is not achievable.

Philosophy of Law

Laws, whether in this country or anywhere else on the planet, comprise little more than the compact to which we tacitly or by implication agree, for the privilege of being part of a larger integrated society. They should reflect the values of at least a majority of each society's members. While we pay a price for the security and other benefits of living together in conformity with these laws, they also protect us from the immoral conduct of scofflaws. The easiest examples are the criminal laws, in almost all cases enacted with the purpose of public protection. By not enforcing these statutes, which are mostly a form of moral code, we risk allowing a few to harm others, or even a greater number whose own conduct otherwise conforms to the law. It also prevents revenge from becoming the right of the wronged, which leads to chaos and escalating lawlessness.

This is not to say that conformity to law necessarily means a loss of freedom; quite the contrary. Laws that protect privacy, speech, association, religion, and the right of private agreements ensure that each member of society can exercise these rights without interference from the larger community. It is only when the views of individuals diverge from those of the majority that conflict arises and constraints appear intolerable. The constraint seems inexcusable when the purpose of the law does not appear to prevent real harm or injury to society, but simply provides a means to impose a majoritarian moral principle that limits or dictates the conduct of individuals, thus impairing liberty. Examples may include laws restricting sexual freedom among adults, archaic "blue laws" limiting commercial activity on certain days of the week that are decreed to be days of leisure or for religious observations only, or curtailing electronic non-defamatory speech that is outside the mainstream of thought. To some, the list seems endless.

For all the good that is attainable through the rule of law, it is an imperfect code of social conduct, and is subject to distortion if manipulated. Perhaps most pernicious is when the rule of law becomes the province of segments of society that use their power to further the goals of that group to the detriment of the larger society. One way that minorities gain this power over the majority is through control of the law-making apparatus. The most obvious tool is the exchange of money for control. Jesse M. Unruh is known to have coined the phrase "Money is the mother's milk of politics," and it is as true today, or even more so, than it was when first uttered in 1962. Political contributions, now cloaked with invisibility by the U.S. Supreme Court's edict in *Citizens United v*

FEC, allow the perversion of the rule of law at the expense of the majority. Examples include the seemingly endless trade and tax laws that favor one industry, group, or cabal of individuals; employment laws that skew the balance of power between employer and employees; and laws limiting personal freedoms to accommodate the vagaries of the influential. Once again, the list seems endless.

Here the courts are powerless. After all, it is not the mission of our judicial system to decide *what* is right, but *who* is right, and this exercise almost always begins and ends with the application of the law as it is written. Expecting more from our judges would simply transfer the power to impose the rule of law to that small group, which to many is as repugnant as allowing any other minority group to do so.

Final Thought

In conclusion, if I were to give advice to a High School graduating class, I would say you are about to embark on what may be a beautiful journey through life, and the choice of pathway is entirely in your hands. But take care to choose wisely--for every door of opportunity that you open, one closes. Steady your gait on your chosen life path by working hard, playing hard, and seek to experience love as deeply as you can. Along the way, remember to treat all living things as you wish to be treated. Life's fulfillment can best be achieved without causing pain or harm.

****

Eric Ewald Anschutz

Raised in Detroit, Michigan, Eric worked for some years in the aerospace business, and went on to work for the US Department of State on arms control, including SALT (Strategic Arms Limitation Treaty), the Nuclear Test Ban and Nuclear Non-Proliferation. He served for four years during the 1970's as a resident US diplomatic representative to the International Atomic Energy Agency, living with his family in Vienna, Austria.

The Beginning

My parents were German immigrants. Both arrived here, separately, in 1924. My father, Erich Karl Anschutz, was 19 at the time he left Germany. Having read glowing accounts of that fantasyland called "Amerika," he came here alone, seeking adventure, and hoping to find some of the gold that was said to litter American streets! My mother, Martha Anna Lehmann, a 16 year old girl at the time, arrived together with her parents.

After some months in Detroit, Dad enrolled in evening classes offered at a local high school to improve his still limited English language skills. He soon took notice of what he always said was the smartest person in the class, a shy and pretty 17-year old girl, also a recent émigré from Germany. Named Martha Anna Lehmann, the girl had come from Weisenfels, a charming small town on the picturesque Salle River, some 40 miles from Leipzig – the city in which my Dad had been born and raised. Both my father and the Lehmann family were lured to Detroit by news of the good jobs and high pay offered by the automobile factories.

My mother recalled that there were some 30 students in the ESL class, including émigrés from various countries; she remembered Italians and Poles, as well as other Germans. Each classroom session was for two hours. During one of the sessions, Martha was sitting in the front of the room with her parents, who were taking the same class, when the teacher, remembered by my mother as Fraulein Williams, asked for a volunteer to read and discuss a passage in English. Martha raised her hand, and correctly performed the reading, thereby eliciting smart-alecky snickers from Erich, seated in the back of the classroom with his friend, Hans Muller, another German.

Despite that rocky start, as the class ended, Erich joined the Lehmanns on the walk to their home, not far from the school. The group stopped at a German bakery, at which my mother was employed as a part-time clerk, bought some goodies, and the senior Lehmanns invited Erich to their home for coffee and cake. As the evening progressed, Erich asked the elders for permission to take their daughter Martha for a ride in his Chevy Coupe to Belle Isle (a then-beautiful local park) on the following Sunday. Permission was granted, the ride took place, and on the following Saturday, the two went to a movie together. Following a two-year courtship my parents were married in December 1927, when the couple were ages 19 and 23, respectively.

Some months after their marriage, Erich, by then earning good wages as a foreman at the Budd Wheel Company, suggested to his young bride that they take a trip to Leipzig so that Martha could meet Lydia and Oskar, her new in-laws, as well as others in the Anschutz family. So, in October 1928, they took off for what was intended to be a one-month trip. Soon after their arrival in Leipzig, however, the young couple realized that Martha was newly pregnant. Local physicians advised her that the return-voyage, scheduled for November when the crossing might be a stormy one, could cause a miscarriage. So it was decided that Martha would remain in Leipzig, staying with the Anschutz parents until the birth, expected the following June – now some seven-eight months hence. Erich, on a five-week leave from his Budd Wheel job, felt obliged to return to America in November, as scheduled. It wasn't until some six weeks after the birth that my mother finally returned to America to rejoin my father. The new baby, born in June 1929, turned out to be me!

My parents soon brought into the world a second child, my sister Dolores Gertrude, born in April 1931. Dolores (the name was taken from Dolores DelRio, a movie star of the time with whom my mother was smitten!) was never known by that name in our house. She was "Loli" then, and remained known to all of us by that name until her demise in 2012. The name "Loli" came from my attempt, at the age of 22 months, to greet my new sister as "girly." I think that the name Loli suited my sister better than any other name would have done!

Throughout the 1930's and early 40's, my sister Loli and I spent the entire summer at the family cottage on Lake Huron, mostly in the care of my grandmother. It was an idyllic childhood, as I look back on it. The Nichols family, close friends of my parents, had built a cottage adjacent to ours, and their three children provided my sister and me with built-in playmates.

My mother, who died in 1999 at the age of 91, was a very special woman. Without doubt, the most intelligent person in our family, she was modest to a fault, wholly unaware of the quality of her mind and the appeal of her gentle charm. Formal education had ended for her, as it had for my father, after eight years of schooling. Yet this woman could quote endlessly from Schiller and Goethe, her two favorite German poets, solve complex mathematical problems in her head, and could win at Scrabble (in English, not her native language) against any of her three offspring, each of whom holds advanced degrees!

Unlike my father, and both of my Lehmann grandparents, who as time went by felt themselves as "American" as anyone else, my mother never fully relinquished her German heritage. In her late eighties, after more than seventy years in America, she said to me "Deutschland war doch meine heimat." "Germany was after all my home." Though she left Germany at age 16, a younger age than any of the others, Mom may have been the one, more than my other elders, who had already developed a sense of personal direction and future happiness in Germany, and therefore left it with reluctance. My father and my Lehmann grandparents, particularly my grandmother, left Germany with enthusiasm, and embraced America as the place where they could achieve their true fullness. They were never disappointed in America. My mother, only 16 when the Lehmanns left Weisenfels, had been valedictorian of her class, had won medals in swimming competition, was popular with her peer group, was being trained to become a manager in the store to which she had been apprenticed, and had already experienced the love of a boy, Heinz Eidner, a budding poet, about whom she spoke to me more than once. For her, departure from Weisenfels was traumatic. Though her life in America turned out to be a good one, a part of her heart remained always in Weisenfels.

My father was a man of gentle nature. He was never "driven" or relentless. He never envied the success of others. While always content, and always quietly self-confident, he always "knew," and so did we, that better times were just around the corner! And he was always on the lookout for ways to turn that corner. My father was diffident in conversation with others. While my grandfather and our male friends discussed loudly and passionately matters of the day, my father took most of it in with a smile, rarely entering into the competition of ideas that characterized social events at our house. Part of the reason for that detachment may be that he abhorred confrontation, possibly because he saw multiple sides of every issue. He seemed to recognize the essential arrogance implied in taking strong positions on matters about which most of us lacked meaningful information.

In 1939, my brother Bob was born. Though ten years younger than me, we two have in our adult years always been close. With his MA in English Literature, he is an accomplished writer and editor. Though he has always lived in Michigan, while my life has been spent in a number of far-off places, we, and our respective families, have seen a good deal of one another. With the advent of email, we are in constant dialog about world events. Bob has been a source of ideas for this book, and has served as editor of much of my writing over the years.

In mid-1942, my father left Budd Wheel to start a small business making parts for the ongoing WW II military buildup. Together with a partner, he founded Quality Tool and Manufacturing Company, which began operations in a rented garage (formerly used for car repair). From that modest beginning, Quality Tool grew rapidly, soon moving into a much larger (still rented) building. By war's end, in mid-1945, Quality Tool was humming day and night, with a work force of more than 100 employees.

In 1946 I entered MIT, majoring in Engineering Management. Soon after graduation, I married a girl that I had met in my senior year. Nancy Hoff was a Phi Beta Kappa student at Wheaton College, in Norton, Massachusetts, graduating at the same time as I did from MIT. Though we remained married for over a decade, and produced a great son, Christopher, the marriage was not meant to be.

In 1951, during the early days of the Korean War, I was drafted into the Army, and because of my science degree was placed into the Scientific and Professional Personnel Program, and assigned to teach elementary physics at the newly formed Army Guided Missile School in Fort Bliss, Texas. Following my discharge from the army, in 1953, I went to work for Sperry Gyroscope Company, and rose through the ranks as a project engineer. After some years, I went to RCA Aerospace Systems and worked on the guidance system for the Apollo program's Lunar Lander.

A New Life

In 1966, two major developments changed my life – and enriched it in ways both personal and professional. Nancy and I were divorced, and I resigned from RCA Aerospace, joining the US Arms Control and Disarmament Agency, an arm of the US Department of State. To begin my work with ACDA, I moved from Lexington, Massachusetts to an apartment in Bethesda, Maryland, a suburb of Washington, D.C. Not long after my arrival in Bethesda, I went for a

Sunday afternoon swim in the apartment house rooftop swimming pool, finding a poolside spot next to a strikingly beautiful woman who had just completed a lengthy swim. Her captivating accent, Norwegian it turned out, her kindly and gentle demeanor and our rambling conversation about such arcane topics as labor unions and foreign affairs (believe it or not!) led to an agreement to meet that evening for dinner and a movie. We have not been apart since! Forty-eight years at this writing.

Sidsel Kari (nee Hesstvedt) was at the time an executive and women's fashion clothing buyer at Woodward and Lothrop, Washington's leading department store chain. We married in March 1967, and soon spawned two wonderful children, Kari Mimi and Eric Sindre. An added bonus is that Sidsel has from the start been a loving friend and step-mother to my son Christopher. All three of our kids have gone on to build productive lives and good families of their own, and between them have produced our seven grandchildren.

Arms Control and Disarmament Agency

During my 16 years in the aerospace world, I rose through the ranks to managerial positions. I was, however, troubled during those years by what seemed to me to be America's growing obsession with armament, and with what seemed to me as excessive spending on military programs. I gradually found my way out of military programs – spending my last several aerospace years on NASA projects.

When JFK was elected to the presidency in 1962, then-Senator Hubert Humphrey urged creation of a new agency of government, dedicated to internationally negotiated reduction of armament levels. President Kennedy agreed, and so was born the Arms Control and Disarmament Agency. Against what seemed to me impossible odds, I was offered, after a series of extensive interviews, a position on the ACDA staff in 1966. The staff was small, about 50 professionals, and 50 support staff. My time with ACDA, from 1966 to 1980, was one of the high points of my professional and personal life. I worked on SALT (Strategic Arms Limitation Treaty), Nuclear Non-Proliferation, and the Nuclear Test Ban. From our studies, my ACDA colleagues and I developed arms control proposals that served as the basis for national arms control policy. I was fortunate several times to be appointed as advisor to the SALT Negotiating Team, variously in Helsinki and Geneva. I also served three times in Geneva, Switzerland as a member of the SALT Standing Consultative Commission.

National War College

In April 1975, I was asked whether I would accept an appointment for a one-year stint at the National War College. Would I ever! The National War College is located at Fort McNair, on the Potomac River, just a few miles from the White House. The year I spent there, as a student (June 1975-June 1976), was another of the high points of my professional life. Most of my (100 or so) classmates were senior military officers, about to be given major commands. Colin Powell, destined to become Chairman of the Joint Chiefs of Staff and Secretary of State, was one of my classmates. For me, the War College was a way-station to my assignment to Vienna, about which more later.

The name "War College" is a misnomer. The War College curriculum is not war, but rather an intense year-long study of geopolitics and international affairs. As an option, War College students are invited to take extra courses in the evening and on weekends at George Washington University, also in Washington, and to receive at the conclusion of the year a Master's degree in International Affairs from GWU. I accepted that invitation, and did get the degree.

At the War College, every single day, no exceptions, from 8-10 AM, the entire student body assembled in our large auditorium, there to hear a presentation from some prominent personage. One day it might be a senator, the next day it might be the Italian Ambassador, and on the third day it might be the Secretary of Agriculture. There was always time left for questions, and there were always many of them. By the end of the school year, we had seen and talked with many of Washington's senior people, including most of the cabinet officers, much of the congressional leadership, and many of the foreign ambassadors.

During my year there, I wrote a lengthy term paper: *Henry Kissinger: Comparison of His Writings as an Academician with his Policies as a Government Official.* The Kissinger paper was ultimately selected as the outstanding paper of the year, and I was invited to present it to the annual meeting of the NWC Alumni Association. That same paper, expanded, served as the basis for my Master's degree thesis at George Washington University

Vienna

I was honored to emerge (in June, 1976) from the one-year National War College program as a "Distinguished Graduate," an award conferred upon each member of the top 10% of the graduating class. Upon returning from the War College to the Arms Control Agency, with my good "report card," I was asked whether I would agree to a move to Vienna, Austria to work with the US Mission to the International Atomic Energy Agency (IAEA). I was both honored and elated upon receiving the offer, and accepted, after discussion with Sidsel. I was sworn in as a Foreign Service Officer (Reserve). We departed Bethesda, Maryland in October 1976, for what turned out to be a four-year Diplomatic Posting to the IAEA in Vienna.

The day after our arrival in Vienna, we went to the local VW dealer, ordered a new Passat station wagon in "Burnt Sienna," which turned out to be a kind of dark pumpkin orange that for some reason we loved, and immediately began our search for housing. Within a few days, we found the best place in town – a newly constructed Bauhaus Style complex of some six small apartment house buildings, with a number of town houses mixed in among them, all built around a swimming pool with sauna, at the edge of the fabled Vienna Woods! Our unit was on the first of three levels, overlooking the pool on one side and the woods on the other, with large balconies on both sides.

Our children, Kari and Eric, were enrolled in the American International School, third grade and kindergarten, respectively. The school was academically good – our kids thrived there. Importantly, too, it functioned as a kind of social center for the American community in Vienna. Parents could meet one another at the almost weekly school-functions, and take part in the frequent school-centered events such as soccer games, picnics, flea market, musicales, scouting for the kids and other such.

The IAEA

The Vienna-based International Atomic Energy Agency is an arm of the United Nations. Its mission is to ensure international compliance with the Nuclear Non-Proliferation Treaty (NPT). To accomplish that important assignment, the IAEA had a field staff (during my time there) of about one hundred inspectors who made periodic visits, both announced and (in limited quotas) unannounced, to the non-military nuclear programs of member states. Inspections were structured to detect any diversion from peaceful programs to military purposes. In support of its inspectorate, IAEA headquarters in Vienna maintained a staff of scientists and technicians responsible for devising inspection techniques and equipment.

Some three months after our arrival in Vienna, President Carter (who came into office in January, 1977) entered into the IAEA picture. Carter was himself an engineer with a considerable background in nuclear technology, gained during his early years in the Navy as a member of Admiral Rickover's nuclear engine design staff. He was also a dedicated believer in the principle of nuclear non-proliferation, and attached great importance to the IAEA in that context. At President Carter's behest, and in his name, the United States undertook an initiative known by the windy name of "International Nuclear Fuel Cycle Evaluation" (INFCE). In early 1978, I was recalled from Vienna to Washington for some ten days to help set up the opening conference and to participate in it. 62 nations sent representatives to the conference, which was held in Washington and opened by President Carter himself. Our purpose in INFCE was to design a proliferation-proof nuclear fuel cycle – that is to design a way to generate nuclear power by means that would make diversion to military use impossible, or at least difficult.

It was decided at the Washington conference that INFCE would be carried out in Vienna, under the auspices of the IAEA, and that each nation would send experts to help in the task. I was designated as the US resident administrator. Eight INFCE working groups were established, and an INFCE Board of Governors was created. Each of the working groups met in Vienna four times annually (on average), for a week or two each time, setting their own timetable and their own agenda, subject only to coordination by and comment from their Board of Governors. As the Vienna-based US INFCE coordinator, and as host to the unending stream of US experts, mine soon became the best job in town.

Department of Energy

My family and I returned from Vienna to Washington in August 1980 where I had accepted a new job at the Department of Energy, as Director of External Nuclear Affairs. Importantly, upon taking that position, I became a member of the newly formed Senior Executive Service (SES). The job was intended to be "liaison with electric utilities and state governments on the political and technical problems attendant to disposal of spent nuclear fuel." I was also to be responsible to work with DOE's national laboratories and with the utility industry in their ongoing research on disposal of radioactive spent nuclear fuel. But, as it turned out, President Reagan won election in November 1980, some two months after I came home from Vienna – having promised during his campaign to abolish the Department of Energy. Though that promise was not fulfilled, I was tagged as a Carter appointee, and it was time for me to move elsewhere.

Naval Aviation

My SES status saved the day. Members of the Senior Executive Service were, by definition, labeled management generalists, able at least in theory to move from management of one department to management of another. I happen to think this is a dumb idea, but it provided for me a way out of the DOE dilemma. From the government's central personnel office, I learned that the Washington-based Naval Air Systems Command (Navair) was looking for a Technical Director of Naval Aviation Field Activities. After a round of interviews, I was offered that position, and accepted immediately (anything to get out of DOE!).

As Technical Director, I became civilian deputy to a Rear Admiral responsible for government operated Naval air engineering and test centers, of which there were nine, located all over the country, employing some 20,000 people, mostly civil service, but including some 2,000 uniformed navy people. The largest of these Navair centers were flight test facilities (for aircraft and missiles), located at Point Magu and China Lake, California, and Patuxent River, Maryland. Other naval aviation engineering and test centers were located in such exotic locations as Hawaii, the Bahamas, and Puerto Rico. Most impressively, there were also several in New Jersey!

Some six months after I took the job, the Admiral to whom I reported retired, and it was decided not to replace him. That is how I, an ex-corporal, became *de facto* head of Navair's nine engineering and test centers, though my title remained Technical Director.

In 1986, some five years after I took the Navair job, we began to hear about the management "guru," W. Edwards Deming, and the effectiveness of his methods of management, which had come to be known as "Total Quality Management," TQM. Japanese automobile and electronics companies, who in the mid-80's were winning increasing market share from their American competitors, credited their success to the Deming methods. American companies, notably Ford, began to practice TQM with apparent success. I joined with other government executives in seeking to learn more about the methods, and in adapting them to our purposes.

I began to realize that my new-found expertise in a "hot" new management method could provide a springboard into a new career following my retirement from Navair, now only a few years away. As Navair's TQM "czar," I traveled widely giving lectures about TQM to win converts. I also organized command-wide TQM training programs, prepared a curriculum and training documentation, and joined with TQM leaders from other parts of the government to develop Best Practices.

Eric Anschutz Associates

Some months prior to my June 1989 retirement from Navair, I went to Washington-based George Washington University (from whom, in 1976, I had been granted a Master's Degree in Foreign Affairs) to seek a TQM teaching position in the University's Center for Continuing Engineering Education. GWU, it turned out, was well aware of TQM's increasing popularity; indeed, the university itself had sponsored several TQM seminars at which Deming himself had been the featured speaker, and had been happily surprised at the huge attendance. We agreed that if all went well, if my course was well attended, I would teach seven courses in the coming year, of four full days each. Fortunately, GWU was just then about to publish its fall catalog, and my course material was included.

The first course, offered in September 1989, drew some 40 people, about double the expected number, which at $1,200 per student greatly pleased the university. But, I too was pleased when at the end of the course, two students asked me to come to their organizations to teach the same course there. Thus was born my TQM consulting practice, which I called Eric Anschutz Associates. My business plan was simple: every TQM course given at GWU was to lead to off-campus courses and TQM consultation at the companies of my on-campus students. The plan worked, and my practice thrived for about five years, with some forty American companies as clients, as well as clients in London, Amsterdam, South America, the Bahamas, and two in Indonesia: a bank in Jakarta and the national Indonesian airline, Garuda, for which I did a four-day seminar in Bali.

Kids

In these last paragraphs I want to say something about my three children. In order of age they are Christopher, Kari and Eric. Chris is married to Nancy Prince; they live in Newton, Massachusetts and have two adult sons: Nathaniel and Nicholas. Kari is married to Jim Stewartson; they live in Manhattan Beach, California, and have three sons: Max, Kai and Soren. Eric and his life-partner, Jennifer Toton, live in San Francisco, and have two daughters: Sonja and Liv.

Son Chris, with a BA in math from Bowdoin College, has had a long and successful career at Medical Information Technology, a leader in development and installation of software for hospitals and physicians worldwide. Chris is Meditech's Senior Vice President for Technology. Daughter-in-law Nancy Prince, also a Bowdoin graduate, worked for some years as Vice-President of Bay Bank, in Boston.

Daughter Kari has two BA degrees, one in anthropology, and another in education, both from the University of Maryland, She worked for some years as a schoolteacher, most recently for the Chinese-American International School in San Francisco, and has for many years been a full-time Mom. Son-in-Law Jim Stewartson is CEO and founder of RIDES.tv, Inc., working at the intersection of technology and interactive entertainment.

Son Eric, with a BA in Sociology and MEd. in Education, also from the University of Maryland, is founder of UpHealth, a Board member at JamBase, and an active angel-investor in several biotech companies. Jennifer, Eric's partner, is a Stanford graduate, holds an MBA from Kellogg, and is a senior marketing executive at Autodesk.

Politics

I have been a lifelong Democrat. For our country to remain in the front rank of nations, our government needs to provide active involvement and support for education, science, infrastructure and the arts – and I believe that progressive policies are far more likely to work toward that end than are those advocated by conservatives. Like most progressives, I think the Second Amendment, "the right of people to keep and bear arms," is meant to apply to members of a militia, not to any punk who may use it to rob gas stations or kill kids in a school. And I identify with those who advocate steeply progressive tax policies, not to take from the rich and give to the poor, but to fund infrastructure and science and education and the arts, thereby enriching all of us.

I have for a number of years, since retirement, written columns for our local newspaper, *The Rossmoor News*, some 150 of them altogether. And I have, in my senior years, written three books, *TQM America*, *Insight and Outrage,* and *Rossmoor: Eden in California.* The latter book was done in partnership with photographer John McCurdy. This book, *November Song,* will be book number four!

Religion

As to religion, I see no evidence of a God, and a good deal of evidence (wars, pestilence, poverty, tornados, murders, floods and other such) that there is no benevolent or omnipresent or omnipotent Supreme Being responsive to prayer. There is, in my mind, no hope of an afterlife. We live on only in our accomplishments and in the hearts and minds of those who knew and loved us.

Though we all know that death is the inescapable price of birth, we would all like to be around for as long as possible – if only to find out what will develop in the next 20 or100 years! And the 1000 after that!

Wars stemming from religious differences have been going on since the days of the Crusades, and are being fought today with greater ferocity and more determination than ever. Why does not God, deemed by believers to be omnipotent and omnipresent, reveal himself, tell all of us which religious doctrine is right, and replace the hatred and violence in people's minds and hearts with love and peace? My answer to that question is that he does not intervene because he does not exist. If he did exist, and if he did love us as believers insist, he would surely put an end to conflict, and steer the world (the world that he is believed to have created) into fruitful and productive and loving and peaceful endeavors.

I do not view religionists as unenlightened or unsophisticated. Indeed, I rather envy them their sense of being a part of the national core group, and their sense of brotherhood with one another. My atheism is not something I think about very much. It is not important to me in the same way that religion is important to a believer. Things that are important to me are family and friends, books, C-Span, PBS, the NY Times, discussion, tennis, golf, voting, writing, music, my home and my community, and my aspirations for the future direction of my country. But these same things can be important to a believer, who would have all that plus his Christianity.

****

Max Ehrman (1872 – 1945) was an American writer, poet, and attorney from Terre Haute, Indiana. His 1927 prose poem, "Desiderata," speaks to all. I include it here, at the end of our "November Song," because it seems to speak especially, and even memorably, to those of us in our November years.

Desiderata
By Max Ehrmann

Go placidly amid the noise and haste,
and remember what peace there may be in silence.
As far as possible without surrender
be on good terms with all persons.
Speak your truth quietly and clearly,
and listen to others,
even the dull and the ignorant;
they too have their story.

Avoid loud and aggressive persons,
they are vexations to the spirit.
If you compare yourself with others,
you may become vain and bitter;
for always there will be greater and lesser persons than yourself.
Enjoy your achievements as well as your plans.

Keep interested in your own career, however humble;
it is a real possession in the changing fortunes of time.
Exercise caution in your business affairs
for the world is full of trickery.
But let this not blind you to what virtue there is;
many persons strive for high ideals.
and everywhere life is full of heroism.

Be yourself.
Especially, do not feign affection.
Neither be cynical about love,
for in the face of all aridity and disenchantment
it is as perennial as the grass.

Take kindly the counsel of the years,
gracefully surrendering the things of youth.
Nurture strength of spirit to shield you in sudden misfortune.
But do not distress yourself with dark imaginings.
Many fears are born of fatigue and loneliness.
Beyond a wholesome discipline,
be gentle with yourself.

You are a child of the universe,
no less than the trees and the stars;
you have a right to be here.
And whether or not it is clear to you,
no doubt the universe is unfolding as it should.

Therefore be at peace with God,
whatever you conceive Him to be,
and whatever your labors and aspirations,
in the noisy confusion of life keep peace with your soul.

With all its sham, drudgery, and broken dreams,
it is still a beautiful world.
Be cheerful.
Strive to be happy.
Find joy wherever you can.

****

Made in the USA
San Bernardino, CA
13 May 2014